The Management of Human Resources in the Asia Pacific Region

Convergence Reconsidered

Editors

Chris Rowley
John Benson

FRANK CASS
LONDON • PORTLAND, OR.

First published in 2004 in Great Britain by
FRANK CASS PUBLISHERS
wn House, 47 Chase Side, Southgate, London N14 5BP

and in the United States of America by
FRANK CASS PUBLISHERS
c/o ISBS, 920 NE 58th Street, Suite 300
Portland, Oregon 97213-3786

Website www.frankcass.com

British Library Cataloguing in Publication Data

The management of human resources in the Asia Pacific Region:
convergence reconsidered – (Studies in Asia
Pacific business)
1. Personnel management – East Asia 2. Personnel management
Asia, Southeastern
I. Rowley, Chris, 1959– II. Benson, John, 1948–III. Asia
Pacific business review
HD70.C5F88 2003
658.3′0095–dc21

ISBN 0 7146 5586 4 (cloth)
ISBN 0 7146 8469 4 (paper)
ISSN 1369-7153

Library of Congress Cataloging-in-Publication Data

The management of human resources in the Asia Pacific Region:
convergence reconsidered
    p. cm. – (Studies in Asia Pacific business)
Includes bibliographical references and index.
    ISBN 0-7146-5586 (hb) – ISBN 0-7146-8469-4 (pbk.)
    1. Personnel management–Asia. 2. Personnel management–Pacific
Area. I. Rowley, Chris, 1959– II. Benson, John, 1948– III. Title. IV.
Series.
    HF5549.2.A75C48 2004
    658.3′0095–dc22

                                        2003017672

This group of studies first appeared in a special issue of
Asia Pacific Business Review [ISSN 1360-2381], Vol.9, No.4 (Summer 2003)
published by Frank Cass and Co. Ltd.

Printed in Great Britain by Antony Rowe Ltd., Chippenham, Wilts.

THE MANAGEMENT OF HUMAN RESOURCES
IN THE ASIA PACIFIC REGION

STUDIES IN ASIA PACIFIC BUSINESS
1369-7153

General Editors: Chris Rowley, Paul Stewart and Malcolm Warner

---

Contents

Notes on Contributors

Chris Rowley is Reader in HRM and Employee Relations at Cass Business School, City University, London. He has written extensively in the area of Asian and Korean HRM in books, journals such as *California Management Review, Journal of World Business, International Journal of HRM*, and for the *Financial Times* 'Mastering Management Online'.

John Benson is an Associate Professor and Reader in the Department of Management, University of Melbourne. He has published widely on industrial relations and HRM issues. His major research interests include Japanese management, the restructuring of Chinese industry, outsourcing and knowledge workers. He was co-editor, with Chris Rowley, of *Globalization and Labour in the Asia Pacific* (Frank Cass, 2000).

Malcolm Warner is Professor and Fellow, Wolfson College, Cambridge and the Judge Institute of Management, University of Cambridge. He is the Editor-in-Chief of the *International Encyclopedia of Business and Management*, the author of a number of books on Asian management, and Co-Editor of *Asia Pacific Business Review*.

Stephen W.K. Chiu received his doctorate from Princeton University and is Professor in the Department of Sociology at the Chinese University of Hong Kong. He is co-author of *East Asia and the World Economy* (Sage, 1995), *City-States in the Global Economy: The Industrial Restructuring of Hong Kong and Singapore* (Westview, 1997), and *The Dynamics of Social Movement in Hong Kong* (University of Hong Kong Press, 2000).

David A Levin has recently retired from the Department of Sociology at the University of Hong Kong. He has written extensively on local industrial relations and is currently working on a large-scale study of the trade union movement in Hong Kong.

Philippe Debroux is Professor of International Management in the Faculty of Business Administration, Soka University, Tokyo, and has been visiting professor at Tsukuba, Brussels and Hanoi Economic Universities. He is currently pursuing research on HRM in multinational companies with an emphasis on South East and East Asia regions including Japan.

Johngseok Bae is Associate Professor of Management at Korea University. He has written in the area of strategic management of human resources and international HRM in books and journals such as *Academy of Management Journal, Industrial Relations, Journal of World Business, International Journal of HRM* and *Human Resource Development Quarterly.*

Christopher Skene is a PhD Candidate in the Department of Politics and Public Administration at the University of Hong Kong. His research interests centre around the study international political economy with a focus on the politics of developing countries, and he has previously published on the relationship between the global economy and labour rights in the Philippines.

David Wan received his PhD from Manchester Business School and teaches at the Department of Management and Organization, NUS Business School, National University of Singapore. His research and teaching involves comparative employment relations, strategic HRM, trade unionism, industrial relations climate, organizational participation, services marketing and hospitality management.

Ying Zhu is a Senior Lecturer in the Department of Management, The University of Melbourne. He completed a PhD at the University of Melbourne, and his research focuses predominately on East Asian countries, including China, Japan, Taiwan and Vietnam. His publications include books, book chapters and journal articles on human resource management, employment relations, labour law and labour market regulation, and economic development in East Asia.

John Lawler is Professor of Labor and Industrial Relations at the University of Illinois at Urbana-Champaign. His research interests focus primarily on human resource management practices in East and South East Asia. He is currently undertaking a multi-country study of employment systems in American multinational firms, funded by a grant from the Society for Human Resource Management.

Vinita Atmiyanandana was Assistant Professor in mass communications at Chulalongkorn University, Bangkok. She is currently employed by the Urbana, Illinois School District.

Dedication

for Florence Benson

without whose unselfish and ceaseless support
nothing would have been possible

Introduction:
Changes and Continuities
in Asian HRM

CHRIS ROWLEY and JOHN BENSON

The years since our earlier collection (Rowley, 1997) have witnessed tremendous and massive economic, social and political change in Asia. There was, *primus inter pares*, the Asian financial crisis which swept though the region in 1997 and 1998, impacting on many countries, albeit in different ways, ferocity and length. It most certainly had an effect in a range of areas, including the style and approach of human resource management (HRM) and how human resources (HR) are dealt with. Some Asian economies continued to open up, restructuring financial sectors and receiving foreign direct investment (FDI). More recent are current economic and political changes that have taken place in Asia, not least China's membership of the World Trade Organization (WTO), with impacts both on China and many other economies. All these developments mean that much of what we know about Asia is outdated and may well be irrelevant. This is particularly the case with HRM, and it is this area that will form the basis of this collection.

This contribution focuses on the importance of the volume and the need to update our knowledge and understanding of Asian HRM. We present a model that can be used for a comparative analysis of HRM, and one that allows the various levels of change to be assessed. This is followed by an overview of the collection's contents, with the common focus being on the changes that have occurred since 1997.

FOCUS AND IMPORTANCE

The focus of this collection is on change and continuity in Asian HRM and how HR are dealt with. This is both within and between Asian economies. The specific aim is to explore and analyse what has happened to HRM in a number of Asian countries since the mid-1990s. A good way to approach this task was to revisit our earlier work and to ask all the contributors to build on our 1997 collection entitled *HRM in the Asia Pacific Region: Convergence Questioned* (Rowley, 1997). This would allow for some precision to be built into the present study and would provide a useful framework for all the authors. Thus, this new collection replicates all the countries analysed earlier, and as far as possible its structure and coverage, in order to give it a framework and base comparison for 'changes' and/or 'continuities' in HRM.

Undertaking this task is important for at least two reasons. First, as mentioned above, the macro level changes that have taken place in this region necessitate such a volume. In particular, globalization, perceived by some as the harbinger of universal HRM and the need for convergence of HR practices to 'one best way', retains profound resonance in a range of areas. There remains a continuing fascination in the management literature and practice for the search for this 'holy grail' of universal (often under the rubric of 'international' or 'global') management, allowing difficult and complex HRM practice to be put on some sort of 'automatic pilot' and so reduce management problems. Furthermore, within some countries particular HRM practices, such as lifetime employment and seniority based pay in Japan and Korea, have moved from 'saint' to 'sinner' in explanations of success. Why is this? Can there be such an easy sea change of practices often presented as former causes of economic success and deeply rooted in cultures (personal, organizational and national) and institutions (see Rowley and Bae, 2003). Also, there has been a varied range of developments across economies, with rebirth (Korea), continuing stagnation (Japan), emergence (China), assimilation (Hong Kong) and competition, to both developed (Singapore, Taiwan) and developing (Thailand, Philippines) ones. The following brief overviews of changes since our previous collection indicates this.

In China rapid economic growth has continued at a faster rate than most of the rest of Asia. While the impact of the Asian crisis was less, there were nevertheless some ripples and increasing unemployment. Japan remains moribund with its general downturn in economic activity, unemployment and low consumer demand reinforced by the collapse of overseas demand for its goods. South Korea (henceforth Korea) faced a likely nemesis when the former shining lights and star performers of the economy, the *chaebols*, collapsed. The economy has, however, strongly bounced back, albeit that the new government is promising closer control and reforms of business. In the Philippines both the crisis and political problems damaged the economy, ending the optimism of the earlier period. Thailand was one of the originators of the crisis when its currency went into free fall, the property bubble burst, unemployment increased, FDI collapsed and the IMF bail came with 'strings'. By 2002 some economic stability had returned albeit in the context of a loss of FDI to China. The earlier prosperity, praise and concern about the post-transfer sovereignty of 'one country two systems' in Hong Kong was replaced as the crisis hit the currency, stock market and property prices. With a continuous deflationary spiral and the consumer price index falling for more than 50 consecutive months (*Economist*, 2003), the earlier decamping of local manufacturing capacity was joined by waves of FDI into China post-WTO, by-passing Hong Kong as its monopoly 'gateway'. Singapore was affected by the crisis, with reduced external demand, although the economy had recovered by 1999. Taiwan initially benefited from the crisis as a 'safe haven' for FDI and continued non-Asian demand for its products. By 1998 the economy had declined, bankruptcies and unemployment rose, whilst by 2002 the economy had recovered, FDI and employment had not.

A second reason why this symposium is important is because we contribute to a number of theoretical debates, not least the resilient key ideas around convergence (universalism) and divergence (contingency) and aspects of cultural and institutional approaches. They remain important as some of the more naïve literature and commentators, such as in the area of international HRM, have ignored or underplayed this. While an improvement on the earlier narrow study of expatriate management, much more is needed. Indeed, such myopia often reduces the subject to the study of multinational companies (MNC) operations void of the complexity involved and detail required.

We can develop such theoretical aspects further by adding another dimension which concerns the ideas of disaggregating different levels within national HRM systems (Rowley and Benson, 2002). Commonly these are the three levels of architecture, policy and practice, to distinguish developments, which may be different, or even contradictory, even within a particular HRM system. This sort of framework provides greater nuance and a more calibrated and sensitive analytical device.

AIDS TO COMPARISONS AND BENEFITS

To assist in the comparisons (temporal, geographical and dimensional) of the selected countries we utilize several analytical devices. First, we again consider the developments in comparison to the HRM dimensions (proposed by Storey, 1992, used in Rowley, 1997). This provides an integrating mechanism for this symposium. We have, however, reduced the earlier twelve dimensions to ten, with some

TABLE 1

ASSESSMENT OF HRM CHANGES AND CONTINUITIES

Dimension	Presence	Change
1. Rules: adherence to	☐	☐
2. Behaviour: common values and norms	☐	☐
3. Key managers: personnel/specialists versus line/general	☐	☐
4. Personnel selection	☐	☐
5. Payment systems	☐	☐
6. Work conditions: harmonized	☐	☐
7. Contracts: individual versus standardized	☐	☐
8. In-house training	☐	☐
9. Right to hire and fire	☐	☐
10. Strategic role for personnel manager	☐	☐

Key: (*Practice*)
   ✓ present
   % present to some degree
   ✗ not present

   (*Degree of change in past 4 years*)
   ++ major change
   + change
   0 none

Source: adapted from Storey (1992).

internal reconfiguration and recompositions.[1] The ten dimensions are listed in Table 1.

Second, we have used many of the original authors where possible (although new authors do bring fresh insights and perspectives on the original works) to cover the same mixed set of economies. These are the developed, large economies of Japan and Korea, the developed, smaller economies of Hong Kong, Taiwan and Singapore, the developing, medium size economies of Thailand and the Philippines and the developing, large sized economy of China.

A third way we encouraged comparison was to be internally rigorous. Thus, as far as possible we have the same structure and format for each of the contributions. This had five main sections with several sub-sections to each. They are as follows.

- Introduction
- Contextual Factors and Issues
  - Political and historical
  - Economic
  - Labour markets
  - 1997 Asian financial crisis and reactions
  - Current economic situation

- Changes in HRM
  - Major changes taking place
  - Table outline of these changes
  - Possible changes in the immediate future
- Discussion
  - Why changes have occurred
  - Convergence or divergence
  - Key issues for HRM
  - Implications for theory development
- Conclusion

Not only did this forced common format and framework help forge each contribution in a similar shape to add consistency of coverage and ease of analysis, but a by-product was that it allows quick direct comparisons between individual aspects of the economies covered – speedy cross-comparisons, for example, of political and historical backgrounds, labour markets, and so on, are rendered easier.

JUST WHERE IS HRM GOING: CONTINUITY OR CONVERGENCE?

A wide range of relevant work has emerged post-1997. Some of this Asian-related literature can be divided into three types: countries/ themes, convergence and divergence. The first group can be single or multi-country. Keeley (2001) in *International HRM in Japanese Firms: Their Greatest Challenge*, examines the integration of local managers into the management process of overseas subsidiaries and parent Japanese MNCs. Kwon and O'Donnell (2001) in *The Chabeol and Labour in Korea: The Development of Management Strategy in Hyundai*, present a fascinating, detailed and historically grounded account of the forces shaping labour and the organization of work.

Bamber and Lansbury (1998) in their latest edition of *International and Comparative Employment Relations*, cover issues and countries relevant to our collection. Bamber et al. (2000) in their *Employment Relations in the Asia Pacific: Changing Approaches*, also include relevant countries.

Kidd et al. (2001) in their *Advances in HRM in Asia*, adopt a thematic approach. This includes indigenous firms, for example, venture business culture and also knowledge workers in R&D in Japan, HR development in Korean *chaebols*, Chinese family businesses in Hong Kong and Thailand, and business culture, career planning and development of managers, and training in Thailand. Western firms in China are also covered, including HR strategy, HR development of

European MNCs, joint ventures and culture. Other volumes include Debrah and Smith's (2001) *Work and Employment in a Globalized Era: An Asia Pacific Focus*, covering, *inter alia*, the Japanese service sector and Chinese job search. Felstead and Jewson (1999) in *Global Trends in Flexible Labour*, touch on a number of Asian experiences. Leisink (1999) in *Globalization and Labour Relations*, covers labour markets and employee relations. Hutchinson and Brown (2001) in *Organising Labour in Globalising Asia*, includes the Philippines garment industry, Chinese joint ventures, and Thai health and safety. Hollinshead and Leat (2003), with their new edition of *HRM: An International and Comparative Perspective*, provide a mix of themes and countries. Jackson (2002) in *International HRM: A Cross-Cultural Approach*, uses a range of models, such as 'The Motivation Organization' (the Japanese model) and 'The Joint Venture Organization' (the Chinese model).

Second, there are those pieces that can be placed broadly within the universal and convergence school. A Special Issue of the American journal *Human Resource Management* in 2002 was on 'best practices' in nine countries: US, Canada, Mexico, Australia, Japan, Korea, China, Taiwan, Indonesia, plus one region: Latin America, composed of Costa Rica, Guatemala, Panama, Nicaragua, Venezuela. This analysis of HRM is in terms of areas including selection, pay and appraisals. The results are somewhat ambivalent. For instance, Drost et al. (2002: 67), on training, state that 'While the results do not indicate any universal practices across all countries studied, they do indicate significant similarities in practices within country clusters' where common practices were influenced by cultural values and industry trends. Therefore, 'While we could find no universal or common practices...we found significant similarities in practices within country clusters' (p.80) due to culture and industry trends.

Yet for many of the others in this volume, this similarity was seemingly less prevalent. Huo et al. (2002: 42) note more divergence than convergence in practices, although this was in the process of converging on ways of recruitment even though selection criteria remained driven by a country's prevalent cultural values. They concluded '...inching toward global convergence, we expect national cultures to continue affecting the hiring practices used...' therefore, cross-national differences will continue to exist. Such divergence was even more obvious in other papers, such as Milliman et al. (2002), on performance appraisals, who state that practices varied significantly between countries, influenced by various contextual factors. Bowen et al. (2002), on strategic HRM, note significant differences in HRM status across countries. In conclusion, for Von Glinow et al. (2002:

123), this project's findings revealed that there were international HRM 'best practices', but somewhat damningly for this school of thought (and actually more worryingly for the neutrality and open-mindedness of the research itself) was their caveat: 'However, they are not as universal as we had hoped.'

Third, from the 'other side' is work confirming the continuity of management differences across countries. Beeson (2002) in *Reconfiguring East Asia: Regional Institutions and Organisations after the Crisis*, notes that apparently universal institutions, including legal systems, while sharing many common features superficially similar to those elsewhere, may operate in very different and distinctive ways. Whitley (1999: 3) in *Divergent Capitalisms: The Social Structuring and Change of Business Systems*, argues that: 'Convergence to a single most effective type of market economy is no more likely in the twenty-first century than it was in the highly internationalized economy of the late nineteenth century.' Differences in systems of economic organization and control are explained in terms of the specific features of institutional environments. This is important as it usefully highlights that '...economic relationships and activities are socially constructed and institutionally variable, such that the ways competitive processes operate, and the nature both of the actors engaged in them and of their outcomes, vary significantly between societal contexts'. (Whitley, 1999: 5). Thus, Venter (2002) in *Common Careers, Different Experiences: Women Managers in Hong Kong and Britain*, using both qualitative and quantitative data, argues that culturally different conceptions of equality and family are key variables underpinning the different work experiences of women managers in Hong Kong and Britain. Therefore, the impact of industrialization was mitigated by cultural constraints and rejected the convergence thesis.

A comprehensive example is the two-volume, 21-country collection by Zanko (2002) and Zanko and Ngui (2003), *The Handbook of HRM Policies and Practices in Asia-Pacific Economies*. All the countries in our volume are contained, *inter alia*, in their collection. They also develop the interesting and important idea of 'regionalism', and its impact on HRM, within an Asian context. It concludes that across the 21 countries in APEC '...there are many ways of managing human resources for success. There was no evidence of a universalist 'one best way' of HRM being followed' (Zanko and Ngui, 2003: 608).

Similarly, of relevance is Cousins (1999: 116), who compared non-standard employment in Europe (Germany, Spain, Sweden, UK) and found that despite similar pressures and direction of change '...these forces for change are mediated through the social, political and institutional structures within each country'. Also, there were clear differences between the extent to which such employment was precarious or stable. Clegg et al. (1999) in *Global Management: Universal Theories and Local Realities,* can be related to this area. A useful collection combining countries and themes is our earlier ten country collection (Rowley and Benson, 2000) titled *Globalization and Labour in the Asia Pacific Region.* Warner (2002) is a useful piece on Asia, and Warner and Joynt (2002) *Managing Across Cultures: Issues and Perspectives,* is a collection with a theoretical background, area studies and cross-cultural issues. Warner's (2003) *Culture and Management in Asia* also covers similar areas.

DIVERGENT CONVERGENCE: LEVELS OF CHANGE

An aspect of this analysis new to this collection is the idea of levels of change in HRM (see Gersick, 1991; Becker and Gerhart, 1996; Kostova, 1999). A model of change (Bae and Rowley, 2001; Rowley and Benson, 2002), had been simplified for use here. Three levels of HRM change can be analysed: architecture, policies and practices. One way of operationalizing these levels is to adopt Storey's (1995) model of HRM (see Table 2). The first level, system architecture (or deep structure), can be measured by differences in 'Beliefs and Assumptions' (Table 2). That is, it is HR that gives a competitive edge, that the aim is not merely compliance but employee commitment, and that employees should be carefully selected and developed. The second level refers to policy choices and mix of policies. These policy options can be measured by 'Strategic Qualities and Managerial Roles' (Table 2),

TABLE 2

OPERATIONALIZING LEVELS OF CHANGE

Levels	Elements	Dimensions
1. Architecture	Beliefs and Assumptions	Rules: adherence to Behaviour: common values and norms
2. Policy	Strategic Qualities and Managerial Roles	Strategic role for personnel manager Key managers: personnel/specialists versus line/general
3. Practice	Key Levers	Personnel selection Payment systems Work conditions: harmonized Contracts: individual versus standard In-house training Right to hire and fire

Source: adapted from Rowley and Benson (2002)

namely that HR decisions are of strategic importance, that HR policies should be integrated into business strategy and that line managers play the critical role in HRM. Finally, the third level refers to the actual HRM practices in the enterprise. These are referred to as the 'Key Levers' (Table 2) and consist of integrated action on selection, training, reward and job redesign that allows for devolved responsibility and empowerment. Of course, these three levels and their corresponding dimensions represent an idealized version of HRM that will not be present even in all Western enterprises. The value of this approach, however, lies in having a common reference point by which to measure changes in HRM.

This framework for analysis leads us to extend the key question of whether change has taken place to include where and at what levels have changes occurred, and whether this change has led to a degree of convergence? These questions are addressed in the contributions that make up this symposium.

OVERVIEWS OF COVERAGE

China

In the past five years, there have been changes in many walks of life, notwithstanding those in the economy and especially in the area of HRM. Once the government embarked on its 'Four Modernizations' and 'Open Door' strategies, the path was decisively mapped out, but the implications for HR only became clearer as the 1980s unfolded. The main impetus for the shifts relate to the changes in the historical, political and macro-economic environments. The main factor has been the unbundling of the economy and its factor-markets that involved the continuing fall in the state sector's share of economic activity and the growth of the non-state sector. This has been accompanied by a change in the outlook of managers and entrepreneurs, as well as in workers' attitudes to reform (some of it voluntary and some of it imposed by circumstance). This contribution explores the relationship between greater marketization and the pragmatic, step-wise adoption of HRM norms and practices, arguing that the faster the former proceeds, the more widespread the diffusion of the latter.

Hong Kong

Enterprise-level HRM practices were developed in the context of an open, competitive, market economy, a colonial regime disinclined to interfere in business decisions or the labour market, and a trade union movement with minimal economic and political clout. The types of employment systems that emerged within this environment, and how changes in the economy and polity impacted on these systems from the late 1970s to the mid-1990s, are outlined. A review of survey evidence on the ways that HRM practices in the private sector have since shifted in response to the Asian crisis and the change of sovereignty is also presented.

Japan

It was reported in 1997 that HRM was best characterized by continuity with some changes to assessment and pay practices. Since then the context of HRM has undergone significant change in four respects. First, very low levels of growth with unemployment rising and firms continuing to shed labour have continued. Second, the labour market is ageing and reduced recruitment of young graduates is occurring. Third, although only indirectly affected by the Asian crisis, the decline in the demand for capital goods from Asia, coupled with a series of financial scandals and a decrease in public spending, contributed to Japan's economic woes. Finally, employers are strongly advocating that HRM reform be undertaken that would see the system move away from uniform employment conditions. What impact these changes have had on HRM is the focus of this piece.

Korea

The operating context of HRM has undergone radical shifts since 1997. These include government change, South–North Korean summit talks, labour market turbulence, corporate bankruptcies, restructuring and downsizing (and even co-hosting, with Japan, the football World Cup). Economic development ground to an abrupt halt and went into reversal when the dark shadow of the Asian crisis was cast over Korea. Yet, the economy confounded the merchants of doom and gloom, and quickly and strongly recovered from 1999. All these factors have undoubtedly influenced the practice of HRM. Therefore, the focus of this piece is to compare the current situation with the past and to delineate the amount and type of such change vis-à-vis continuity in HRM.

Philippines

The purpose of this piece is three-fold: to build on the 1997 study, to demonstrate differences in HRM practices in the import substitution industrialization (ISI) and export-oriented industrialization (EOI) sectors and to highlight changes, if any, since the mid-1990s. This contribution agrees with the earlier position that suggested there was a trend towards the adoption of more sophisticated and more Western HRM practices. However, it also contends that the overall findings may be of limited value as the earlier study focused more on a small number of Philippine-owned ISI sector firms. To better capture the diversity between sectors this study draws a comparison between HRM practices in the ISI and EOI sectors. These two sectors have been very different in terms of their history, design and operating rationale.

Singapore

This contribution traces the development of HRM from the mid-1990s with particular reference to the impact of the Asian crisis. In particular, it explores the changes in HRM since 1997. National HRM concerns and strategies to maximize human capital as Singapore transforms itself into an innovation and knowledge economy are highlighted. The issue of convergence versus divergence in the management of HR is also considered. Current and future HRM challenges that are most likely to impact on the country's competitiveness and economic performance are also explored.

Taiwan

The changes in the macro-economic environment, due to the Asian crisis, have been an important stimulus to organizational and HRM changes in Taiwanese enterprises. This contribution tackles these responses by looking at individual firms, using a case study approach. The pattern of organizational responses introduced in these companies has exhibited a variety of different characteristics. Most have implemented strategies towards enhancing the competitiveness of individual firms. The situation has changed since 1997, marked by differences between a period of economic boom and recession. Consequently, as key economic and labour market conditions have changed so have HRM practices evolved.

Thailand

The Asian crisis, which severely impacted on the economy, and its aftermath, was the product of a number of forces, but management practices in Thailand played a major role. The period since has seen efforts at innovation and reform in the managerial arena, including changes in HRM policies and practices. To date, these shifts are still incomplete, particularly in locally owned companies. Companies surveyed in the post-crisis period tend to exhibit approaches to HRM more consistent with flexible, high-performance work systems (HPWS) than with more traditional approaches. Although subsidiaries of MNCs are generally ahead of locally owned companies in this respect, data presented in this contribution show that Thai companies (at least larger, globally active ones) are seemingly more apt in using HPWS methods, though adapted in many ways to the Asian context.

CONCLUSION

There have been tumultuous changes in the operating context of HRM in Asia and its HR practices and policies since our earlier collection. This issue continues to attract much management and academic debate, especially under the rubric of 'globalization'. Indeed, elements of former 'traditional' HRM systems and models have been weakened and different practices introduced. It is the impact of this change and the inter-play with the existing systems that interests us. Has this resulted in convergence towards some sort of 'stereotypical' Western, or perhaps Asian, model of HRM given the common overarching label of 'Asian' and geographical proximity? In what areas and at what levels? It is this theme that informs the following pieces and which in turn shed light on HRM practices in Asia.

NOTE

1. We reproduce below the earlier Table for the sake of completion and comparisons

ORIGINAL TABLE 1:
ASSESSMENT OF HRM CHANGES AND CONTINUITIES

DIMENSION	PRESENCE	CHANGE
Adherence to rules	☐	☐
Common values and norms	☐	☐
Transformational managerial role	☐	☐
Importance of line managers	☐	☐
Freedom in personnel selection	☐	☐
Individual performance-related pay	☐	☐
Harmonisation of work conditions	☐	☐
Individual contracts	☐	☐
In-house training	☐	☐
Standardised contracts	☐	☐
Right to hire and fire	☐	☐
Strategic role for personnel manager	☐	☐

Key: (*Practice*)
    ✓ present
    % present to some degree
    ✗ not present

(*Degree of change in past 4 years*)
    ++ major change
    + change
    0 none

Source: adapted from Storey (1992).

REFERENCES

Bae, J. and Rowley, C. (2001), 'The Impact of Globalization on HRM: The Case of South Korea', *Journal of World Business*, Vol.36, No.4, pp.402–28.

Bamber, G. and Lansbury, R. (eds.) (1998), *International and Comparative Employment Relations: A Study of Industrialised Market Economies*. St Leonards, NSW: Allen & Unwin.

Bamber, G., Park, F., Lee, C., Ross. P. and Broadbent, K. (eds.) (2000), *Employment Relations in the Asia-Pacific: Changing Approaches*. London: Thomson Learning.

Becker, B. and Gerhart, B. (1996), 'The Impact of Human Resource Management on Organizational Performance: Progress and Prospects', *Academy of Management Journal*, Vol.39, No.4, pp.779–801.

Beeson, M. (ed.) (2002), *Reconfiguring East Asia: Regional Institutions and Organisations After the crisis*. London: Routledge.

Bhopal, M. and Rowley, C. (2002), 'The State in Employment: The Case of Malaysian Electronics', *International Journal of Human Resource Management*, Vol.13, No.8, pp.1166–85.

Bowen, D.E., Galang, C. and Pillai, R. (2002), 'The Role of HRM: An Exploratory Study of Cross-Country Variance', *Human Resource Management*, Vol.41, No.1, pp.103–22.

Clegg, S., Ibarra-Colado, E. and Bueno-Rodriques, L. (eds.) (1999), *Global Management: Universal Theories and Local Realities*. London: Sage.

Cousins, C. (1999), 'Changing Regulatory Frameworks and Non-Standard Employment: A Comparison of Germany, Spain, Sweden and the UK', in A.Felstead and N. Jewson (eds.), *Global Trends in Labour*. Basingstoke: Macmillan, pp.100–20.

Debrah, Y. and Smith, I. (eds.) (2001), *Work and Employment in a Globalized Era: An Asia Pacific Focus*. London: Frank Cass.

Drost, E.A., Frayne, A., Lowe, B. and Geringer, J.M. (2002), 'Benchmarking Training and Development Practices: A Multi-Country Comparative Analysis', *Human Resource Management*, Vol.41, No.1, pp.67–88.

Economist, The (2003), 'A Survey of Asian Finance: The Weakest Link', 8 Feb.

Felstead, A. and Jewson, N. (eds.) (1999), *Global Trends in Flexible Labour*. Basingstoke: Macmillan.

Gersick, C. (1991), 'Revolutionary Change Theories: A Multilevel Exploration of the Punctuated Equilibrium Paradigm', *Academy of Management Review*, Vol.16, No.1, pp.10–36.

Hollinshead, G. and Leat, M. (2003), *HRM: An International and Comparative Perspective*. Harlow: Pitman.

Huo. Y.P., Huang, H.J and Napier, N.K. (2002), 'Divergence or Convergence: A Cross-National Comparison of Personnel Selection Practices', *Human Resource Management*, Vol.41, No.1, 31–44.

Hutchinson, J. and Brown, A. (eds.) (2001), *Organising Labour in Globalising Asia*. London: Routledge.

Jackson, T. (2002), *International HRM: A Cross-Cultural Approach*. London: Sage.

Keeley, T. (2001), *International HRM in Japanese Firms: Their Greatest Challenge*. Basingstoke: Palgrave.

Kidd, J.B., Li, X. and Richter, F.J. (eds.) (2001), *Advances in HRM in Asia*. Basingstoke: Palgrave.

Kostova, T. (1999), 'Transnational Transfer of Strategic Organizational Practices: A Contextual Perspective', *Academy of Management Review*, Vol.24, No.2, pp.308–24.

Kwon, S.H. and O'Donnell, M. (2001), *The Chaebol and Labour in Korea: The Development of Management Strategy in Hyundai*. London: Routledge.

Leisink, P. (1999), *Globalisation and Labour Relations*. Cheltenham: Edward Elgar.

Milliman, J., Nasan, S., Zhu, C. and De Ceri, H. (2002), 'An Exploratory Assessment of the Purposes of Performance Appraisals in North and Central America and the Pacific Rim', *Human Resource Management*, Vol.41, No.1, pp.87–102.

Rowley, C. (1997), 'Comparisons and Perspectives on HRM in the Asia Pacific', *Asia Pacific Business Review*, Vol.3, No.4, pp.1–18

Rowley, C. and Bae, J. (2002) 'Globalisation and Transformation of HRM in South Korea',

International Journal of Human Resource Management, Vol.13, No.1, pp.522–49.

Rowley, C. and Bae, J. (2003), 'Culture and Management in South Korea', in M.Warner (ed.), *Culture and Management in Asia*. London: Taylor and Francis, pp.187–209.

Rowley, C. and Benson, J. (eds.) (2000), *Globalization and Labour in the Asia Pacific Region*. London and Portland, OR: Frank Cass.

Rowley, C. and Benson, J. (2002), 'Convergence and Divergence in Asian HRM', *California Management Review*, Vol.44, No.2, pp.90–109.

Storey, J. (1992), *Developments in the Management of Human Resources*. Oxford: Oxford University Press.

Storey, J. (ed.) (1995), 'HRM: Still Marching On, Or Marching Out?', *HRM: A Critical Text*. London: Routledge, pp.3–32.

Venter, K. (2002), *Common Careers, Different Experiences: Women Managers in Hong Kong and Britain*. Hong Kong: Hong Kong University Press.

Von Glinow, M.A., Drost, E.A. and Teagarden, M.B. (2002), 'Converging on IHRM Practices: Lessons Learned from a Globally Distributed Consortium on Theory and Practice', *Human Resource Management*, Vol.41, No.1, pp.123–40.

Warner, M. (2002) 'Globalization, Labour Markets and Human Resources in Asia-Pacific Economics', *International Journal of Human Resource Management*, Vol.13, No.3, pp.334–8.

Warner, M. (ed.) (2003), *Culture and Management in Asia*. London: RoutledgeCurzon.

Warner, M and Joynt, P. (eds.) (2002), *Managing Across Cultures: Issues and Perspectives*, London: Thomson Learning.

Whitley, R. (1999), *Divergent Capitalisms: The Social Structuring and Change of Business Systems*. Oxford University Press.

Zanko, M. (ed.) (2002), *The Handbook of HRM Policies and Practices in Asia-Pacific Economies*. Vol.1. Cheltenham: Edward Elgar.

Zanko, M. and Ngui, M. (eds.) (2003), *The Handbook of HRM Policies and Practices in Asia-Pacific Economies*. Vol.2. Cheltenham: Edward Elgar.

China's HRM Revisited:
A Step-wise Path to Convergence?

MALCOLM WARNER

China has changed significantly over the past five years. Writing prior to that time (see Warner, 1997), we noted that it had experienced substantial economic reforms since 1978, the date of Deng Xiaoping's 'Open Door' policy initiative, let alone 1949 when the People's Republic was set up. The rate of change in the 'Middle Kingdom' since the original assessment was completed has accelerated even further, as the country experienced further sustained economic growth and a 'deepening' of reforms in the run-up to entry into the World Trade Organization (WTO).[1]

In the present overview, we revisit the earlier collection published in 1997 (see Rowley, 1997). We now look for both continuity and change in human resource management (HRM) practices here since the time the contribution on the People's Republic of China (PRC) was written (in 1996, one year earlier) and whether relative convergence been taken one – or more steps – further. The main theoretical proposition we will explore below is the relationship between greater marketization and the pragmatic, step-wise adoption of HRM norms and practices, arguing that *the faster the former proceeds, the more widespread the diffusion of the latter.*

As far as continuity is concerned, we can readily note that there is much that has remained fairly stable, given the length of China's history (see Fairbank and Goldman, 1998). This state of affairs should be predictable given the brevity of the number of years covered and the nature of Chinese society and its determinants. The organizational inertia of the original, Soviet-based work institutions (see Laaksonen, 1988; Kaple, 1994; Lu and Perry, 1999) had left a residue of entrenched practices that were hard to change and that enhanced continuity rather than diluted it. The Soviet-inspired command economy had been accompanied by a lifetime employment and welfare system known as the 'iron rice bowl' (*tie fan wan*) that was enterprise based (see Walder, 1986) with earlier roots in Japanese-occupied Manchuria (see Warner, 1992; 1995), in the Nationalist regime and in the early Communist liberated areas prior to 1949 (see Frazier, 2002).[2]

Looking for change is on the other hand no difficult task, for even in five years there have been shifts in many walks of life, notwithstanding in the economy and especially in the area of HRM. Once the Chinese government embarked on its 'Four Modernizations' and 'Open Door' strategies, the path was decisively mapped out but the implications for human resources (HR) only became clearer as the 1980s unfolded. Whether the Chinese rulers had a coherent strategy in mind at the outset is moot but it is clear that they pressed ahead pragmatically (Korzec, 1992; Naughton, 1995). The nature of the reforms was then to roll further forward in the 1990s (Lee et al., 1999). The background as far as HR policies were concerned has already been fully set out by the present author (see Warner, 1995; 1997). Since then, the period 1997 to 2001, and indeed subsequently, has seen further progress in this domain.

CONTEXTUAL FACTORS AND ISSUES

The main contextual dynamic has been the consolidation of Deng's legacy by President Jiang Zemin and Prime Minister Zhu Rongji; both ultimately stood down in late 2002. More will be set out in detail under a number of headings, for example, historical and political and so on, in the next sections. Suffice it to say that the economic reforms have been further 'deepened' in the late 1990s and the period after 2000.

Political and Historical

The political changes that have been seen in China in the last decade have been significant but it is too early to anticipate their full historical implications. Whilst it is true that the events of June 1989 made a profound impact on many people's hopes for a 'new' China, both at home and abroad, it was not to be. Whether a 'victory' for the students would have led to this is moot but it is clearly the case that the liberal reform faction(s) suffered a serious setback. Human rights, particularly for labour activists, worsened even further in the aftermath of the Tiananmen Square events.[3]

Outside pressure was slow to make its impact but economic growth assuaged some of the pain and a new generation of students made their way in the world, many preferring to train for a management career through the MBA (Master of Business Administration) or undergraduate business degree rather than through the Party School route.

Since 1996, we have seen a significant degree of 'perestroika' and no little 'glasnost' but there has been no far-reaching breakthrough in terms of political reforms. The replacement of Deng Xiaoping as 'paramount leader' by Jiang Zemin had not led to a politically 'freer' China in Western terms but there is now a little more political 'space' for its citizens than in earlier days in terms of a less restrictive life on a day-to-day basis.

Economic

The PRC has now enjoyed two decades of economic growth since Deng launched the Open Door policy in 1979. It has enjoyed faster economic growth and performance than the former Soviet Union (see Nolan, 1995). It has also been lauded as a potential 'economic superpower' by international bodies like the World Bank since then. By the year 2020, it may even supplant Japan as second in the world economic rankings, after the USA (see Newton and Subbaraman, 2002).

Living standards have risen greatly in recent years but the distribution of benefits has been uneven. Those living in towns have done better than those in the country; most of the urban workers have benefited vis-à-vis most of the peasants. A new middle class has also emerged, particularly in Beijing and Shanghai as well as in many of the big eastern coastal towns and cities. However, income inequality has grown and the 'Gini Coefficient' (defined as the ratio of poor to rich income) is now larger (around 0.4) than it was under Mao (around 0.2) and apparently converging with that of other East Asian countries (see Ng and Warner, 1998: 166).

China has undergone further economic growth since the mid-1990s. The growth rate has continued to remain high but a little less so than in the previous decade (it grew at nearly 10 per cent per annum over the past two decades). Whilst the management of the economy has not been without its difficulties with continuing corporate indebtedness especially in the state sector and ongoing deflation in the marketplace, the PRC has grown faster than most of its Asian neighbours, many of which have not fully recovered from the 1997 financial crisis (see Ip et al., 2000).

Gross Domestic Product (GDP) per capita is now much greater than in 1995 (see Table 1). Between 1995 and the end of 2000, GDP per capita went up from 4772 to 6985 in yuan (Renminbi, or RMB) at current market prices. In nominal terms, GDP was less than US$1,000 in 2000 but much higher than this in purchasing power – possibly three to four times higher, according to World Bank estimates. It was even higher in prosperous cities, like Shanghai. But elsewhere, private consumption had also risen considerably over the period as a percentage of GDP.

TABLE 1

KEY INDICES FOR THE PRC ECONOMY, 1997–2001

	1997	1998	1999	2000	2001
Population, mill.	1230.1	1248.1	1259.1	1265.8	1275.8
Labour-force, mill.	705.8	714.1	719.8	730.1	750.5
Unemployment, %	3.1	3.1	3.1	3.1	3.4
Nominal GDP, US$bill.	898.2	946.5	991.4	1080.0	1157.3
GDP, US$ per capita	656.6	758.2	787.4	853.2	907.1
Real GDP growth, %	8.8	7.8	7.4	8.0	7.3
Utilized FDI, US$bill.	44.2	43.8	38.8	38.4	42.5

Sources: Goldman Sachs, IMF, Lehman Brothers, World Bank etc, 1987–2001.

Labour Markets

China is now much closer to a fully operative labour market than it was five years ago. Under the 'iron rice bowl' system, mobility between firms was close to zero (see Warner 1995; White, 1996). This situation gradually changed as the Dengist labour reforms were introduced in the mid and late 1980s (see Cook and Maurer-Fazio, 1999). Whilst one could earlier speak of a 'nascent' labour market, one is now closer to 'real' labour markets in many parts of the urban economy. In big cities at least, the mobility of workers, technicians and managers has reached levels never before seen in the PRC. But in many parts of China, particularly in the interior provinces, changes have been slower. In areas of high economic growth, people may move from their job; but where there is stagnation they do so much less, unless they have to, that is to say, they are dismissed.

1997 Asian Financial Crisis and Reactions

China played a role in the economic troubles of the region in the 1990s because of the devaluation of its currency, preceding the crisis in 1994 when the RMB/US$ rate was brought down by 50 per cent from 5.82 to 8.72 (Newton and Subbaraman, 2002: 39). It is said that this may have led to competitive devaluations in other Asian countries. However, the 1997 Asian financial crisis did not have a significant impact on the Chinese economy, as it did on others in Asia, especially on the Overseas Chinese (Nanyang) business community (see Ip et al., 2000). The main reason for this was the fact that the PRC was less closely coupled with foreign economies in terms of both imports and exports. China had one of the lowest degrees of economic openness in Asia in the mid-1990s. Exports of goods and services were only 21 per cent of GDP in 1996 (26 per cent in 2000), whereas they were 171 per cent for Singapore (180 per cent in 2000) and 142 per cent for Hong

Kong (150 per cent in 2000). The negative multiplier impact for the internal market in China was lower then than in the rest of Asia, although this may change as it enters the WTO. The rise in unemployment was very limited in 1997, although it could potentially grow with greater trade interdependence in future years. The 1997 crisis was not then as much of a major crisis internally in the PRC, either economically or politically, as in the rest of Asia but there were secondary ripples; for example, foreign direct investment (FDI), especially from overseas Chinese investors, into Guangdong province declined after mid-1997 and its exports were affected by competitive devaluations from Asian competitors (see Huang, 2000).

Current Economic Situation

Economic growth has continued to bless the Chinese economy in the first few years of the new millennium. The rate had been on average over 7 per cent in the five years since 1996 (and recently per annum around 8 per cent since 2000). The economy was not without its troubles, as deflation and unemployment were still major concerns in 2002. The aggregate balance of payments surplus should continue to burgeon and hopefully further FDI will increase to take up the slack in the current account surplus, putting pressure on the yuan to appreciate somewhat. The winding-down of the still heavily indebted state-owned enterprise (SOE) sector continues apace.

The SOEs ('owned by the whole people', in the official jargon) were for a long time the mainstay of Chinese industry ever since the 1950s (see Schurmann, 1966; Walder, 1986; Warner, 1995). These were and are still mainly found in large industrial cities like Beijing, Chongqing, Dalian, Guangzhou, Shanghai, Shenyang, Wuhan, and so on. Large and medium-sized SOEs in this sector once produced the bulk of total gross value of industrial output – nearly 80 per cent in 1978 but now down to under 25 per cent of this total.

Employing over 100 million workers in all by the late 1990s, SOEs were generally seen as inefficient and over-manned. But they still provide work for a sizeable minority of urban workers. One in two state firms admitted losses at the end of the last decade; it is hard to be sure of the current picture but many still are 'in the red' and now have had to be sold off or made bankrupt. Bad loans accounted for 40–50 per cent of GDP; there is a largely unfunded pension system; also, there is a good deal of official corruption.

Unemployment has been growing in the PRC since the early 1990s and the number out of work may be over one in eight in many large cities; joblessness may even be as high as over one in five in parts of the 'rust-belt' in the North East (*dongbei*). The 'official' unemployment figure of around 3 per cent in the late 1990s has long been regarded as an underestimate.

A leading figure in the Chinese Academy of Social Sciences (CASS) recently described joblessness as the biggest challenge currently facing the PRC; Professor Hu Angang, a CASS labour economist, cited figures to show that between 1993 and 1997, laid-off workers rose from 3 million to 15 million (with two in three from the SOEs). He estimated around 10–15 million had been thrown out of work by the start of the new millennium. The 'rust-belt' provinces and cities have been the worst hit. The highest reported joblessness cited is in Liaoning Province with over 22.4 per cent, followed by Hunan with 21.3 per cent; at city-level, Chongqing at 18 per cent and Tianjin with 17 per cent, both had noteworthy high levels of unemployment (see Documentation/*China Quarterly*, 1999). By 2000 and 2001, the jobless rate rose considerably and may even have been higher, due to the pressures of globalization and structural reform. The entry into the WTO is likely to make life even more difficult. During 1999, 6 million SOE workers lost their jobs (World Bank, 2000: 4). About 8 million workers were laid off from SOEs by the end of 2000 (World Bank, 2000: 4). On the assumption that there are over 15 million surplus workers yet to be made redundant, SOE restructuring may have further negative impacts (see Newton and Subbaraman, 2000: 42).

The White Paper on Employment and Social Welfare issued by the State Council in April 2002 stated that more than 25.5 million people were laid off from SOEs in China from 1998 to 2001, of which 16.8 million had been re-employed, leaving 8.7 million still without new employment. Wang Dongjin, Vice-Minister of Labour and Social Security, noted that the number of urban jobless would rise to more than 20 million over the next four years (O'Neil, 2002). The problem would be exacerbated by China's entry to the WTO, with farmers likely to flock to cities to find work. China will therefore face serious structural imbalances, with an abundant supply of low-skilled workers but also great demand for skilled professionals.

China defines the jobless in a distinctive way, however. According to the State Statistical Bureau, unemployment officially covers the urban registered unemployed who (a) possess non-agricultural residence, (b) are within a certain age range (16 to 50 for males and 16 to 45 for females), (c) are able and willing to work, and (d) have registered with the local labour bureau for employment (Chinese Labour Statistical Yearbook, 1997: 588). Only the very blatantly unemployed qualify for what are known officially as 'unemployment benefits'. In fact, another form of joblessness is perhaps more pervasive – this is the category of 'hidden' unemployment – referring to workers, often in the SOE sector, who have been 'laid-off' (*xiagang*). The Chinese State Statistical Bureau defines 'laid-off' workers to be 'workers who have left their posts and are not engaged in other types of work in the same unit, but still maintain a ... relationship with the unit that they have worked for' (Chinese Labour Statistics Yearbook, 1997: 588). Workers who have been 'laid-off' are only provided with basic living subsidies (*shenghuofei*) at subsistence levels, in place of unemployment benefits, and are not counted in the registered unemployment rate. This official practice may account for the perception of a low rate of joblessness in Chinese cities.[4]

In light of the vast number of people made redundant and the inadequacy of the insurance system and social assistance available, re-employment has required substantial local mobilization. All SOEs that make workers redundant are obliged to set up re-employment service centres. Loss-making enterprises can apply for state co-financing: the Ministry of Finance and local sources such as the unemployment fund each provide one third, the enterprise provide the remaining third. Making a realistic estimate, we may say that around a quarter to a third of the jobless who have sought help through these routes may have been helped to re-enter formal employment; the others have either gone into the informal economy or remained out of work.

CHANGES IN HRM

Major Changes Taking Place

There have been major changes in 'people-management' in the PRC since the mid-1990s (see Child, 1994; Chan, 1995; Warner, 1999). A life-time employment system, once acclaimed with pride, was believed by a number of influential Chinese economists to be associated with weak management, factor-immobility and inefficiency (see Warner, 1995). The general view of many of these economists working on China as an academic field of study (but mainly overseas) was that the status quo that Deng sought to reform was highly wasteful and held back economic development (see Naughton, 1995). The Chinese paramount leader launched the management reforms of 1984 for example and later the 1992 personnel policy innovations to deal with these constraints. Managers were to be henceforth allowed more autonomy, particularly in SOEs, to hire and fire; decision-making was to become more decentralized in not only personnel but also marketing and purchasing domains (Child, 1994). The most important reforms were certainly designed with factor-rigidities in HR allocation in mind. But whether this has resulted in a full-blown HRM model is not yet clear outside joint ventures (JV) and wholly owned foreign firms of a reasonable size (see Goodall and Warner, 1997). Research by the present author and colleagues (see Ding et al., 2000) based on a sample of 62 SOEs and JV firms has underlined this point. Size, ownership and location, it was pointed out, were very important in how people were managed. It was clear that HRM had a different meaning in different kinds of firms. It was more likely to be implemented in larger firms as opposed to smaller ones, the same study showed, whether they were in the North or in the South and whether firms were state, joint, or foreign owned.

The use of the HR model (see Poole, 1997) can be distinguished from straightforward personnel management (PM) as follows. HRM translates into Chinese pinyin as '*renli ziyuan guanli*' (with the same Chinese characters as in Japanese) which signifies 'labour force resources management'. But many – both managers and academics (and most students) – often employ it as a synonym for 'Personnel Management' (*renshi guanli*) and treat it as an achieved usage. The reality is that the form of older practice still lingers on in many Chinese firms, especially in SOEs where a more conservative air endures (see Ding et al., 2000; 2001; 2002). PM is even the norm in many JVs, as one HR Director noted 'we are still the policemen of the *danwei*'. She meant that their role was robustly applying personnel rules and regulations to 'police' employee behaviour. Thus, apart from its usage in the large JVs and wholly owned multinational corporations (MNCs) in China, it is still very far from the initial concept of HRM as understood in the international academic HRM community (see Goodall and Warner, 1997; Pange, 1999) due to organizational inertia in most of these cases. The importance of older practices in China, however, cannot be underestimated. It may still pervade the residual elements of the institutional framework and the attitudes associated with the *danwei* (see Francis, 1996).

The larger foreign-funded enterprises, whether JVs or wholly owned, associated mainly with MNCs, are often much admired, pattern-setting employers and are predominantly the firms following HR practices, in the shape of HRM borrowed from the west (see Verburg, 1996; Ding et al., 2000; 2001; 2002). Already, many JVs and non-state firms have incorporated some new personnel practices, if not a whole package, into their own management systems. Most foreign-funded, as well as Town and Village Enterprises (TVEs) as privately-owned ones (see Garnaut et al., 2001), had much more autonomy in their people management compared with their state-owned equivalents. This freedom to take decisions has helped boost motivational energies, for example, as rewards became more performance-linked. But full HRM was only found on the ground in larger TVEs and/or privately-owned firms (see Ding et al., 2002).

Under the old system, it was said 'we pretended to work and they pretended to pay us' (anonymous). A Western-inspired workplace practice, amidst all this, adopted nationwide since the mid-1980s, has been the implementation of 'labour contracts' (see Korzec, 1992; Warner and Ng, 1999). Initially these were 'individual' contracts but soon they became supplemented by 'collective' ones. The trade union in an enterprise is empowered by the 1994 Labour Law (implemented in 1995 in fact) to sign 'collective labour contracts' with the 'employer' on behalf of the 'employees' (see Josephs, 1995; Warner, 1996). Such contracts supplement 'individual' ones introduced on an experimental basis earlier and set out in the *Temporary Regulations* of the Ministry of Labour of 1986. The collective version may be described as a 'framework agreement' for the myriad individual contracts in the enterprise. But whether such contracts are harbingers of the onset of 'collective bargaining' and a 'labour market' in the Western sense has yet to be seen.

By defining the duration of the contract, the nature of employment has changed in the PRC. The period of contract is now clearly defined and hence displaces, by implication, the previously hallowed practice of permanent 'lifetime employment' referred to earlier. If this practice was near-universal in urban, mainly state-owned, enterprises in 1978, in two decades it has become the exception in legal terms although in practice it often persists. Almost all firms had adopted individual formal labour contracts by the year 2000, as this was a legal requirement. The incidence of collective labour contracts is restricted to larger firms, most of which are SOEs and a minority of JVs (see Ng and Warner 1999; Ding et al. 2000; 2001; 2002).

By the start of the new millennium, it was claimed by the Chinese official trade unions that there were over 300,000 collective contracts signed in the PRC. However, most of these were in union branches in SOEs and if this figure were to be true, they would be found in approximately half of the All China Federation of Trade Unions (ACFTU) branches in existence (Ng and Warner, 1998). In an empirical study we found that the incidence of *both* individual and collective contracts together was also more likely to be found in the North and North East of China, whereas the presence of individual contracts alone were more likely to be extant in firms in the South and South-East (see Ding et al., 2000). Three variables shaped the pattern of industrial relations, namely ownership (SOE v. JV), employee size (large v. small) and location (north v. south) (Ding et al., 2000).

It is not yet clear if this has led to the introduction of a Western-style system of collective bargaining but there are undoubtedly 'family resemblances' between the Chinese and foreign systems of such bargaining. It would be unreasonable to find a replication of industrial relations (IR) and HRM overnight here, either as a result of greater convergence, whether relative or otherwise, as China entered the WTO in late 2001.

Essentially, a collective contract may be reminiscent of the classic notion of 'common rules' engendered by collective bargaining. However, it does not commit, as analogous to Western practice, the individual to the 'buying and selling of labour' (see Warner and Ng, 1999). Instead, the actual exchange in the PRC is now left to the regulation by the individual labour contract and the appropriate provisions of the 1994 Labour Law. The state is evidently anxious to institute a workplace system of IR that fits its international commitments under the WTO. It is designed to cement a mutual and stable dialogue between management and the union, acting as a representative agent and deputizing for the workforce. A collective bargaining institution helps push forward the ACFTU's steps towards modern unionism by the use of 'benchmarking' against Western IR practices (Ng and Warner, 1998). This trend is likely to grow further as China tries to show it is modelling its IR and HRM on Western lines but the irony may be that Chinese officialdom cannot control its unions without the present apparatus of power, and this fact may ease its entry into the WTO.

In the international IR arena, there is also the state's effort to appease foreign criticism about industrial conditions at the workplace level as they match up with international norms of labour standards, especially on matters of collective bargaining and labour protection, as declared by the International Labour Organization (ILO) in its codified body of international labour standards. Such a position of workplace enlightenment may help in dealing with international political pressures concerning external trade negotiations and issues (see Warner, 2002) like China's entry into the WTO that was finalized at the end of 2001. Indeed, in May 2001, the government of the PRC – through the Ministry of Labour and Social Security – and the ILO signed an accord – a *'Memorandum of Understanding'* – vis-à-vis cooperation and partnership, 'based on the ILOs goal of *'Decent Work'* to support national reform and social progress worldwide' (ILO, 2001: 1). According to the Director-General of the ILO (Juan Somavia), this was 'only a beginning' (Address to Press Conference, 2001, see ILO, 2001). The topics to be covered were labour rights, employment services, re-employment and training and so on (ILO, 2001: 3). In addition, tripartite consultation, as well as collective bargaining mechanisms, labour contract legislation, labour dispute settlement and 'capacity-building of the social partners' were covered in the Memorandum (ILO, 2001: 4–5].

The dual role of Chinese trade unions as both bargaining agent and state agency presents problems for freedom of association, as part of a package of ILO standards in the twenty-first century. There is little evidence that this contradiction is being adequately resolved as it appears that the independence of unions in the PRC is a 'non-negotiable' issue to date. Whilst union membership is optional in law, it is hard to evade in large SOEs, although much of the non-state sector is non-unionized and the ACFTU has less and less chance of entering firms as the non-state sector in the economy expands, such as TVEs and privately-owned firms (see Ding et al., 2001: 2002). An outline of these changes is set out in Table 2, from which it can be seen that some changes have been discernable.

If we return to the six enterprises discussed in the study five years ago (Warner, 1997), we find that the movement in the direction of HRM practices (cases 1, 2 and 4) have been consolidated further, whereas in the other three firms (cases 3, 5 and 6) which exhibited more conservative characteristics there has been relatively more change towards market-driven practices (see Table 3).

It is clear that there is now much greater overlap between the recognizably HRM-oriented firms compared with those that were

TABLE 2
ASSESSMENT OF HRM CHANGES AND CONTINUITIES

Dimension	Presence	Change
1. Rules – adherence to	✓	+
2. Behaviour– common values and norms	✓	+
3. Key managers – personnel/specialists versus line/general	%	%
4. Personnel selection	✓	%
5. Payment systems	✓	+
6. Work conditions – harmonized	%	+
7. Contracts – individual versus standardized	✓	++
8. In-house training	✓	+
9. Right to hire and fire	✓	++
10. Strategic role for personnel manager	%	+

Key: (Practice)
    ✓ present
    % present to some degree
    ✗ not present

    (Degree of change in past 4 years)
    ++ major change
    + change
    0 none

Source: adapted from Storey (1992).

more associated with PM/IR, than in 1996, both in general and the six firms we then surveyed (see Warner, 1997). But one must not exaggerate the degree of 'convergence' and if there has been an evolution it has only been relative. It is, however, the case that all firms in China now have to comply with a number of legally required practices, as laid down in the post-1995 Labour and Trade Union Law frameworks (see Josephs, 1995; Ng and Warner, 1998), across the board. This compliance will thus tend to even out original differences between firms, including the six cases that we originally examined. The 'iron rice bowl' is now both *de jure* and *de facto* virtually broken; rewards are now increasingly performance based; social insurance is now contributory; trade unions and works congresses are having to accommodate to market forces, and so on. Individual employment contracts are de rigueur; collective ones are to be found in many large firms, including the ones examined. Hence, we can see a further advance in HRM 'with Chinese characteristics' (that is, as adapted to local circumstances) but there is weaker evidence of 'strategic HRM' as defined in western terms (see Mabey et al., 1998).

Possible Changes in the Immediate Future

The immediate future will see the non-state owned sectors expand and the SOEs shrink further, correspondingly, as the impact of WTO entry leads to more competition in internal markets making it more difficult for formerly feather-bedded firms to survive. The deepening of structural reforms will mean that bad loans will be, albeit slowly and painlessly, dealt with amongst other matters. The implications for the micro-economic level is greater marketization that will lead to more market-driven HRM practices, such as even more performance-driven rewards, more contributory social insurance and less unionization vis-à-vis the status quo reported in the earlier study that was our then point of departure, (Warner, 1997: 25–7).

TABLE 3

SUMMARY OF CHINESE CASE STUDIES: 1996 COMPARED WITH 2001

Company Name	Firm Type	Change over period, 1996–2001
Case 1: Beijing Jeep	JV	wholly HRM
Case 2: Guoxing Electronics	JV	moderate shift
Case 3: Schindler Elevators	JV	wholly HRM
Case 4: Peony TV	SOE	almost wholly HRM
Case 5: Beijing Transformers	SOE	moderate shift
Case 6: Beijing Pharmaceuticals	SOE	moderate shift

Source: Adapted from Warner (1997)

DISCUSSION

Why Changes Have Occurred

The main impetus to the changes we have noted above relate to the changes in the historical, political and macro-economic environments we have taken note of earlier. The main factor has been the unbundling of the Chinese economy and its factor markets that involved the year on year fall in the state sector's share in economic activity and the growth of the non-state sector.[5] This has been accompanied by a change in outlook of Chinese managers and entrepreneurs, as well as a shift in workers' attitudes to reform, some of it voluntary and some of it imposed by circumstance (see Goodall and Warner, 1997; Warner, 1999).

Convergence or Divergence

In the earlier essays (Warner, 2000; 2002; 2003), we spoke of 'relative convergence' as being the main feature of Chinese HRM; this remains largely the case.[6] It may be suggested that when these prominent nationally known SOEs were reformed with a shift towards financial autonomy, 'the state attempted to introduce a new format perhaps analogous to the 'limited company' system in Western economies. This shift of policy has been seen as the 'corporatization' of the SOEs' that has brought in its train the possible 'Westernization' of their labour–management relations and HRM. However, as Guthrie's research (1999) has pointed out, classical economics do not dominate decision-making completely; social considerations still do count. Even so, practising managers should note that a number of prominent Chinese firms are adopting potentially 'convergent' policies, among them performance measurement, already for years a norm elsewhere in Asia, for example, Hong Kong.

The practice is apparently imitative of the HRM model commonly present among enterprises in Western market-based economies, where the latter are concerned with an explicit agenda to streamline *business performance* by stressing *human performance,* assessing it individually rather than collectively (Ng and Warner, 1998). There is evidence that Chinese workplaces are moving towards individual performance-based rewards systems but more often than not, they tend to award group bonuses, as in past days (Takahara, 1992; Warner, 1995; Ding et al., 2000).[7]

Key Issues for HRM

The key issues for people management in China are mainly linked to completing the 'long march' from PM towards full-blown HRM. They relate to the elimination of the 'iron rice bowl' and the transition to market-driven employment practices, not just in large firms but also across the wide range of businesses now to be found in China (see *The Economist*, 2002). The weight of tradition and inertia has to date been a drag on such a process but the change is now more and more in evidence, particularly as the state sector withers away.

Recruitment is now much more dependent on the market, not allocation by the labour bureaux. Selection is now done using meritocratic criteria for the most part. Rewards systems are now as complex as ever but more performance-driven. Motivation is now increasingly and unambiguously based on material rewards rather than a pledge of job security and benefits in kind. Training is now more systematic, at least in larger firms, even if development is less de rigueur.

Diffusing reformed HR practices to those SOEs, mainly those in the North East and other 'rust-belt' regions still in the rut is perhaps the key issue here. As the state sector declines, the non-state sector has less of a burden of out-of-date practice to carry but its smaller firms and *Nanyang* JVs may not rise beyond the personnel paternalism found in comparable businesses in the rest of East Asia and adopt international HRM standards.

Implications for Theory Development

The implications for theory development are less clear (see Warner, 2003). There has not been much mention of the PRC in most texts on HRM theory to date; nor conversely, has HRM theory appeared much in past writings on Chinese management, for the most part. In the 1990s, attempts were made to see the Chinese way of managing people through an HRM theoretical prism, most notably in the *International Journal of HRM* (see Warner, 1993; Warner, 1996; Ding et al., 2000). Quite clearly, Asian practice needs to be absorbed into HRM theory; if China becomes more like its neighbours, then we can begin to understand its norms and routines in relation to theirs (see Warner, 2002).

If we find evidence of greater relative convergence in the Chinese case, we may be able to conclude that HR theory is adequately generalizable across social contexts that were – and still are to some extent – very different from the Western institutional backgrounds from which its basic concepts sprung (see Child, 1994; Poole, 1997; Mabey et al., 1998).[8]

That is to say, we can then meaningfully compare Chinese norms and practices with those outside that country in HRM terms. But Rowley (1997: 198) noted that 'the evidence supporting convergence in this collection is actually mixed and equivocal, with caveats often used'. Indeed, in earlier writings, the present writer had been cautious in seeing HRM as being as yet firmly established in current Chinese practice across the board (see Warner, 1995; 2000; 2003). The researcher must therefore look for 'internal convergence' (advanced sectors in the PRC vis-à-vis backward ones), as much as 'external convergence' (Chinese firms matching up to foreign HRM standards). We may, however, now be entering a new phase, as China has now entered the WTO and has a truly 'Open Door' to the world.[9]

CONCLUSION

To sum up, we have now reviewed the pragmatic, step-wise path to HRM in China that has characterized the five years following our earlier assessment (Warner, 1997). Then, we spoke of 'relative convergence' as being the main feature of Chinese HRM; this remains largely the case. As we see the non-state owned sectors expand and the SOEs shrink correspondingly, the impact of WTO entry is predicted to lead to more competition and greater marketization.[10] The greater the impact of these changes on Chinese firms, the more PM will be replaced by HRM, year by year. The speed of this trend will however depend on how far the new norms become institutionalized and how far managers' as well as workers' attitudes absorb and integrate them.

NOTES

1. The impact of China's entry into the WTO has yet to be seen, as it only signed up in late 2001 and will not experience significant consequences for a couple of years at least.
2. Frazier's book (2002) is a fascinating account of how the roots of the 'iron rice bowl' are to be found in the 1920s, 1930s and 1940s, as much as in later decades. He explores in scholarly detail the continuities between the Nationalist and Communist regimes.
3. For a more detailed account of labour activism and trade unions in China, see Chan's (1995) view.
4. It is very difficult to compare Chinese unemployment statistics with Western ones but this may improve as China conforms more closely to ILO norms in the coming years.
5. For an up to date account of this shift, see Newton and Subbaraman (2002).
6. We have sometimes used the terms 'soft' and 'relative' convergence interchangeably; this does not imply 'soft' meaning 'comfortable', rather 'less sharply defined', as opposed to 'hard' convergence being 'clear-cut'.
7. The persistence of 'red-eye disease' as it became known, that is to say 'jealousy' has often meant group rather than individual bonuses are the norm, even now.
8. We can maybe include Japanese HRM together with Western norms and practice here.
9. Estimates of how open the door will be are contained in Newton and Subbaraman (2000: 76). Estimates vary from 0.5 per cent to 4.1 per cent extra GDP growth in the short-term.
10. The exposure to world economic forces on such a scale will, it is hoped, lead to much greater exposure to outside ideas, with wider institutional and political reform in China anticipated.

REFERENCES

Chan, Anita (1995), 'The Emerging Patterns of Industrial Relations in China and the Rise of the Two New Labour Movements', *China Information: A Quarterly Journal*, Vol.9, No.4, pp.36–59.

Child, John (1994), *Management in China During the Age of Reform*. Cambridge: Cambridge University Press.

Chinese Labour Statistical Yearbook (1997), Beijing: State Statistical Bureau.

Cook, Sarah and Maurer-Fazio, Margaret (1999), 'Introduction', in *'The Workers' State Meets the Market: Labour in Transition'*, Special Issue, *Journal of Development Studies*, Vol.35, No.3, pp.1–15.

Ding, Daniel Z., Goodall, Keith and Warner, Malcolm (2000)' 'Beyond the Iron Rice Bowl: Whither Chinese HRM?', *International Journal of Human Resource Management*, Vol.11, No.2, pp.217–236.

Ding, Daniel, Z., Lan, Ge and Warner, Malcolm (2001), 'A New Form of Chinese Human Resource Management? Personnel and Labour-management Relations in Chinese Township and Village Enterprises: A Case-study Approach', *Industrial Relations Journal*, Vol..32, No.4, pp.328–43.

Ding, Daniel Z., Lan, Ge and Warner, Malcolm (2002), 'Beyond the State Sector: A Study of HRM in Southern China', Working Paper. Cambridge: Judge Institute of Management, University of Cambridge, 20pp. (forthcoming in *International Studies in Management and Organization*).

Documentation (1999), *China Quarterly*, No.160, p.1106.

Economist, The (2000), 'A Survey of China', 8 April, 18pp.

Economist, The (2002), 'A Survey of China', 15 June, 16pp.

Fairbank, John K. and Goldman, Merle (1998), *China: A New History*. Cambridge, MA: Harvard University Press.

Francis, Corinna B. (1996), 'Reproduction of Danwei Institutional Features in the Context of China's Market Economy: the Case of Haidian District High-Technology Sector', *China Quarterly*, No.147, pp.839–59.

Frazier, Mark K. (2002), *The Making of the Chinese Industrial Workplace: State, Revolution and Labor Management*. Cambridge: Cambridge University Press.

Garnaut, Ross, Song, Ligang, Yao, Yang and Wang Xiaolu (2002), *Private Enterprises in China*. Canberra: Asia Pacific Press.

Goodall, Keith and Warner, Malcolm (1997), 'Human Resources in Sino-Foreign Joint Ventures: Selected Case Studies in Shanghai and Beijing', *International Journal of Human Resource Management*, Vol.8, No.5, pp.569–94.

Guthrie, Douglas (1999), *Dragon in a Three-Piece Suit: The Emergence of Capitalism in China*. Princeton, NJ: Princeton University Press.

Huang, Cen (2000), 'Diaspora Chinese Enterprises in Guangdong Province: Problems and Governmental Responses During the Asian Crisis' in Ip, David, Lever-Tracey, Constance and Tracey, Noel (eds.), *Chinese Business and the Asian Crisis*. Aldershot: Gower, pp.131–46.

ILO, Press Releases (2001), Geneva: International Labour Organization, May.

Ip, David, Lever-Tracey, Constance and Tracey, Noel (eds.) (2000), *Chinese Business and the Asian Crisis*. Aldershot: Gower.

Josephs, Hilary K. (1995), 'Labour Law in a "Socialist Market Economy": the Case of China', *Columbia Journal of Transnational Law*, Vol.23, No.3, pp.561–81.

Kaple, Dorothy (1994), *Dream of a Red Factory: The Legacy of High Stalinism in China*. (Oxford: Oxford University Press).

Korzec, Michael Z.(1992), *Labour and the Failure of Reform in China*. London: Macmillan and New York: St Martin's Press.

Laaksonen, Oiva (1988), *Management in China During and After Mao*. Berlin: de Gruyter.

Lee, Grace M., Wong, Linda and Mok, Ka-Ho (1999), 'The Decline of State-Owned Enterprises in China: Extent and Causes', Occasional Paper, no.2, Hong Kong: City University, Dec., 79pp.

Lu, X. and Perry, Elizabeth (1997), *Danwei: The Changing Chinese Workplace in Historical and Comparative Perspective*. Armonk: NY and London: M.E. Sharpe.

Mabey, Chris, Salaman, Graham and Storey, John (1998), *Human Resource Management: A Strategic Introduction*. Oxford: Blackwell.

Naughton, Barry (1995), *Growing out of the Plan: Chinese Economic Reform 1978–93*. Cambridge: Cambridge University Press.

Newton, Alastair and Subbaraman, Robert (2002), *China: Gigantic Possibilities, Present Realities*. London: Lehman Brothers.

Ng, Sek-Hong and Warner, Malcolm (1998), *China's Trade Union and Management*. London: Macmillan and New York: St Martin's Press.

Nolan, Peter (1995), *China's Rise, Russia's Fall*. London: Macmillan and New York: St Martins Press.

O'Neill, Mark (2002), 'China warns of 20 million urban jobless', *South China Morning Post*, 30 April, p.1.

Pange, Lee (1999), '"Human Resistance or Human Remains?"– How HR management in China must change', *China Staff: The Human Resources Journal for China and Hong Kong*, Vol.V, No.8, July/Aug., pp.8–11.

Poole, Michael (1997), 'Industrial and Labour Relations' in M.Warner (ed.), *IEBM Concise Encyclopedia of Business and Management*. London: International Thomson Business Press, 264–82.

Rowley, Chris (1997), 'Reassessing HRM's Covergence', *Asia Pacific Business Review*, Vol.3, No.4., pp.197–210.

Schurmann, Franz (1966), *Ideology and Organization in Communist China*. Berkeley, CA: University of California Press.

Storey, J. (1992) *Developments in the Management of Human Resources*. Oxford: Oxford University Press.

Takahara, Akio (1992), *The Politics of Wage Policy in Post-Revolutionary China*. London: Macmillan and New York: St Martin's Press.

Verburg, Robert (1996), 'Developing HRM in Foreign-Chinese Joint Ventures', *European Management Journal*, Vol.14, No.5, pp.518–25.

Walder, Andrew G. (1986), *Communist Neo-Traditionalism: Work and Authority in Chinese Industry*. Berkeley, CA: University of California Press.

Warner, Malcolm (1992), *How Chinese Managers Learn*. London: Macmillan and New York: St Martin's Press.

Warner, Malcolm (1993), 'Human Resource Management "with Chinese Characteristics"', *International Journal of Human Resource Management*, Vol.4, No.1, pp.45–65.

Warner, Malcolm (1995), *The Management of Human Resources in Chinese Industry*. London: Macmillan and New York: St Martin's Press.

Warner, Malcolm (1996), 'Chinese Enterprise Reform, Human Resources and the 1994 Labour Law', *International Journal of Human Resource Management*, Vol.7, No.7, pp.779–96.

Warner, Malcolm (1997), 'China's HRM in Transition: Towards Relative Convergence?' *Asia Pacific Business Review*, Vol.3, No.4, pp.19–33.

Warner, Malcolm (ed.) (1999), *China's Managerial Revolution*. London and Portland, OR: Frank Cass.

Warner, Malcolm (ed.) (2000), *Changing Workplace Relations in the Chinese Economy*. London: Macmillan and New York: St Martin's Press.

Warner, Malcolm (2002), 'Globalization, Labour Markets and Human Resources in Asia-Pacific Economies: An Overview', *International Journal of Human Resource Management*, Vol.13, No.3, pp.384–8.

Warner, Malcolm (ed.) (2003) *The Future of Chinese Management*. London: Frank Cass.

Warner, Malcolm and Ng, Sek-Hong (1999), 'Collective contracts in Chinese Enterprises: A New Brand of Collective Bargaining under "Market Socialism"', *British Journal of Industrial Relations*, Vol.37, No.2, pp.295–314.

White, Gordon (1996), 'Chinese Trade Unions in the Transition from Socialism: towards Corporatism or Civil Society?', *British Journal of Industrial Relations*, Vol.34, No.4, pp.433–57.

World Bank (2000), Annual Report, Washington, DC.

HRM in Hong Kong
since 1997

STEPHEN W.K. CHIU and DAVID A. LEVIN

Enterprise-level employment practices were developed in postwar Hong Kong in the context of an open competitive market economy, a colonial regime disinclined to interfere in business decisions or the labour market, and a trade union movement with minimal economic and political clout. We review briefly the principal types of employment systems that emerged within this environment and how changes in the economy, the polity and the labour market impacted on these systems from the late 1970s to the mid-1990s. We then examine how HRM practices in both the private and public sectors[1] have changed since 1997 in response to two critical events occurring that year: the onset of the Asian Financial Crisis and the change of sovereignty over Hong Kong when, after 150 years of British colonial rule, Hong Kong became a Special Administrative Region (SAR) of the Peoples' Republic of China (PRC) in July, 1997. Our discussion section summarizes changes in HRM practices and takes up the issue of convergence in these practices. We consider in the concluding section whether the claim that Hong Kong represents a hybrid case of HRM practices is as applicable today as it was five years ago (Ng and Poon, 1997: 55).

Our review differs from the overview of Hong Kong's HRM in the previous collection in two ways (Ng and Poon, 1997). First, we emphasize macro-trends rather than case studies and refer for this purpose to findings from government-sponsored surveys as well as surveys undertaken by the Hong Kong Institute of Human Resource Management (HKIHRM). Second, we focus on the civil service as well as the private sector. One reason for doing so is that the government is Hong Kong's largest employer. Another is the historical contrast in human resource (HR) policies and practices between the public and private sectors due to the different institutional contexts in which they operate (Levin and Chiu, 2000). A key question is whether the two critical events noted above are bringing about convergence in HRM practices between these two sectors.

CONTEXTUAL FACTORS AND ISSUES

Political and Historical

Hong Kong's export success in manufacturing from the late 1950s to the early 1980s rested on flexibility of manufacturing and competitive prices on the basis of low production costs. Flexibility was inherent in an industrial structure comprised of 'networks of small firms, networking and subcontracting among themselves on an ad hoc basis, following the orders channelled by small firms specializing in export/import' (Castells, 1992: 47–8; 1996: 160–61).

Flexible employment practices accompanied flexible manufacturing practices. Cantonese-owned and managed factories typically divided their jobs into primary and secondary internal labour markets. Those assigned to the primary internal market were likely to be male, to be paid monthly, to enjoy relatively higher employment security and receive fringe benefits such as accommodation and meal allowances. Those assigned to the secondary internal labour market were known as long-term casual workers (*cheung saan-kung*) or casual (temporary) workers (*saan-kung*). They received fewer fringe benefits, their positions were less secure, and they had less chance of promotion than permanent staff. They were more likely to be female and were often paid on a piece-rate basis (Levin and Ng, 1995: 129).

One other distinctive private sector employment system was found in large privately owned British companies, some of prewar origins, in gas, electricity, communications, transport and the dockyards. These companies shared a number of characteristics:

> Western technology, sheltered product markets (some were monopolies), large workplaces, and professional expatriate managers... [they] used labour contractors, apprentices, and employed labour on a permanent or temporary basis [but] their particular characteristics resulted in them adopting a more formal approach to existing practices (England and Rear, 1981: 73).

These employers invested more resources in the training of 'core' employees and designed their personnel practices to encourage these employees to remain with the enterprise by giving them permanent status, placing them on incremental wage scales and providing other benefits including accommodation (England and Rear, 1981: 74). Some established joint consultation bodies.

Although similar in some ways to the large-scale private sector firms, the employment system of the Hong Kong Civil Service differed firstly by offering permanent employment until retirement age for most staff. Second, it had a highly structured internal labour market that was reorganized in the early 1970s by creating an occupation-based system with well-defined ports of entry, career paths, and seniority pay scales linked to occupation and rank. Unionization subsequently spread, especially among white-collar civil servants who were dissatisfied with their occupational pay scales and promotion prospects. In response to the cumulative 'bureaucratic insurgency' of the late 1970s and recognizing that previous arrangements for settling pay and structural problems were no longer working, the Government set up the Standing Commission on Civil Service Salaries and Conditions of Service in January 1979 to advise on matters affecting civil servants (excluding those in the directorate scale and those employed by the judiciary and the disciplined services) (Levin and Chiu, 2000: 145–8). Third, the number of joint consultation committees increased from the late 1970s. Civil Service management has been more tolerant of union representation and participation in these committees than large private sector firms with similar bodies (Levin and Chiu, 1997).

Political power in colonial Hong Kong was formally concentrated in the hands of the Governor, appointed from England, who was advised by a nominated Executive Council. An appointed Legislative Council (LegCo) served as the law-making body. In the post-war period, as in the pre-war, a symbiotic relationship developed between government and key business leaders who were co-opted into consultative policy–advisory networks and LegCo while the trade union movement was largely excluded from this formal political structure. These institutional arrangements combined with the colonial state's belief in the virtues of the self-regulating market which allowed employers a relatively free hand to design their HRM practices within the constraints set by markets, finances and technologies. Employers were able to exercise power over the labour process and employment relations (ER) since the two main trade union federations were numerically weak relative to employment, fragmented and largely powerless at the enterprise, industry and societal levels (Chiu and Levin, 1999; Levin and Chiu, 1993).

While the government avoided intervening in matters concerning trade, the movement of capital and labour, and business decisions, it nevertheless promoted services supportive of business activities. It also expanded its role during the postwar period in the provision of land for development, general and vocational education, and investment in social infrastructure (hospitals, schooling, housing, social welfare) that bear on the maintenance and development of HR. Castells (1992) argues that these measures helped enable manufacturers to remain price competitive through what were in effect wage subsidies. The government affected employment practices more directly through the 1968 Employment Ordinance which has been continuously upgraded and now provides a statutory set of employment benefits for workers including provisions governing the time, manner and place of payment of wages, end of year payment, deductions from wages, protection of female employees from dismissal during maternity leave, provision of rest days, protection against acts of anti-union discrimination, severance payment, long-service payment, sickness allowance, statutory holidays with pay and annual leave with pay.

The framework of political governance began to change in the mid-1980s due to three major political events:

1. The restructuring of LegCo to include some seats filled by elections;
2. The 1984 Sino-British joint declaration under which Hong Kong was to become a SAR under the sovereignty of the PRC from 1 July 1997; and
3. China's drafting of the Basic Law as the mini-constitution under which Hong Kong would be governed after China resumed sovereignty (Levin and Chiu, 1994).

Both the Colonial government and the government of the PRC recognized the importance of Civil Service continuity for the maintenance of stability during the transition to 1997. This did not, however, preclude the Colonial government from instituting changes. In the late 1980s, it outlined a new strategy for public sector reform with stress on financial and management reforms 'aimed at bringing about long-term improvements to the efficiency and management of the public sector, and better service and accountability to the community' (Howlett, 1996: 24).

The greatest uncertainty facing the civil service, however, was what would happen to existing HRM policies and practices after the handover. On the one hand, the key documents relating to Hong Kong's future status – the 1984 Sino-British Joint Declaration and the 1990 Basic Law, the mini-constitution for post-1997 Hong Kong – emphasized the maintenance of continuity in the systems governing civil service HRM practices (with the exception of the privileged treatment accorded to expatriates) including existing systems of recruitment, employment, assessment, discipline, training and management, as well as the maintenance of special bodies for appointment, pay and conditions of service (Chan and Clark, 1991: 165–209). An academic observer predicted, however, that the Mainland Chinese authorities would come to play an 'intimate role in the public personnel process' by setting general personnel policy including recruitment criteria, and wages and training policy as well as by supervising the appointment of senior government personnel, approving their transfer and promotion, and supervising their appraisal (Burns, 1988: 223). As 1997 approached therefore, uncertainty remained over whether existing institutions governing civil service ER would be maintained, altered or scrapped.

Economic

By the 1980s, the manufacturing sector was facing problems of rising labour costs, a growing labour shortage and rising land costs. The opening of China's economy after 1979 to external industrial investment, especially in the newly created special economic zones (SEZs) close to Hong Kong, provided an opportunity for Hong Kong manufacturers to transfer their more land- and labour-intensive industrial activities into Mainland China, especially the Pearl River Delta region. This emergent regional industrial division of labour gave a new lease of life to many Hong Kong manufacturers but at the same time led to de-industrialization within Hong Kong as labour-intensive production processes were relocated to South China and other lower cost areas of Asia. The number working in manufacturing fell from 990,365 in 1981 to 768,121 in 1991 and from 41.3 to 28.2 per cent of the total working population. Employment fell in all Hong Kong's main industries between 1980 and 1990 with the exception of printing (Chiu et al., 1997: 53).

Labour Markets

This 'hollowing out' process continued into the 1990s but it did not result in mass unemployment since the tertiary sector was also expanding rapidly (Ng and Poon, 1997). The proportion of the working population in import/export, retail and wholesale, restaurants and hotels increased from 22.3 to 26.3 per cent between 1986 and 2001; community, social and personal services from 18.4 to 25.5 per cent; and financing, insurance, real estate and business services from 6.4 to 16.1 per cent (Census and Statistics Department [hereafter abbreviated C&S], 1996: 32; C&S, 2001: 55).

1997 Asian Financial Crisis and Reactions

With the onset of the Asian financial crisis in mid-1997 and a higher risk premium in the region, as well as the Hong Kong Government's decision to maintain the existing link between the Hong Kong and US dollar, local interest rates were raised and their volatility increased. Hong Kong banks tightened their credit, causing asset prices, notably of stocks and property, to fall. A wave of speculative attacks on local financial markets during the third quarter of 1998 caused asset prices to plunge even more. As the adverse impact spread, domestic demand fell sharply. Aggravating the economic downturn was a marked decline in exports to recession-hit economies in East Asia, to mainland China and the US (Financial Services Bureau, 1999).

Overall economic growth turned negative in the first quarter of 1998 (for the first time since the third quarter of 1985) and worsened in the ensuing three quarters. Real gross domestic product (GDP) fell by 5.3 per cent in 1998 but then grew at 3 per cent in 1999, a strong 10.5 per cent in 2000, and then just 0.1 per cent in 2001. The average annual rate of change in GDP for the period 1991–2001 was 3.9 per cent. For the five year period 1996–2001 it fell to 2.5 per cent (Chiu and Levin, 2000a; Financial Services Bureau, 2002: 72–3).

CHANGES IN HRM

Major Changes Taking Place

We turn below to a more detailed discussion of the impact of the economic downturn since 1997 on:

1. Employment security,
2. Compensation practices,
3. Skill formation,
4. Work reorganization, and
5. ER.

We discuss the private sector first and then the case of the Civil Service.

The Decline of Employment Security

The Asian Financial Crisis impacted immediately on job security. The seasonally adjusted unemployment rate rose dramatically from 2.1 per cent in September 1997 (quarterly average) to 5.2 per cent by September 1998 and peaked at 6.3 per cent in September 1999. It then declined to 4.5 per cent for the quarter ending March 2001 but subsequently rose from 5.3 per cent in September 2001 to 7 per cent for the first quarter of 2002 and remained at roughly this level for the rest of the year. The underemployment rate rose from 2.6 per cent in the fourth quarter of 2000 to 3.0 per cent in the fourth quarter of 2001 (C&S, various years).

By January 1998 redundancies had been reported across the board – in the hotel, retail and service industries, in the transport and communications sector, the finance and real estate sectors and in manufacturing and construction. Major lay-offs announced during 2001 included QPL International Holdings/ASAT Limited (600 technicians, craft workers and clerks in March), Triumph International (Hong Kong) (400 craft workers in July), a bus company (500 drivers in July), KK supermarket (525 staff in June), The Bank of China (Hong Kong) (450 clerks and elementary workers in September), ASAT Ltd (about 600 in July) and PCCW (506 from senior to elementary occupations in December). Major redundancies announced in the first three months of 2002 included Phoenix TV (over 400 in January), Motorola Semiconductor Hong Kong Ltd. (700–800 engineers and employees from production and business development in January), and PCCW (858 in March). The effects of the economic downturn on employment security are reflected in the rise in the number of claims (alleged breaches of contractual employment terms or statutory provisions) involving termination of contract/dismissal that were handled by the Labour Relations Division of the Labour Department from 20,494 in 1997 to 30,204 in 1998 (Commissioner for Labour, various years).

A more detailed picture of the effects of the economic downturn on employment security by industry and occupation is available from a government-commissioned survey, based on a representative household sample, carried out during April to June 2000 (C&S, 2000). Some 538,100 employed persons or 18.3 per cent of the total of about 3.12 million employed were affected by what the survey labelled 'corporate consolidation' in 1998 and 1999. By industry, 24.9 per cent of the employed population in construction and 21.3 per cent in manufacturing were affected by corporate consolidation compared with a low of 14.5 per cent of those working in community, social and personal services. By occupational category, the group with the highest proportion affected by corporate consolidation were craft and related workers (24 per cent) and plant and machine operators and assemblers (21.2 per cent). Managers, professionals and associate professionals were less affected (16.7 per cent).

A follow-up survey question asked about the nature of this impact. As shown in Table 1, of those reporting an impact, some 12.1 per cent indicated having been laid off/dismissed and 12.6 per cent were facing the risk of being laid off/dismissed. Also worth noting is the high proportion (40.6 per cent) reporting having to work for more flexible/longer hours. This suggests downsizing may have been accompanied by heavier workloads for those who remained employed.

TABLE 1

EMPLOYED PERSONS AFFECTED BY CORPORATE CONSOLIDATION
IN THE ECONOMY IN 1998 AND 1999

Type of impact	No. ('000)	%
More flexible/longer working hours	218.5	40.6
Salary/wage cuts	179.9	33.4
Slackwork	81.9	15.2
Reduction in fringe benefits	80.2	14.9
Facing the risk of being laid off/dismissed	68.1	12.6
Had ever been laid off/dismissed	65.3	12.1
Other	19.3	3.6
Overall	538.1	100.0

Note: multiple answers were allowed

Source: Census and Statistics Department, Hong Kong. *Thematic Household Survey Report No. 1: Employment Concerns and Training Needs* (Printing Department, 2000), p.59.

The impact on employment security is also suggested by the response to a question in this survey about the challenges/problems faced by their current industry. Most frequently cited was keen competition among companies within the industry (31.1 per cent) followed by corporate downsizing (26.1 per cent) and contraction of business (21.9 per cent). When asked about challenges/problems faced by their current occupation category, some 20.6 per cent mentioned reduction in the number of posts. These two findings suggest that a significant minority of the employed perceived themselves to be at risk of losing their job.

Compensation Practices

Corporate consolidation impacted immediately on pay levels and other benefits for workers. Trade unions reported being swamped with workers' inquiries about labour laws and with complaints about employers forcing employees to accept cuts in pay and benefits (as well as extending their work hours) (*South China Morning Post* [hereafter abbreviated SCMP], 1998).[2]

The April–June 2000 government survey of the impact of corporate consolidation on employees found that about one-third of the employed had experienced pay cuts while 14.9 per cent reported a reduction in fringe benefits (Table 1). The most frequently cited item, in response to a question about challenges/problems faced by current occupation category, was salary/wage cuts (28.9 per cent). The number of claims handled by the Labour Relations Division of the Labour Department over non-payment/deduction of wages not surprisingly rose, from 4,303 cases in 1997 to 6,146 cases in 1998, accounting for

20.4 per cent of all claims. Their number continued to rise to reach 7,612 in 2000 (26.6 per cent of all claims in that year).

Another change appears to be an increase in the use of various types of incentive pay schemes. According to a 1994 HKIHRM survey, 72.1 per cent of responding companies reported having an incentive pay scheme with the most frequently mentioned type of scheme a discretionary bonus (51.6 per cent for managerial/professional, 46 per cent for clerical/supervisory and 34 per cent for manual/technician). In the September 2001 HKIHRM survey, the proportion having incentives schemes had risen to 78 per cent (of 186 responding companies). The individual 'performance bonus' was most common for managerial/ professional (72.2 per cent) followed by clerical/supervisory (60.4 per cent) and manual/technician (46.5 per cent). Some 24.3 per cent of companies reported having a group bonus for managerial/professionals. Just over a third (34 per cent) of companies reported having a stock option/share scheme for managerial/professionals compared with 16 per cent for clerical/supervisory and 9 per cent for manual/technician. Sixteen out of 183 responding companies had a flexi-benefit scheme (Tang et al., 1996: 43–5; Cheung, 2001: 37–41).

An HKIHRM 2002 Hong Kong Pay Trend Survey carried out in early 2002 and covering 40 large companies and 56,000 workers who had their salary reviewed in January found that 97 per cent of all employees had their salaries frozen for 2002. Twenty-seven companies reported an across the board salary freeze while three cut pay by 2 per cent. Ten recorded a less than 1 per cent overall increase in salary. This survey also found with respect to bonuses that 21 firms operated a non-guaranteed bonus paying policy during January and February, covering 32 per cent of total employee sample. Some companies have proposed scrapping the customary year-end double pay and replacing it by a business and individual performance-linked discretionary bonus. Wharf New T&T announced in February, 2002, that middle and senior staff would have their 13-month double pay converted to a performance-linked bonus while basic rank staff would have an option to choose a contractual-bound double pay or a performance linked bonus (HKIHRM, 2002a). The Hong Kong Shanghai Banking Corporation cancelled the year-end bonus in 2001 and adopted a performance-linked discretionary bonus (HKIHRM, 2002b).[3]

Skill Formation

HKIHRM surveys find that from 70 to 75 per cent of responding companies in 1994 and 2001 reported having a training and development policy but these findings are not representative of employers as a whole (Tang et al., 1996; Cheung, 2001). A more accurate current picture is available from the government's survey in 2000 of establishments' manpower training and job skills requirements. This survey found that out of 265,163 establishments surveyed, only 9.5 per cent had training plans (and a similar percentage a training budget). The industry with the highest proportion of establishments having training plans was electricity and gas (41.7 per cent), followed by construction (23.5 per cent) and financing, insurance, real estate and business services (17.3 per cent). The industries least likely to have a training plan include manufacturing (only 6.6 per cent of establishments), transport, storage and communications (7.2 per cent) and wholesale, retail and import/export trades, restaurants and hotels (7.8 per cent). Size of establishment is strongly correlated with whether an establishment has a training plan and training budget. Of the 4,321 large establishments in the government's survey, 55.4 per cent reported having training plans and 46.1 per cent having a training budget compared with 25 and 22.9 per cent respectively for medium-sized establishments and 6.6 and 7.0 per cent respectively for small firms.

Work Reorganization

It is necessary to infer from fragmentary pieces of information what trends are occurring in work reorganization. One indirect source of evidence is findings from the 2000 Census and Statistics survey asking employed persons about changes experienced in their job requirements during the previous three years. Substantial numbers reported increasing use of computer and machinery/equipment (20.1 per cent), higher intensity of work (19.2 per cent), skill upgrading (14.5 percent), job straddling/multi-skilling (14.2 per cent), higher academic qualification (11.2 per cent) and higher/multiple language skills (5.8 per cent) (Table 2). This seems to indicate that employees are being expected to work harder, upgrade their skills, and become more functionally flexible.

There are substantial differences by industry. Increasing use of computer and machinery/equipment was mentioned by 32.1 per cent of those in financing, insurance, real estate and business services, 22.2 per cent of those in manufacturing, to a low of 16.6 per cent of those in transport, storage and communication. The industry variation for the item higher intensity of work ranged from a high of 23.2 per cent of those in construction to a low of 16.4 per cent for those employed in community, social and personal services. Skill upgrading ranged from a high of 19.4 per cent in financing, insurance, real estate and business services to a low 11 per cent in whole, retail and import/export, restaurants and hotels. Job-straddling/multi-skilling

TABLE 2

EMPLOYED PERSONS BY CHANGE IN JOB REQUIREMENTS
IN THE PAST THREE YEARS

Type of change in job requirement	No. ('000)	%
More flexible/longer working hours	789.6	26.9
Increasing use of computer & machinery/equipment	589.2	20.1
Higher intensity of work	562.9	19.2
Skill upgrading	425.7	14.5
Job straddling/multi-skilling	416.1	14.2
Higher academic qualification	327.6	11.2
Higher/multiple language skills	169.4	5.8
Others	32.1	1.1
No change	632.2	21.6
Don't know	8.4	0.3

Source: Census and Statistics Department, Hong Kong. *Thematic Household Survey Report No. 1: Employment Concerns and Training Needs* (Printing Department, 2000), pp.48–9.

was highest among those in construction (19.7 per cent) and lowest among those in transport, storage and communication (11.6 per cent). Higher academic qualification was mentioned by 17.3 per cent in financing, insurance, real estate and business services followed by 12.3 per cent of those employed in community, social and personal services. Higher/multiple language skills was above the overall average for wholesale, retail, and import/export, restaurants and hotels sector.

Another relevant question from this survey asked employed persons about the challenge/problems faced by current occupation category. After salary/wage cuts, the next three items in terms of frequency cited all suggest work reorganization of some kind: higher job requirements (21.4 per cent), reduction in the number of posts (20.6 per cent) and increasing use of computer and machinery/equipment (18.8 per cent). A follow-up question asked whether they could meet the change in job requirements comfortably. Although relatively few reported being unable to meet the change in job requirements, over three-fourths reported being able to 'just meet' the change in job requirements.

The importance of work reorganization is also reflected in two findings from the HKIPM 2001 survey. The first concerns the rationale for having training and development policies. In the survey, the importance of factors shaping the companies' training and development activities was assessed using a 3-point scale (with 1=low and 3=high). The highest mean importance rating was given to response to product changes (2.6) followed by response to technological changes/changes in workplace equipment (2.5), response to organization changes/re-engineering (2.4), expansion of skill range of employee (2.3), and to fill the current skill/language gap (2.3) (Cheung, 2001: 25). This suggests the importance of the impact of work reorganization as a motivation for skills development.

The second finding concerns respondents' identification of change in importance of 19 HR activities in the previous three years. Majorities of the 170 valid returns considered five items to be more important: training and development management (60 per cent), organization change (56 per cent), changes in work organization (52.9 per cent), manpower planning (52.4 per cent) and performance appraisal (50.6 per cent). Majorities considered the following activities to be less important: formulating and monitoring other HR policies (51.8 per cent), job analysis and evaluation (52.9 per cent), workplace safety, health and welfare (62.9 per cent), discipline/grievance management (61.8 per cent), payroll and benefits administration (61.2 per cent), HR outsourcing strategy (62.9 per cent), and management of HR vendors (66.5 per cent) (Cheung, 2001: 46). These results would seem to indicate that the traditional functions of the HR manager are being superseded by more responsibility for facilitating organization restructuring. The decreasing importance of HR outsourcing and management of HR vendors may reflect the impact of declining voluntary turnover since the Asian crisis.

Employment Relations

Given the government's voluntarist approach to ER, it has been difficult for trade unions interested in bargaining collectively to gain employer recognition for this purpose. For this reason, several trade unionists elected to LegCo in the mid-1990s supported a bill before the handover that would establish the right to collective bargaining. The Employee's Rights to Representation, Consultation and Collective Bargaining Ordinance passed LegCo and was gazetted on 30 June 1997, the last day of colonial rule. Had it remained in effect, it would have introduced a major change to the voluntarist system of ER by providing a legal mechanism whereby trade unions could represent workers in wage bargaining. It would have potentially affected 900,000 employees working in enterprises with 50 or more employees.

The pre-handover LegCo was disbanded on 30 June 1997 and replaced by a Provisional LegCo which excluded those from the democratic camp. On 16 July 1997, the Provisional LegCo passed a bill to suspend until 31 October 1997, three labour bills passed by the pre-handover LegCo, including the collective bargaining bill. A government review was undertaken of these three ordinances and, on the basis of this review, the matter was then considered by the Labour

Advisory Board (LAB), a tripartite body appointed by the Chief Executive to advise the Commissioner for Labour on labour matters. A majority of the LAB members deemed it inappropriate to bring the collective bargaining ordinance into operation. With this advice, the Administration decided to seek repeal of the collective bargaining ordinance. In October 1997, the Provisional LegCo passed the Employment and Labour Relations (Miscellaneous Amendments) Ordinance which repealed the collective bargaining ordinance (SCMP, 1997a, 1997b).

Another post-handover development related to ER has been occasional instances of organized resistance to mass lay-offs and attempts by large private firms to cut wages or benefits following the Asian crisis. This is particularly the case in large firms where labour was relatively well organized. One illustration is Hong Kong Telecom. In mid-September 1998, Hong Kong Telecom (which had close to 15,000 employees at the time, probably Hong Kong's largest private employer) announced it would cut wages for its 13,800 staff by 10 per cent for one year, with effect from 1 November, and that those who refused to accept the cut would be sacked. Staff unions first proposed that the pay cut be suspended for a year but the company rejected this. Faced with the threat of industrial action by the staff unions as well as an outpouring of public criticism over a pay cut – the company was sitting on HK$15 billion (about US$2 billion) in cash and had just received HK$6.7 billion in compensation from the government for surrendering its monopoly on international calls – the company backed down by withdrawing its original proposal and reopened discussions with staff. In mid-November, the company came up with a modified proposal, pledging no salary reduction and no forced redundancy for at least 13 months but replacing the existing bonus scheme for staff earning more than HK$10,000 a month with a new profit-related bonus scheme, under which profits would have to rise by at least 3 per cent for workers to receive a half-month bonus). Following opposition and further negotiations, the company offered a revised version under which the majority of workers would receive a quarter of their month's bonus as long as the company registered growth in operating profit in the coming year. All except about 100 employees eventually accepted the new pay package (Chiu and Levin, 2002).[4]

Civil Service Reform

Employment in the Civil Service has traditionally been considered an 'iron rice bowl' (jobs for life), but public sector reform and more recently civil service reform have begun to change this practice. With the government running a large deficit, pressure mounted to privatize government activities. One example is hiving-off estate maintenance and management from the Housing Authority, affecting some 9,000 caretakers, managers, and technicians working at the 165 public rental estates. In August 1999, the Alliance of Housing Department Staff Unions threatened a week-long strike over being excluded from a working group studying the privatization and a taskforce that would approve changes. Perhaps in response to this union protest, the Chief Executive, in his policy address in October 1999, tried to assure civil servants that the Administration would attempt to avoid redundancies 'as far as possible' when pushing ahead with civil service reforms and cost-cutting targets through inter-departmental redeployment, secondment and employee retraining (SCMP, 1999a, 1999b).

In March 1999, the Civil Service Bureau published a consultation document proposing a major restructuring of civil service employment practices that would make the Civil Service operate more flexibly. As a result of feedback received during the first stage of consultation with staff, the government drew up more detailed proposals for detailed discussion with the Staff Sides and department/grade management through working groups with staff representatives. Of the many reforms implemented, only those concerning entry and exit and pay are reviewed here (Civil Service Bureau, 2002a).

In June 2000, the government introduced a new entry system of terms of appointment for new recruits in line with its aim of increasing flexibility of the appointment system. Under the new system, most recruits are appointed initially on probationary terms and/or agreement terms for a specified period before being considered for appointment on prevailing permanent terms. Departmental and grade management is responsible for monitoring and managing probationers and agreement officers.[5] In July 2000, the government introduced a Voluntary Retirement (VR) Scheme to enable existing staff of 59 grades with surplus staff (or anticipated surplus) to retire voluntarily with pension benefits and compensations. At the close of the three-month option period in October 2000, about 11,000 applications were received and about 9,400 were approved. A management initiated retirement scheme was introduced in September 2000 for directorate civil servants on pensionable and permanent terms. The scheme is viewed as a 'management tool that allows the injection of new blood by creating space in the directorate ranks, and helps to maintain the quality of senior management'.

With respect to pay, the Administration commissioned the Standing Commission on Civil Service Salaries and Conditions of Service to conduct a review of starting salaries in the Civil Service in 1998. The results showed that civil service entry pay had outstripped that in the private sector. To bring the Civil Service closer in line with the labour market, benchmarks for most of the 12 Qualification Groups of the civilian grades were lowered by 6 to 31 per cent and those for disciplined grades by 3 to 17 percent. The new benchmarks and starting salaries took effect on 1 April 2000 for new recruits and serving staff on transfer.

During the first two years of the Asian crisis, pay levels for serving civil servants were frozen. In 2001, civil servants were given a pay rise following the upturn of the economy in 2000. As the economy deteriorated towards the latter half of 2001, however, legislators from the business sector pressured the government for a review of the pay system and pay levels. In December 2001, for example, the leader of a pro-business political party stated in LegCo that 'many people have criticized the remuneration and fringe benefits of civil servants as being far better than those of employees of comparable ranks in the private sector' and asked the government what it intended to do about this. In his reply to this question, the Secretary for the Civil Service noted that the government was in the process of drawing up proposals on this matter and that its 'initial thinking is to cover the total remuneration package, including salaries and fringe benefits, in the exercise' (Government Information Bulletin, 2001).[6] On 18 December 2001, the government announced it had decided to carry out a comprehensive review of the pay policy and system for the Civil Service covering the fundamental principles underpinning civil service pay policy (especially the principle of broad comparability with private sector pay), the methodology for determining pay levels in the civil service, the rationalization of the grading structure and salary structure of some 400 grades and over 1,000 ranks in the civil service, an improved and more flexible salary system, and the annual pay adjustment mechanism. A Task Force was formed in January 2002 to conduct the review.

PWC Consulting Hong Kong Limited was appointed by the Task Force to carry out a study on the latest developments in civil service pay administration in five countries: Australia, Canada, New Zealand, Singapore and the UK. It submitted its Interim Report to the Task Force in April 2002 (PWC Consultancy, 2002). The Task Force then presented its own preliminary findings and observations based on the consultant's report and issued a *Consultation Paper on the Review of Civil Service Pay Policy and System* in the same month. The Task Force asserted in this Consultation Paper that it believed 'the community would like to see a thorough rethinking of the basic principles of the existing pay system 'of the Civil Service'. It is very likely that some major changes will be made to the existing pay policies, system and structure but the exact forms these take will depend on the reaction of civil servants and the wider public to them as well as the future financial situation of the government.

The evidence discussed above suggests that HRM practices in Hong Kong have been shifting away from organization-oriented to more market-oriented practices or to put it slightly differently, from rule-bound forms of personnel administration to more flexible forms in the broader context of the Asian financial crisis and, in the case of the public sector, increasingly stringent budget constraints rather than from intervention by Mainland authorities. These changes, as summarized in Table 3, are thus most relevant to the public sector and in large-scale firms in the private sector. Declining employment security, pay and bonuses increasingly linked to performance rather than seniority and the outsourcing of some HRM functions are among the more important examples of these changes.

Possible Changes in the Immediate Future[7]

HRM practices that may spread in the near future include the outsourcing of HRM functions (recruitment, payroll), the greater use of software for such functions as employee selection, more flexible benefit packages (in large companies), encouragement of early retirement of long-serving employees, and employer branding in order to better align employees with the company's mission. Retention of

TABLE 3

ASSESSMENT OF HRM CHANGES AND CONTINUITIES

Dimensions	Presence	Change
1. Rules: adherence to	%	+
2. Behaviour: common values and norms	%	+
3. Key managers: personnel/specialists v. line/general	%	+
4. Personnel selection	✓	+
5. Payment systems	%	+
6 Work conditions: harmonized	✗	0
7. Contracts: individual v. standardized	✓	0
8. In-house training	%	0
9. Right to hire and fire	✓	0
10. Strategic role for personnel manager	✗	0

Key: (*Practice*)
　　✓ present
　　% present to some degree
　　✗ not present

　　(*Degree of change in past 4 years*)
　　++ major change
　　+ change
　　0 none

Source: Adapted from Storey (1992).

valued employees is likely to be given greater priority than recruitment and selection. At the same time, firms are also likely to pursue downsizing vigorously in order to cut cost and focus on core operations. Relocation of back office functions to low-cost areas such as China is also likely to spread even in the service sector.

Compliance issues are likely to become more salient in future as a result of new legislation. Under the Mandatory Provident Schemes Ordinance, first enacted in 1995 and put into effect in 1998, a number of employers (typically small companies) have been fined for failing to pay required Mandatory Provident Fund (MPF) contributions for their employees or for failing to enrol an employee under their employ for at least 60 days in an MPF scheme. There are also compliance issues relating to sex, ethnicity and age. The passage of equal opportunity legislation and the creation of the Women's Commission have been accompanied by increasing awareness of gender discrimination in the workplace as well as discrimination against minority groups and age discrimination. There have been demands from concerned community groups to extend equal opportunity legislation to these other social status categories. Yet another area where compliance issues will arise is workplace surveillance. A Code of Practice on Monitoring and Personal Data Privacy drafted by the Privacy Commissioner for Personal Data was issued in March 2002, for a three-month consultation.

DISCUSSION

Why Changes Have Occurred

We can also view changes and their causes from the perspective of the main HRM challenges facing businesses. A 1996 survey report on HRM in Hong Kong identified four challenges facing business and human resource professionals in the context of the 'more turbulent and tougher environment' of the 1990s:

1. Intensified business competition from newly industrialized countries in Asia as well as the PRC;
2. The outflow of managerial and professional talent due to rising anxieties as 1997 approached;
3. High labour turnover in the context of a tight labour market that added to recruitment and other employment costs; and
4. Growing tensions between employers and employees due to the 'rising expectations from the workforce on issues like compensation and benefits, equality and rights' and better organized and visible union activities (Tang et al., 1996: 7; see also Enright et al., 1997: 204–12).

The challenge of improving labour productivity has become even greater since the Asian financial crisis as the business environment grows more uncertain and complex due to globalization and liberalization of trade and investment, the rapid development of information technology and e-commerce, and China's accession in late 2001 to the World Trade Organization. Cost controls remains a high priority for many firms. One evolving strategy for raising productivity appears to involve a combination of downsizing with greater demands on employees (longer working hours, skill upgrading requirements). One example of greater demands on employees is that front-line workers in banking are now expected to be more customer oriented and to be able to market a greater range of products. Another strategy, following that already practised by manufacturing, is to relocate low-value added service-related activities to mainland China as at least one bank and one airline have already done.

The challenge of loss of managerial and professional talent and high labour turnover has by contrast diminished as anxieties over the possibility of radical changes to Hong Kong's way of life after the political handover have subsided. Nor is high labour turnover any longer a major problem as job opportunities began to dry up with the onset of economic recession. On the other hand, tensions between employers and employees have been exacerbated by the Asian financial crisis as employers downsized and sought to reduce compensation without prior consultation with employees in many cases.

Convergence or Divergence

On the issue of convergence between public and private sector HRM practices as well as between local and overseas practices, the evidence suggests this has indeed been occurring. Public sector reforms over the past decade, civil service reforms since 1999, and the more recently proposed comprehensive review of the civil service pay system provide ample evidence that the Hong Kong government is searching for 'best practices' in the private sector as well as overseas to achieve a leaner and more efficient government.[8] The reasons for doing so are both financial and political in that they reflect an attempt to curb the long-run trend of growth in public expenditure and to meet the increasing demands for accountability and value for money from the LegCo and the wider community. The huge budget deficit announced by the Financial Secretary in March 2002 and the long time anticipated before the budget will be back in balance is likely to add further pressure on the government to find ways to maximize output while mininizing costs, that is, to follow the lead of the private sector in finding creative ways to adapt to a more complex and tougher environment. More generally, as noted above, HRM practices in Hong Kong have been undergoing a transformation from organization-oriented to more market-oriented practices as part of the process of enhancing flexibility in the use of HR. In this respect, Hong Kong HRM practices are converging towards those common in large firms in the US and Britain.

Key Issues for HRM

Even though there is no longer an overall labour shortage, this does not mean there are no skill shortages. At the managerial level, there are problems of developing leadership skills, especially at the middle management level where training tends to focus on skill development in employees' current roles rather than preparing successors for senior management levels. Training for line managers in performance management is likely to become more critical given cost consciousness of companies and declining tolerance for poor and average performers.

Another issue that HRM companies will have to pay more attention to is improving communication with employees. This may occur in order to forestall ER problems and to understand better what motivates employees.[9]

Surveys of HR managers' own perceptions about what they consider to be the most important HR activities in the future are also relevant. The HKIHRM 1994 and 2001 surveys asked respondents an open-ended question about the three most important HR activities in the next three years. Of the 545 responses in the 1994 survey (out of 192 valid returns), 21.3 per cent considered training the most important HR activity in the next three years, followed by organization and management development (14.3 per cent), recruitment/retention (12.5 per cent), manpower planning/succession planning, career planning (12.3 per cent) (Tang, 1996: 53–4). Of the total of 468 responses from 158 valid returns in the 2001 survey, 16.9 per cent of the responses concerned training and development/career development, 10.9 per cent change management, and 10.7 per cent retention of talent and high calibre (Cheung, 2001: 50–1). Training and management development are likely to continue to rank among the top three activities considered most important in future.

Implications for Theory Development

In their focus on the impact of de-industrialization and recommercialization on HK's HRM prior to 1997, Ng and Poon (1997: 55) argued that Hong Kong represented the emergence of a hybrid case, 'composed of both converging patterns analogous to the West, Japan and other Asian Societies, as well as divergent practices which are probably distinctive to Hong Kong'. In particular, an Asian approach inspired by a Confucian heritage had been found resilient vis-à-vis market forces generated from the restructuring process. While we agree that a culturally specific set of HRM practices is still discernible in Hong Kong, the dominant trend since 1997 has been to converge towards a model that is not too dissimilar from the Anglo-American model, with its concomitant emphasis on performance and the bottom line. Since 1997, most large-scale enterprises that previously exhibited many traits of a 'Confucian' internal labour market have already instituted changes to enhance their flexibility and performance. The stability in employment highlighted by the previous review appears to be evaporating in the face of the continuing deep recession after the Asian financial crisis. Even the public sector, the quintessential model employer, is pursuing a wide ranges of changes in its HRM practices that, if successfully implemented, will radically transform the face of its HRM.

The Hong Kong case is certainly important for the broader theoretical understanding of the relationship between cultural values and their structural and institutional environment in a small open economy that is highly sensitive to turbulence in the external environment. The regulatory framework, the balance of power between labour and management, and the overall structure and pace of economic growth, all mediated the effects of culture. We still do not have a good mapping of all these relations in Hong Kong because the lack of good data necessarily limits our understanding. We do not yet have a good survey of enterprise-level HRM practices that covers a reasonable range of firms in sufficient numbers. Case studies are also relatively scarce. Moreover, we also need a better understanding of the social construction of HRM practices through the activities of professional organizations, management training institutes, and the diffusion of international best practices.

CONCLUSION

We are not arguing that complete convergence, 'wiping out' any cultural traits, will occur in the near future but we anticipate that Hong Kong is likely to be the economy to move the fastest in this direction (see Rowley and Benson, 2002). Owing to its colonial past and the dominance of laissez-faire ideology, the local labour market has always been the most lightly regulated relative to other Asian economies (Chiu and Levin, 1999). Global and market-driven changes are therefore much easier to institutionalize in Hong Kong. This accounts for the swift response of the labour market to industrial restructuring (Chiu et al., 1997) and is also the reason why most of the changes documented in this study could be traced to the pre-1997 era and were identified in the previous review. Nevertheless, they have all been pushed to new levels since 1997. Perhaps an unmistakable continuity amidst all these changes is the increasing emphasis on HRM in competitive strategies, be it cost-cutting labour utilization, flexible deployment of HR, and the transformation of internal HRM in face of the erosion of a stable internal labour markets. The challenge for HR professionals and academics alike is therefore to understand the role of HRM in sustaining the competitive and performance advantage of the firm in these turbulent times.

NOTES

1. We focus in this article on the Civil Service as one major component of the 'public sector'. The latter includes three types of body: government bureaux and departments (the Civil Service), subvented organizations, and statutory bodies of which the government is the shareholder. Terms and conditions of employment for those in subvented organizations are generally modelled on those of civil servants although without some of the fringe benefits.

2. In response to complaints that some employers were imposing wage reductions on their employees without their consent, the Labour Department drafted guidelines which were approved by the Labour Advisory Board in October 1998 and issued as *Guidelines on What to Do if Wage Reductions and Retrenchments are Unavoidable*. These guidelines state that employers should notify staff at least 7 to 14 days before any pay-cut decisions. They called on employers who cut pay to give written guarantees that if any lay-offs follow, severance pay will be calculated on the original, higher salary before the cut. The guidelines also recommended that higher-rank staff should receive proportionately higher pay cuts than lower-paid staff..

3. A comparison of the HKIHRM 1994 and 2001 surveys suggests that two compensation-related practices have remained largely unchanged. First, the method of determining pay for managerial/professional, clerical/supervisory and manual/technical continues to be primarily a unilateral decision by management or negotiations with individual employees; relatively few cases involve negotiations with trade unions or staff associations. Second, a substantial majority of firms continues to review wages and salaries annually although there was a drop in the number doing so every 6 months.

4. Another example of strong union opposition to pay cuts leading to management concessions occurred at Cathay Pacific Airways during 1999–2000. Disputes between the management and the unions flared up again in 2000 extending to 2002 over a number of issues including rostering, overtime pay compensation, the two-tiered pay system (pilots joining Cathay after 1993 are on a lower pay scale), plans for retirement-age captains whose contracts are extended to be put on the lower pay scale and salary increases (SCMP, 2001a; 2001b). This dispute remains unresolved as of June 2002.

5. In July 2001 the Executive Council approved the design principles of a new Civil Service Provident Fund Scheme in place of the pension system for recruits offered appointments to the Civil Service on or after 1 June 2000 under the new entry terms and when they subsequently progress to permanent terms of appointment.

6. At about the same time, a motion was put to the LegCo on reviewing the pay adjustment mechanisms of publicly-funded and statutory bodies. In January 2002, the government announced it was hiring a consultant to determine if the pay packages of about 100 senior executives of nine statutory bodies were in line with the median pay of their private-sector counterparts.

7. We are grateful to Ms Selma Lai for sharing with us her knowledge of current HRM

challenges facing large firms in Hong Kong.

8. For example, in the Interim Report released by the Task Force on the Review of Civil Service Pay Policy and System in April 2002, the systems of civil service pay of Australia, Canada, New Zealand, Singapore, and the United Kingdom were reviewed. See http://www.info.gov.hk/jsscs/en/report/tf/interim/content.htm.

9. Tensions in the Civil Service have risen as a result of a decision by the Chief Executive in Council on 28 May 2002, that civil service pay be reduced by 4.42% for the directorate and upper salary band, 1.64% for the middle salary band, and 1.58% cent for the lower salary band, with effect from 1 October 2002. The Government had to seek legislative approval for this pay reduction through the 'Public Officers Pay Adjustment Bill', which was not supported by civil service unions, because the contractual employment arrangements between the Government and most serving civil servants do not contain an explicit provision authorizing the Government to reduce pay. For details of the Government's rationale for this, see the 'Speech by SCS on Second Reading of the Public Officers Pay Adjustment Bill' (Civil Service Bureau, 2002b).

REFERENCES

Burns, John P. (1988), 'The Chinese Civil Service System' in I. Scott and J.P. Burns (eds.), *The Hong Kong Civil Service and its Future*. Hong Kong: Oxford University Press, pp.204–26.

Castells, Manuel (1992), 'Four Asian Tigers with a Dragon Head: A Comparative Analysis of the State, Economy, and Society in the Asian Pacific Rim' in Richard P. Appelbaum and Jeffrey Henderson (eds.), *States and Development in the Asian Pacific Rim*. [??? 2]Sage, pp.33–70.

Castells, Manuel (1996), *The Information Age*. Vol.1. *The Rise of the Network Society*. London: Blackwell.

Census and Statistics Department (1996), *1996 Population by census: Summary Results*. Hong Kong: Government Printer.

Census and Statistics Department (1998), *Quarterly Report of Employment, Vacancies and Payroll Statistics*. Hong Kong: Printing Department.

Census and Statistics Department (2000), *Thematic Household Survey Report*, No. 1. *Employment Concerns and Training Needs*. Hong Kong: Printing Department.

Census and Statistics Department (2001), *2001 Population Census: Summary Results*. Hong Kong: Printing Department.

Census and Statistics Department (various years), *Quarterly Report on General Household Survey*. Hong Kong: Printing Department.

Chan, Ming K. and Clark, David J. (eds.) (1991), *The Hong Kong Basic Law: Blueprint for 'Stability and Prosperity' under Chinese Sovereignty?* Hong Kong: Hong Kong University Press.

Cheung, Sara F.Y. (2001), *Human Resource Management Strategies and Practices in Hong Kong*. Research Report 2001. Hong Kong: Hong Kong Institute of Human Resource Management.

Chiu, S.W.K. and Levin, D.A. (1999), 'The Organization of Industrial Relations in Hong Kong: Economic, Political and Sociological Perspectives' in *Organization Studies*, Vol.20, No.2, pp.293–322.

Chiu, S.W.K. and Levin, D.A. (2000a), 'Unemployment in Hong Kong: Causes, Characteristics and Policy Measures' in J.S. Lee (ed.), *Recent Developments in Involuntary Unemployment in Asian Countries: Causes and Policies*. National Central University, Research Center for Taiwan Economic Development, pp.119–67.

Chiu, S.W.K. and Levin, D.A. (2002), 'Hong Kong in the Twenty-First Century: Challenges and Opportunities for Labour' in T. Hanami (ed.), *Universal Wisdom Through Globalization*. Tokyo: The Japan Institute of Labour, pp.318–329.

Chiu, Stephen W.K., Ho, K.C. Ho and Lui, Tai-lok (1997), *City-States in the Global Economy: Industrial Restructuring in Hong Kong and Singapore*. Boulder: Westview Press.

Civil Service Bureau (2002a), 'Civil Service Reform', accessed at www.csb.gov.hk/hkgcsb.

Civil Service Bureau (2002b), 'First and Second Readings of Public Officers Pay Adjustment Bill', accessed at www.csb.gov.hk/hkgcsb.

Commissioner for Labour (various years), *Report of the Commissioner for Labour*. Hong Kong: Printing Department.

England, Joe and Rear, John (1981), *Industrial Relations and Law in Hong Kong*. Hong Kong: Oxford University Press.

Enright, Michael J., Scott, Edith E. and Dodwell, David (1997), *The Hong Kong Advantage*. Hong Kong: Oxford University Press.

Financial Services Bureau, Economic Analysis Division (1999), *1999 Economic Prospects*. Hong Kong: Printing Department.

Financial Services Bureau, Economic Analysis Division (2002), *2002 Economic Prospects*. Hong Kong: Printing Department.

Government Information Bulletin (2001), 'LCQ3: Civil Service Pay Policy and System', 12 Dec.

Hong Kong Institute of Human Resource Management (2002a), News *Digest*. 10 Jan.

Hong Kong Institute of Human Resource Management (2002b), News *Digest*. 5 March.

Howlett, Bob (ed.) (1996), *Hong Kong 1996: A Review of 1995*. Hong Kong: Government Printer.

Levin, D.A. and S.W.K. Chiu (1993), 'Dependent Capitalism, a Colonial State, and Marginal Unions: the Case of Hong Kong' in Stephen Frenkel (ed.), *Organized Labor in the Asia-Pacific Region: A Comparative Study of Trade Unionism in Nine Countries*. Ithaca, NY: ILR Press, pp.187–222.

Levin, D.A. and Chiu, S.W.K. (1994), 'Decolonization without Independence: Political Change and Trade Unionism in Hong Kong' in J.R. Niland, R.D. Lansbury and C. Verevis (eds.), *The Future of Industrial Relations: Global Change and Challenges*. Thousand Oaks: Sage Publications, pp.329–48.

Levin, D.A. and Chiu, S.W.K. (1997), 'Empowering Labour? The origins and practice of joint consultation in Hong Kong' in R. Markey and J. Monat (eds.), *Innovation and Employee Participation Through Works Councils: International Case Studies*. Aldershot: Avebury, pp.280–306.

Levin, D.A. and Chiu, S.W.K. (2000), 'Bureaucratic Insurgency: The Public Sector Labour Movement' in S.W.K. Chiu and T.L. Lui (eds.), *The Dynamics of Social Movement in Hong Kong*. Hong Kong: Hong Kong University Press, pp.139–83.

Levin, D.A. and Ng, S.H. (1995), 'From an industrial to a post-industrial economy: challenges for human resoruce management in Hong Kong' in A. Verma, T.A. Kochan and R.D. Lansbury (eds.), *Employment Relations in the Growing Asian Economies*. London: Routledge, pp.119–57.

Ng, S.H. and Poon, C. (1997), 'Economic Re-structuring and HRM in Hong Kong', *Asia Pacific Business Review* Vol.3, No.4, pp.34–61.

PWC Consultancy (2002), 'Consultancy Service for an Analytical Study on the Latest Developments in Civil Service Pay Administration in Other Governments', Interim Report to the Task Force on the Review of Civil Service Pay Policy and System.

Rowley, Chris and John Benson (2002), 'Convergence and Divergence in Asian Human Resource Management', *California Management Review* Vol.44, No.2: 90–109.

South China Morning Post (1997a), 'Board scraps "frozen" labour laws passed by former legislative council', 16 Aug.

South China Morning Post (1997b), 'EXCO decides to scrap two out of five pre-handover labour laws', 1 Oct.

South China Morning Post (1998), 'Disputes rise as workers exploited', 24 May.

South China Morning Post (1999a), 'Housing staff protest over shake-up', 19 April.

South China Morning Post (1999b), 'Public housing staff win greater say', 25 Aug.

South China Morning Post (2001a), 'Chaos looms after pilots' vote: Cathay fliers overwhelmingly endorse industrial action from July 1 in battle for improved pay', 21 June.

South China Morning Post (2001b), 'Pilots put battle plan into action', 4 July.

Storey, J. (1992) *Developements in Management of Human Resources*. Oxford: Oxford University Press.

Tang, Sara F.Y., Lai, Edmond and Kirkbride, Paul S. (1996), *Human Resource Management Strategies and Practices in Hong Kong*. Research Report. 2nd edn. Hong Kong Institute of Human Resource Management.

Flexible Labour Markets and Individualized Employment: The Beginnings of a New Japanese HRM System?

JOHN BENSON and PHILIPPE DEBROUX

In an earlier essay, we reported that human resource management (HRM) in Japan was best characterized by continuity with some changes to assessment and pay practices (Benson and Debroux, 1997). There is, however, nothing particularly 'Japanese' about the slowness of change in HRM practices. Studies of Western companies have also revealed that renewal processes in HRM are not a one-shot affair but continuous. In Western countries, despite the fact that various HRM policies and tools have been debated for years, there is little indication that much of this has been implemented and even less evidence that there is any strategic integration of HRM policies with corporate plans (Gratton, et al. 1999).

The ambiguous character of HRM as to its assumed cause–effect relationships, strategies, and personnel practices leads to the conclusion that there is no universal model of HRM (Legge, 1995). Storey (1989) makes the broad distinction between 'hard' and 'soft' models of HRM, whereby the former reflects a kind of 'utilitarian instrumentalism' that attempts to integrate business strategy, organizational systems and human resource policies in a coherent and goal-focused way. In this case, human resources (HR) are simply reduced to one of the factors of production. In contrast, 'soft' models place emphasis on individuals and are based on a kind of 'developmental humanism' (Legge, 1995). Trust, self-regulated behaviour and commitment are at the centre of this approach where employees are considered the key assets or the source of competitive advantage (Storey, 1989).

It is now over five years since we mapped out the changes taking place in Japanese HRM. This study reviews some of the changes over this period and considers the future directions of HRM. The study commences with an outline of the important contextual factors and issues underpinning HRM, including employer proposals for reform. The next section then explores changes taking place in employment, remuneration and evaluation. This is supplemented by a more general assessment of the key changes occurring in Japanese HRM. The study concludes with a discussion on why such changes are occurring, whether the changes constitute a convergence towards the Western model and the implications for HRM and theory development.

CONTEXTUAL FACTORS AND ISSUES

Historical and Political

In the aftermath of the Second World War a welfare corporatist system developed. Large Japanese companies replaced the state in wealth redistribution in support of the post-war egalitarian social bias and the economic catch-up strategy (Dore, 1973). This mix of pre-modern patterns of thought and economic rationalism was predicated on job security for the regular members of the company and cooperative industrial relations. Building on the legacy of the Confucian culture in Japan, a system of well defined networks of mutual obligations developed in the modern enterprise (Koizumi, 1989). Management aimed at a steady growth and emphasized long-term recognition of the economic and social needs of its members and their families. In return the company could expect strong employee commitment and acceptance of rapid organizational and technological change (Moore, 1987.

The stability of the system was ensured by the corporate control mechanism system that arose from the institutionalization of long-term employment and collaborative industrial relations, and from the business transactions and cross-shareholdings in companies belonging to industrial groups (Dore, 2000). The rationale of this system was socially legitimized by an education system based on meritocracy, with those with the best academic credentials entering the best and largest companies (Rohlen, 1983). Despite employing only 20 to 25 per cent of the total salaried population, large companies have exerted a massive influence on employment practices, the markets, civil society and the family and its distinctive social composition during the past 50 years.

In this environment, workers were confident that their jobs would be preserved and incomes would rise. This made it possible to avoid labour and other social conflicts and to steadily increase both savings and consumption. Differentials in wages and fringe benefits remained large but the prosperity of large companies trickled down to the smaller companies. Female workers were employed on less favourable terms and conditions than their male counterparts. Nevertheless, until recently, the distinction in employment conditions between males and females were generally accepted by the majority of men and women (Hunter, 1993). The success of the Japanese economy, not only in terms of growth but also the rise in the standard of living, vindicated the idea that business systems and social institutions are linked and that organizational structures and strategies cannot be contemplated in isolation from their institutional contexts (Granovetter, 1985).

Economic

The post-war Japanese economy experienced high and sustained economic growth of about 10 per cent up to the early 1970s. After that time, and for the next 20 years, economic growth of about 5 per cent occurred, although this period was characterized by declining real gross domestic product (GDP) growth and a series of economic cycles. With this lower growth, tension developed between the business environment and traditional management practices, and Japan entered into a period that Hasegawa (1996) described as 'contrived compatibility'. That is companies manipulated the system so as to retain as much of the previous organic compatibility despite the changing business environment. This partly explains why companies continued to invest heavily after returns fell well below the levels achieved in other developed countries. By the mid-1980s, before the bubble-induced investment spree, the ratio of non-residential capital stock to economic output was 40 per cent higher than the equivalent US figure (Ostrom, 1999). As capital accumulated, returns fell. The increased use of capital relative to other inputs such as labour led to decreasing returns. Moreover, capital was poorly utilized. Detailed examination of specific industries and production processes found that inefficiency, rather than diminishing returns, accounted in the most part for Japan's pattern of declining returns (McKinsey, 1996).

For most of the 1990s, the Japanese economy alternated between periods of recession and extremely low rates of economic growth. Only in 1996 did real GDP growth reflect the conditions that prevailed a decade earlier and much of this growth was due to substantial spending on government projects (Ostrom, 1999). Details are presented in Table 1. For an economy based on, and accustomed to, high growth this economic downturn had a serious effect on employment. In 1995 regular employment fell for the first time in 20 years and in manufacturing there was a fall of 1.9 per cent from the previous year (*Ministry of Labor*, 1996). Unemployment, which was 2.1 per cent in 1991, had by August 2002 risen to 5.6 per cent (*Nihon Tokei Geppo*, 2002: 2).

TABLE 1

GDP GROWTH, 1990–2001

Year	GDP (billion yen)	Real GDP Growth %
1990	469,781	5.5
1991	481,661	2.5
1992	483,376	2.2
1993	485,498	0.4
1994	490,731	1.1
1995	502,794	2.5
1996	520,054	3.4
1997	521,315	0.2
1998	517,204	–0.8
1999	526,950	1.9
2000	535,690	1.7
2001	521,650	–1.3

Source: Nihon Tokei Kyoki, 2002

Labour Markets

Twentieth century Japan was marked by a sustained expansion of the workforce. The growth was largely a product of demographic changes; a tripling of the working age population and declining birth rates that led to rising participation by women in the labour market. For a long time the seniority-based pay system was in accordance with the structure of the population. The number of older people was relatively small and was in line with the limited number of managerial positions. There was an ample supply of young people available to perform the day-to-day operational tasks.

Demographic factors will in the twenty-first century, however, lead to a declining workforce. By 2005, the workforce is expected to peak at 68,530,000 and then decrease to about 66,730,000 by 2010. The youngest section of the labour force (15 to 29 years old) is expected to decrease significantly by 2010 with a reduction of approximately 4,000,000 from the peak of 16,310,000 recorded in 1998. At the opposite end of the age spectrum, the older workforce (55 and older) is expected to increase dramatically; from 23.1 per cent in 1998 to about 29 per cent by 2010 (Ministry of Labour, 2000).

The ageing of the labour force will have implications for HRM practices. Pension and medical insurance systems, premised on a growing population, will need to be re-examined. Moreover, some companies may have difficulty meeting the liabilities of retirement allowances without an influx of young workers. Pressure is also building up to increase the average retirement age from the current norm of 60 to 65 years. In addition, the prospect of importing foreign labour has emerged (United Nations, 2000). Nevertheless, a massive increase in immigration into what remains a relatively closed and socio-culturally homogeneous society would likely give rise to large-scale social problems.

It may, however, be premature to assert that Japan will suffer from a labour shortage in the future. Extensions of the mandatory retirement age and the better utilization of women may counter the demographic trends (Ministry of Health, Labour and Welfare, 2002). Moreover, Japanese companies are likely to increase their foreign direct investments considerably in the coming years. Already, the internal demand for labour in the manufacturing sector is decreasing and the rate of import of components made in Asia by Japanese multinational corporations has substantially increased (Ministry of Economy, Trade and Industry, 2001). Increases in productivity may also be used to offset the decline in the supply of labour (Goto, 2001). Consequently, if a more efficient use of capital investment, deregulation and technological progress, is achieved then this would compensate for the 0.7 per cent annual decline in the working-age population (Economic Planning Agency, 1999).

Nevertheless, the ageing of the workforce, coupled with a seniority pay system, is placing pressure on the cost of the employment system. In the past it was possible to maintain a seniority-based pay system without increasing total payroll costs as the exit of older employees matched the entry of younger and less expensive workers. This situation has changed dramatically. The ratio of employees aged 55 or over among full-time regular male employees at companies with 1,000 or more employees increased from 22 per cent in 1979 to 36 per cent in 1998 (Ministry of Labour, 1999). The loss of job opportunities for young people due to the growing cost of maintaining the employment of middle-aged and elderly workers is creating a displacement effect between those two segments of the population (Genda, 2001).

During the first part of the 1990s, no significant changes in working hours, pay and unemployment rates were observed. The primary and secondary labour markets continued to move in relatively close harmony. Despite the subdued business environment, the ratio of openings to applicants stayed quite high for professional and technical occupations. The large companies that formerly recruited many high school graduates had started to reduce their employment of this group, shrinking their employee numbers by transferring manufacturing abroad and resorting to new employment policies that relied on non-regular workers (Ministry of Labour, 1996). By the end of the decade poor economic conditions coupled with an acceleration of the restructuring process brought about a fall in labour demand and reduced recruitment of young graduates from both high schools and universities.

1997 Asian Financial Crisis

It is difficult to separate the impact of the Asian financial crisis from the downturn in economic activity that has occurred in Japan over the last decade. This period, as discussed earlier, was characterized by periods of recession and extremely low rates of economic growth. Unemployment rose steadily during this time. When the currency crisis developed in Thailand in 1997 Japan was suffering from low consumer demand. This had been partly offset by the high consumer demand elsewhere in Asia. The crisis swiftly spread to other Asian countries including Indonesia, Malaysia, Taiwan, Hong Kong, the Philippines and Korea. Japanese companies were hard hit as sales of consumer products fell and orders for Japanese capital goods declined.

The combined effect of poor domestic demand and the impact of the Asian financial crisis led to a fall in GDP in 1998. Although the crisis had a severe impact on many of the Asian economies at the time, by 2002 most of these economies had recovered. This was not the case in Japan.

Current Economic Situation

A series of financial scandals in the latter part of the 1990s, a 67 per cent increase in consumption tax in 1997, and a decrease in public spending added to the economic difficulties facing Japan. The lack of a clear set of objectives saw a reversal in some of these public policies and the use of public money to provide support to the ailing banking system. Moreover, several important reforms implemented in 1998 and subsequent years, such as financial and telecommunications deregulation, meant that that the economy would take some time to recover. These factors led to a record decline in real GDP growth and unemployment in 2001.

Employer Proposals for Reform

An important part of the context of Japanese HRM reform is the proposal by the peak employer body, Nikkeiren (1995), to establish a new Japanese HR model. Nikkeiren argued that the current employment model has placed too much restraint on quantitative flexibility. As a consequence enterprises have had to rely on qualitative flexibility in the internal labour market. This, according to Nikkeiren, entails a loss of freedom of choice and independent decision-making by the employee. They suggested that one option would be to limit qualitative flexibility and to increase quantitative flexibility as a whole.

In the present employment system only two options exist: regular full-time employment, which includes job security and qualitative flexibility; and non-regular employment, which simply creates quantitative flexibility. Nikkeiren (1995) argued that it is necessary to replace this dual employment system with various employment models with different combinations of flexibility.

Underpinning this argument is the fact that all economies face a trade-off between unemployment, the level of wages (and other employee benefits) and productivity. In Japan, until recently, the employment rate and wages were high. The price paid for this was low productivity. In many industries and for particular groups of employees, namely the producers of non-tradable goods, the tertiary industries and white-collar workers, this pushed up costs, bringing down living standards and adversely affecting Japan's position in the world economy (Tselitchtev, 2000). Such a trade-off is not sustainable in the long run in a more competitive global market. Japanese companies face the dilemma of either cutting employment and withholding implicit obligations regarding employment stability, or bringing down the level of wages and benefits, or doing both. The second alternative is the most plausible but as the Japanese authorities are unlikely to accept much higher levels of unemployment, especially without the strong welfare state safety net that exists in other countries, there is no option but to limit and cut wages and benefits (Nikkeiren, 2002).

Cutting wages for all employees will not, however, solve the problem as it would not provide for new work incentives that are necessary to boost Japanese productivity. These arguments have led Nikkeiren (1995) to propose three types of employee. First, a core or 'elite' group of long-term members of the company. Second, a contractor group of specialists catering to specific and usually short-term problems, and third, a peripheral group of employees that undertake simple, routine tasks, and that do not expect long-term employment with the company. This argument is not particularly original and is similar to what Herriot and Pemberton (1995) hypothesized in a Western context. Over 30 years ago, Ujigawa and Uemura (1970) were discussing the transformation of the Japanese employment system in their book *Salaryman Kakumei* (The Salaryman's Revolution). They argued that creativity would become increasingly important and they advised employees to become more autonomous and less committed as long-term job guarantees would, in the future, be reserved for only a small group of managers and specialists. The 'three worlds' model presented by Nikkeiren (1995) is a step in that direction. It supports the development of a multiple-track personnel system to accommodate the three strata of personnel.

Each of these tracks will feature distinct recruitment, remuneration, welfare, training and promotion schemes.

CHANGES IN JAPANESE HRM

Major Changes Taking Place

In our earlier essay, we concluded that HRM in Japan was best characterized by continuity with some changes to assessment and pay practices (Benson and Debroux, 1997). This finding was supported by later case study research by Dalton and Benson (2002). It is these issues we now explore in more detail. The previous section on contextual factors and issues provides the background for this analysis.

Employment and Remuneration: New Opportunities and Diminishing Expectations

Seniority-related wages and promotions are relatively high in Japan. With the increasing age of the working population wage systems based on age and the number of years of tenure have an automatic cost driver built into them (OECD, 1997). The Nikkeiren proposal aims to increase flexibility by allowing companies to have greater ability to adjust their labour costs according to short and long-term economic trends. How far has the Nikkeiren 'three worlds' model of employment been adopted by enterprises?

The preserved elements of the conventional Japanese management system is found in the 'first world' of regular, full-time employment. Whilst the percentage of workers in this group has declined it remains a significant group that will serve as a social and economic buffer against changes that might have a destabilizing effect on Japanese society. Increasingly, however, within this group workers are being rewarded for individual efforts. 'High flyers' are offered more rapid promotion and remuneration packages based on assessments of their individual contributions. These elite employees are expected to take the lead in enhancing productivity with more sophisticated individual assessment systems being implemented to ensure adequate rewards and incentives.

The 'second world' group of contractors and specialists are growing in numbers as companies realize the need for expertise to be brought in at various levels of the company. Whilst some of these will stay with the enterprise for many years others will move on after their contracts have expired. Companies are, however, increasingly relying on the 'third world' group of temporary and part-time workers. For those employees belonging to the 'second and third' worlds the transformation will lead, in most cases, to deterioration in their wages, working conditions and employment stability. The elite regular employees will also be affected as stronger limits will be placed on wage increases and other parts of the remuneration package such as allowances and bonuses. This may mark the beginning of what Krugman terms 'the age of diminishing expectations' (Krugman, 1993).

These trends can be seen in recent wage settlements. The average total monthly nominal wage in Japan for all industries fell from 421,400 yen in 1997 to 396,300 yen in 1999. In the same period the average wage fixed by labour agreements fell from 316,000 to 306,000 yen (Nihon Tokei Geppo, 1999). This represents the first fall in nominal wages since the mid-1950s. Case-study evidence supports these figures. Japan Air Line reduced wages for its 12,000 regular employees by 3 to 4 per cent in 2000 and is planning to reduce retirement benefits by 20 per cent. Hitachi Shipbuilding reduced the basic wage for 1,500 employees temporarily transferred to Kyushu Hitachi Shipbuilding by an average of 10 per cent. Even companies in the growing industries with comparatively high profit rates have become cautious about basic wage increases. One example is NTT DoCoMo, which froze its basic wages for 2,000 employees despite good financial results (Tselichtchev, 2000). Kobe Steel, Sumitomo Metal, and Alps Electric announced plans to reduce employee wages for one to two years beginning in the fiscal year 2002 (*Nikkei Weekly*, 15 Oct. 2001a).

While this trend has been driven, to some extent, by the poor financial performance of companies, it has now become more widespread. For example, many companies that achieved an operating surplus in 2000 did not distribute the surplus in the form of basic wage increases (Ministry of Health, Labour and Welfare, 2001). This confirms that companies were more likely to distribute surpluses through lump sum payments (Kawamoto, 2002). More than 80 per cent of companies that increased their payments to employees did so mainly or exclusively through increases in bonuses. This is consistent with the shift towards a performance-based wage system. Bonuses can be varied within the same age group, and from one period to another, depending on the individual or group's performance.

The Shift towards a Performance Based Evaluation System

There has been a gradual shift towards an economically rational merit-based appraisal system for wages and promotion in Japanese companies. In the early 1970s many companies introduced 'Management by Objectives' (MBO) on a limited scale for specific categories of employees, such as salespeople and traders. This was seen as a partial answer to the growing number of Japanese employees who wanted to have their needs reflected in the content of their work. Evaluation systems were also introduced in response to the increasing demands of HRM departments for schemes that would provide an evaluation of employees' level of achievement. Nevertheless, the principles underpinning lifetime employment remained so deeply ingrained in the socio-political and economic fabric of society such schemes were more in name than substance.

Recent studies across industries show that companies are increasingly adopting evaluation schemes that seek to measure the contribution of individual employees. Such evaluation schemes underpin individualized HRM practices such as internal job vacancy advertising, annualized wages and performance-based pay. This allows for short-term achievements to be reflected in wage levels and for long-term contributions to be recognized in retirement and severance pay. So far, however, the skill-grading system has not been abolished. A survey conducted in 2001 showed the skill-grading wages system is still the dominant pay system (Nihon Shakai Keizai Seisansei Honbu, 2001). Among the respondent companies the skill-grading wages system was used for 82 per cent of managerial level employees and 87 per cent for non-managerial personnel. Respondents did, however, expect these figures to fall substantially over the next three years.

Similarly, performance is increasingly becoming an important factor in promotion. The Romu Gyosei Kenkyujo (1999) found that over 80 per cent of companies based their decisions on promotion to the position of sub-section chief (*kakaricho*) on ability and performance. Nevertheless, seniority was also important in nearly half the companies. For promotion to the rank of section chief (*kacho*), the figures were higher for ability and performance and lower for seniority. These figures demonstrate the higher the position the less important is seniority. It was also found that an increasing number of companies had introduced a specialists' track.

The Tokai Sogo Kenkyujo (2001) has projected the evolution of company appraisal systems up to 2004. Details of the expected changes over the three-year period are provided in Table 2. A shift away from the skill-grading system for most ranks is predicted and confirms the attempts to establish 'professional' job grades with pay and promotion based on merit. This was particularly the case for those in managerial positions. The findings, however, indicated that companies were not willing to adopt performance as the sole criteria for evaluation of work duties. Instead some form of individual ranking is likely to be established that will incorporate all three criteria. For instance, at Sumitomo Corporation, some executives who have reached a given status according to the skill-grading system may still be subject to a seniority system. Nevertheless, further promotions and wage increases will be based on an assessment of performance (Nabeta, 2000).

TABLE 2

PROJECTED EVOLUTION OF APPRAISAL SYSTEM 2001–04

Rank	System		
	Skill	Job	Contribution
Division Chief	75–35	11–7	7–54
Section Chief	78–37	9–8	6–50
Ass. Sect. Chief	82–69	9–9	4–19
Non-executive	84–76	7–14	3–11
Specialists	7–43	10–28	7–23

Source: Tokai Sogo Kenkyujo (2001)

The problems of reforming performance appraisals are well illustrated in the case of Fujitsu which abolished its seniority-based pay system in 1992. Employees were then to be evaluated on the degree to which they achieved their operational targets. But many employees, especially the younger ones, were not satisfied with the new evaluation method because the relative rating system was preserved. This led to Fujitsu in 1998 removing the relative ranking system with the result that much larger wage differentials appeared. In this process, however, employees tended to set less challenging targets and developed a short-term attitude. Some were reluctant to help colleagues and concentrated narrowly on their own targets. Once again Fujitsu decided to change its system in 2001. Not only results but also the efforts of employees and way of achieving targets are now taken into consideration (Suzuki, 2001).

At this stage, many companies are proceeding on a 'trial and error' basis to recreate a stable and fair evaluation system. What is clear, however, is that there is a growing heterogeneity in the type of systems being developed. This ranges from job-grading systems based on a thorough job analysis and job description to competency-based systems with more individual accountability. Nippon Hewlett-Packard, for example, undertook an analysis of all jobs in the company and devised about 800 distinct job descriptions. At Takeda Pharmaceuticals and Sakura Bank, a system based on job weight ranking, using the Hay Consultants method, has been introduced (Kinoshita, 2001).

Departure from Age and Tenure

These reforms show a clear departure from age and tenure. Whilst this has been a trend for the past two decades the process has accelerated over the past five years. On the whole, age–wage profiles are becoming flatter. As the labour force ages, promotion is occurring later. The 'baby boomers' generation has now reached the age level for managerial posts, and the supply of appropriate workers outnumbers the demand for middle and upper-middle managers. In a survey conducted by Yatabe (2000) three-quarters of the companies reported that age was no longer a consideration in determining remuneration. Nearly half of the companies reported this was also the case for their ordinary employees. These figures increased when companies were asked to consider their future plans. The shift was clearly over to performance-based systems with more than three-quarters of the companies surveyed claiming this was their major reason for the reforms. It is now not unusual for younger employees to be promoted over senior colleagues and to receive higher remuneration (Debroux, 2001).

One example of the breakdown of age and tenure as key factors in remuneration has been the introduction of annualized pay schemes (*Rosei Jiho*, 2002). A survey conducted by the Central Labour Standards Commission in 2001 found that 35 per cent of companies with over 1000 employees had adopted annualized pay schemes. Among these companies 85 per cent had introduced the scheme for their managers. This change is illustrated by the scheme introduced for store managers in a leading supermarket chain. The total compensation for these managers consists of three parts; the basic wage, a store target related amount, and a bonus related to individual performance. At the beginning of the period targets are set for the store and at the end of the period store performance and an assessment of the manager's performance is made. Extra amounts are awarded based on these assessments that can vary between zero and the amount of the base wage. These amounts are then annualized over the following year. Managers now in effect have up to 50 per cent of their income determined by performance. In addition, if managers do not reach the targets set they can also be demoted (Nabeta, 2000).

The case of NEC is an example of changes in the wages system for both managerial and non-managerial personnel. Until 2001 the basic wage consisted of a 'duties–qualifications' component based on the grade of the employee's job and the employee's estimated ability, and a base component that increased according to evaluations of job performance. NEC has recently introduced a new wage scheme that has eliminated all existing job grades. Instead, qualifications and the nature of work have been combined to produce four categories: complex administrative and technology-related work involving high degrees of discretion and judgement; lower level administrative and technological work; production-related and inspection jobs; and other general work. Wage levels vary depending on the category and the evaluation of individual performance. Increases in the basic monthly wage and the qualifications grade are based on individual evaluation, which depends on the level of achievement and the level of skills required (Japan Labor Bulletin, June 2001).

At the present time the situation varies between companies and between industries. Moreover, seniority elements in wages continues to exist for some categories of workers although, within stricter limits. Some leading companies have also attempted performance-based wage systems for non-executive personnel. This has often had a reverse effect as individual workers attempt to improve their own performance at the expense of collaborative efforts. The result has been loss of information and productivity. This has led to companies such as Fujitsu to rethink their performance-related pay system for non-executive personnel. Fujitsu has stated it will reintroduce a seniority element (Suzuki, 2001). Likewise, Matsushita Electric Works has reached an agreement with its union concerning a dual pay system for rank-and-file employees from 2002. Employees who are in charge of planning and decision-making will get paid according to their performance, while those involved in clerical work and manufacturing processes will be paid by seniority (*Nikkei Weekly*, 17 Dec. 2001b).

The Restructuring of Japanese HRM

The foregoing discussion illustrates the changing nature of Japanese HRM. Our assessment of change since our 1997 essay is that the speed of change has increased and what may have been considered unique practices five years ago have become more firmly established. Nevertheless, HRM reform is still ostensibly at the level of practice with little indication that the change has occurred at the policy or architectural level (Rowley and Benson, 2002). Table 3 provides a summary of our assessments based on our continuing research, the recent literature, government and business reports, and the reform agendas of the key parties. Although aspects of this assessment are contestable its value lies in being able to indicate broad trends rather than universal application of particular HRM practices.

In general, there has been a loosening of the rigid requirements of the traditional Japanese employment system: employees are provided with more flexibility in recruitment, work conditions and payment systems. This has led to a more individualized employment system where performance will now, partially at least, determine remuneration and promotion. These reforms have led to an increase in the importance of the role of personnel managers as firms grapple with the introduction of new remuneration strategies and the need to recruit more specialist staff. While permanent employment is still the norm increasingly more contract employment is occurring.

TABLE 3

ASSESSMENT OF HRM CHANGES AND CONTINUITIES

Dimensions	Presence	Change
1 Rules: adherence to	✓	+
2 Behaviour: common values and norms	✓	+
3 Key managers: personnel/specialists v. line/general	✓	+
4 Personnel selection	✓	+
5 Payment systems	%	+
6 Work conditions: harmonized	✓	+
7 Contracts: individual v. standardized	%	+
8 In-house training	✓	+
9 Right to hire and fire	✓	0
10 Strategic role for personnel manager	✓	0

Key: (*Practice*)
  ✓ present
  % present to some degree
  ✗ not present

  (*Degree of change in past 4 years*)
  ++ major change
  + change
  0 none

Source: adapted from Storey (1992).

DISCUSSION

Why Changes Have Occurred

Increased globalization, the poor state of the Japanese economy and demographic pressures related to an ageing workforce have served as a catalyst for HRM reform. Yet beyond these macro conditions lie a number of other factors important in any analysis of the changing nature of Japanese HRM. The first of these factors is the increasing mismatch of traditional HRM and business needs. Team organization is more effective in the contexts of product specialization and standardized volume production. In industries where complex production systems can be broken down and programmed systematically, the monitoring of group activity becomes a more transparent and less costly activity (Hart and Kawasaki, 1999). Such an environment fits the traditional efficiencies and capabilities of the Japanese system. This no longer satisfies the growing demand for highly skilled creative specialists. Under current practices, new ideas may never surface or, at best, will be implemented less than wholeheartedly (Hart and Kawasaki, 1999). Changes are more necessary now, even in mature industries, after the late 1970s micro-electronics and other high technology innovations led to significant deskilling and thus invalidated the connection between length of service and technical capability. In such conditions, delays in promotion may incur a cost increase caused by the inappropriate assignment of able employees to tasks where they are unable to realize their productive capabilities.

A second factor has been the gradual shift away from seniority and towards meritocracy. To manage the incentive system effectively, companies must also be in a position to offer sufficient opportunity for promotion to the best performers. The traditional skill-grading system provided a reliable guide for workers and management as to what levels of performance could be expected. But it was correlated highly with seniority as abilities were assessed in terms of training undertaken and experience in the firm. Many Japanese companies relied upon the assessment of performance by the work group with little external control. A shifting balance occurred between the intention of management to retain discretionary power over evaluation and reward, and the intention of employees to limit any uncertainty affecting their remuneration. Management discretion was thus eroded over time with the result that seniority became the key factor (Kinoshita, 1999).

A third factor is the changing attitude towards the organization and work by younger Japanese. The best performers accepted the system until recently since they could expect to reap long-term benefits. But with traditional employment practices in doubt younger workers are far less willing to make such an investment. As Dore (2000) pointed out, younger workers believe that the long-term merits of lifetime employment are an illusion. They are convinced that they will never recoup their investments, as their elders were able to do. They have neither faith in, nor affection for, an escalator type of career, nor do they have any confidence in companies' eventual ability to pay them a retirement allowance. In addition, the orientation of younger people is towards more individualism (Sugimura, 1997). The current generation has developed a new set of work values appropriate to the affluent and sophisticated society in which they have been raised and are working. These attitudinal changes have led to the belief that flexible, short-term ability-based remuneration will leave them better off.

A final factor is the loss of faith in the traditional model of HRM. Entry into a good company with long-term secure employment and good promotional prospects was worth the sacrifice of individual freedom. Large-scale dismissals in the electronic and telecommunications industries (*Nikkei Weekly*, 17 Dec. 2001b) and the demise of large companies such as Yamaichi Securities and Takushoku Bank created anxiety in all segments of the working population and illustrated the risks of company-specific skills. Workers are also aware of the inability of unions to protect jobs. In short, no position is secure for life nor is promotion guaranteed. This has led to a significantly higher proportion of young Japanese workers changing employers before the age of 30 than in the US or Germany (Nabeta, 2000). In addition, the traditional compensation model is premised on a traditional family structure. Now with many adults choosing to remain single or childless the traditional model has little relevance (Sorifu, 1999).

Convergence or Divergence

Japanese companies are faced with the need to undertake change if they are to meet the changing expectations of workers and the increased competition of the global society. Unlike in previous downturns, however, companies have less flexibility now to undertake change through peripheral modifications of the HRM system. This coupled with the increased pressure brought on by globalization means that Japanese companies will need to consider some radical reforms. This is emerging as a constant theme in the Japanese media where the main issues are now the need for increased competition and for company restructuring. As companies restructure, a number of similarities between the new HRM practices emerging in Japan and those existing in the dominant Western paradigm can be detected.

The transitional nature of these changes (Dalton and Benson, 2002), however, means that it is too early to draw conclusions as to the degree of change or to what the final outcomes will be. The level of experimentation taking place, for example with the introduction and subsequent rejection of new appraisal and reward systems in some leading companies, means that many of these changes have not penetrated the basic architecture of Japanese HRM. Dismissal laws represent another clear case of this transition. A doctrine of abusive dismissal appears to be slowly evolving. The rules are likely to be relaxed for workers deemed to have sufficient bargaining power and capability to negotiate to their advantage with management and to find another job on the external labour market (Ouchi, 2002). However, the basic principle of protecting employees from dismissal remains deeply entrenched and dramatic changes cannot be expected in the foreseeable future.

There is also growing opposition to the restructuring of HRM. This is particularly the case among middle-aged and elderly workers concerning their security of employment. Despite a desire to introduce reforms many companies feel obliged to honour their long-term employment guarantee to the older workers. A number of influential corporate opinion leaders continue to defend traditional Japanese practices and maintain that the existing system can survive the current poor economic situation and be rejuvenated. They recognize that the certainty and reassurance of the past may have gone, and that radical changes are necessary but they remain convinced that the fundamental characteristics of the multiple stakeholder system with its emphasis on human capital can be preserved (Kinoshita, 2001).

One interpretation of the trends outlined above is of a convergence towards some idealized Western HRM system. It is, however, not possible to argue that simple convergence is taking place. As with most transitional stages the final outcomes may differ substantially. Experimentation with Western practices will continue but will be modified to suit the unique needs of a different system. This is the principle underpinning the Nikkerien style of moving towards a more market-driven approach but with a strong core of workers enjoying a more traditional system. This, of course, could also be seen as convergence with the system under which most Japanese work. In short, many of the changes are now more closely aligned with the practices that exist in small firms, contractors and sectors outside the large manufacturing firms or government employment.

Key Issues for HRM

While transitionary and evolutionary change is occurring in HRM there are some that argue the Japanese economy needs a radical deregulation of the general corporate environment to enable a new genre of Japanese companies to flourish. This line of thought is becoming popular among influential academics such as Nakatani (1997) and Yashiro (1999) and opinion leaders such as Ohmae (1995) and Sakaiya (1998). Such a position is also strongly advocated by those reflecting the opinions of the influential consulting companies and private research centres (Tanaka and Asakawa, 2001).

The argument for more radical reform reinforces the idea that the traditional practices in large companies such as lifetime employment and seniority wages were indeed no more than a transitory phenomenon. For these proponents Japan is now entering the modern age after 60 years of economic development under benevolent paternalistic rule. Whilst past HRM practices blended with the work values of the time they are no longer attuned to the needs of the modern world. Egalitarianism has become a drag on creativity, stultifying the competitive drive, and the desire to work hard and to excel (Nakatani, 1997). In short, the relational psychological contract must be replaced by a more transactional type of organizational commitment, free of any socio-cultural connotations linked to the norms of employee–employer relations (Sakaiya, 1998). A report by

Keizai Doyukai (1999) confirms that corporate leaders favour a radical departure from 'Japanese style' employment practices and a shift towards a new HRM system based on results and performance.

The implications for HRM are clear. If the present process of gradual reform continues HRM will involve considerable experimentation. Not all experiments will work and not all will simply be the adoption of western practices. A large degree of uncertainty will exist and ad hoc schemes will arise to fill the vacuum left by managerial experiments. This transitional stage may extend for many years with little clear direction as to the final outcome. On the other hand, if more radical reform is undertaken, and extended beyond HRM, then the transitional period will become more uncertain and more difficult to manage. Workers will be alienated in this process and Japanese companies will not be able to appeal to the wider norms and values of society to gain the necessary commitments.

It is difficult to predict what approach will dominate the reform process and what the final outcomes will be. Major management associations themselves are also divided on this issue. With the merger of Nikkeiren and Keidanren in May 2002 to form the Japan Business Federation (JFB) a more united employer approach would be expected. Yet, even in this case the two organizations do not share the same opinion concerning a number of issues related to the restructuring process and the search for a new deal between labour and management (*Japan Labor Bulletin*, Feb. 2002).

Implications for Theory Development

The case of Japan and the processes of reform have a number of implications for the development of HRM theory. Three issues stand out. First, the concept of convergence has limited use in understanding the processes of change and the likely outcomes. It assumes the one best way of doing things and is void of the influences that national cultures and institutions, and company norms can have as barriers to change. Moreover, as the Japanese HRM system is diverse it is necessary to go beyond the stereotypical practices that are referred to as the Japanese model.

A second issue is that change can occur in a variety of ways and at a variety of levels. The approach outlined by Rowley and Benson (2002) offers one way to analyse what is happening in Japan. The distinction made between HRM architecture, policy and practice points to a clear need to focus on the level at which change is occurring. Only by doing so can some sense be made of the transitional arrangements that are evolving. The final issue relates to the general unitary approach underpinning HRM. The Japanese case points to the problems that will arise as more market-based processes are put in place. Can it be assumed that a more individualistic approach is also good for employees and that they will not have to carry a disproportionate burden of the reform? In short, HRM will need to accommodate a more collective focus if it is to be useful in analysing events in Japan over the next decade.

CONCLUSION

In 1997 we suggested that 'a Japanese model with a more individualistic focus is one possible strategy' for the future (Benson and Debroux, 1997: 79). This study has illustrated that the changes in HRM since then have moved in this direction. It is, however, difficult to conclude that these changes represent a long-term trend as many of them are transitional and experimental. At this stage there appears to be developing a hybrid model that is inherently unstable and contradictory. Yet, there is little evidence to suggest that the basic architecture of Japanese HRM has been reformed. Such reform will depend not on ad hoc changes to employment practices but on wider changes to society, institutions, and corporate governance.

REFERENCES

Benson, J. and Debroux, P. (1997), 'HRM in Japanese Enterprises: Trends and Challenges', *Asia Pacific Business Review*, Vol.3, No.4, pp.62–81.

Dalton, N. and Benson, J. (2002), 'Innovation and Change in Japanese Human Resource Management', *Asia Pacific Journal of Human Resources*, Vol.40, No.3, pp.345–62.

Debroux, P. (2001), Unpublished Survey on New Appraisal, Remuneration and Career Development Practices in Japanese Companies.

Dore, R. (1973), *British Factory–Japanese Factory: the Origins of National Diversity in Industrial Relations*. Berkeley: University of California Press.

Dore, R. (2000), *Stock Market Capitalism versus Welfare Capitalism*. Oxford: Oxford University Press.

Economic Planning Agency (1999), *Keizai Hakusho* (Economic Survey of Japan), 1998–1999: Challenges for Economic Revival. Tokyo: Economic Planning Agency.

Genda, Y. (2001), 'The Unhappiness of Middle-aged and Older Workers', *Japan Labor Bulletin*, May, pp.6–10.

Goto, J. (2001), 'Aging Society and the Labour Market in Japan: Should the Fertility Rate Be Raised Now ? No !' *Japan Labour Bulletin*, September, pp.6–11.

Granovetter, M. (1985), 'Economic Action and Social Structure: the Problem of Embeddedness', *American Journal of Sociology*, Vol.91, No.3, pp.481–510.

Gratton, L., Hailey, V., Stiles, P. and Truss, C. (1999), *Strategic Human Resource Management*. Oxford: Oxford University Press.

Hasegawa, H. (1996), *The Steel Industry in Japan: A Comparison with Britain*. London: Routledge.

Hart, R. and Kawasaki, S. (1999), *Work and Pay in Japan*, Cambridge: Cambridge University Press.

Herriot, P and Pemberton, C. (1995), 'A New Deal for Middle Managers', *People Management*, Vol.4, No.12, pp.32–5.

Hunter, J. (1993), *Japanese Women Working*. London: Routledge.

Japan Labor Bulletin (2001), 'Reassessing Job-ability Qualification Systems', June, pp.2–3.

Japan Labor Bulletin (2002), 'New Employers' Association, JTF Inaugurated through Unification of Keidanren and Nikkeiren', Feb., p.3.

Kawamoto H. (2002), 'A Review of the 2002 Shunto', *Japan Labor Bulletin*, July, p.14.

Keizai Doyukai (1999), 'Dai 14 Kai Kigyo Hakusho' (14th Company White paper), Tokyo: Keizai Doyukai.

Kinoshita, T. (1999) *Nihonjin no Chingin* (The Wages of Japanese People). Tokyo: Heibonsha Shinsho.

Kinoshita, T. (2001), 'Chingin Seido no Tenkan to Seikashugi Chingin no Mondaiten' (The Conversion of the Wages, Personnel System and the Issue of the Result Principle Wages), *Annual Review of Labor Sociology*, No.12, Nov., pp.55–72.

Koizumi, T. (1989), 'Management of Innovation and Change in Japanese Organizations', *Advances in International Management* Vol.4, pp.245–54.

Krugman, P. (1993) *Pop Internationalism*. Cambridge Mass.: MIT Press

Legge, K. (1995), *Human Resource Management: Rhetoric and Realities*. Basingstoke: MacMillan.

McKinsey (1996), *Capital Productivity*. Washington DC: McKinsey Global Institute.

Ministry of Economy, Trade and Industry (2001). White Paper on International Trade, Tokyo: Ministry of Economy, Trade and Industry.

Ministry of Labour (1996), *White Paper on Labour*. Tokyo: Japan Institute of Labour.

Ministry of Labour (1999) *White Paper on Labour*. Tokyo: Japan Institute of Labour.

Ministry of Labour (2000), *White Paper on Labour*. Tokyo: Japan Institute of Labour.

Ministry of Health, Labour and Welfare (2001), *White Paper on Labour*. Tokyo: Japan Institute of Labour.

Ministry of Health, Labour and Welfare (2002), *Rodo Keizai Hakusho* (White Paper on Labour Economy). Tokyo: Japan Institute of Labour.

Moore, J. (1987), Japanese Industrial Relations", *Labour and Industry*, Vol.1, No.1, pp.140–155.

Nabeta, S. (2000), *Korekara no Jinji ga Kawaru Nihon* (Japanese Human Resource Management will Change from Now On). Tokyo: Kenkyujo.

Nakatani, I. (1997), A Design for Transforming the Japanese Economy, *Journal of Japanese Studies*, Winter, 1997.

Nihon Shakai Keizai Seisansei Honbu (2001), *Nenpan Nihonteki Jinji Seido no Genjo to Kadai, Nihon Shakai Keizai Seisansei Honbu Jinjiiin – Noryoku, Jisseki nado nom Hyoka. Katsuyo ni Kansuru Kenkyukai Saishu Hokoku* (Current Situation and Topics Cocerning the Japanese-style Human Resource Management, Yearbook, Human Resource Committee, Final Report of the Study Group on Competency, Appraisal of Performance). Tokyo: Nihon Shakai Keizai Seisansei Honbu.

Nihon Tokei Geppo, Aug. 1999, p.3.

Nihon Tokei Geppo, Sept. 2002, pp.2–5.

Nihon Tokei Kyokai (2002) *Japan Statistical Yearbook*. Tokyo: Mainichi Shinbunsha.

Nikkei Weekly (2001a), 'Serious Changes Hit Labor Market', 15 Oct. pp.3–5.

Nikkei Weekly (2001b), 'Wage System Needs Re-examination', 17 Dec. p.7.

Nikkeiren (1995), *Nihonteki Keiei no Shin-jidai* (A New Era for Japanese-Style Management). Tokyo: Nikkeiren.

Nikkeiren (2002), *Rodo mondai Kenkyu Iinkai Hokoku* (Report from the Labour Issues Committee). Tokyo: Nikkeiren Shuppanbu.

OECD (1997), *Employment Outlook*. Paris: Organization for Economic Co-operation and Development.

Ohmae, K. (1995), 'Letter from Japan', *Harvard Business Review*, May–June, pp.154–63.

Ostrom, D. (1999), *The Competitive Debate Comes to Japan*. Tokyo: Japan Economic Institute.

Ouchi, S. (2002), 'Change in Japanese Employment Security: Reflecting on the Legal Points', *Japan Labor Bulletin*, 1 Jan., pp.7–11.

Rosei Jiho. (2002), 5 January.

Rohlen, T. (1983), *Japan's High Schools*. Berkeley: University of California Press.

Romu Gyosei Kenkyujo (1999), *Koyo Kanri no Jitsumu* (Practice of Employment Management). Tokyo: Rodosho Seisaku Chosabu.

Rowley, C. and Benson, J. (2002), 'Convergence and Divergence in Asian Human Resource Management', *California Management Review*, Vol.44, No.2, pp.90–109.

Sakaiya, T. (1998), 'Japan is Changing', *Japan Echo*, Vol.25, No.6, pp.34–7.

Sorifu (Prime Minister's Office) (1999), *Kokumin Seikatsu ni Kansuru Yoron Chosa* (Survey on Citizens' Life-Style) www.sorifu.go.jp/survey/kokumin index.html/

Storey, J. (1989), 'Introduction: from Personnel Management to Human Resource Management' in John Storey (ed.), *New Perspectives on Human Resource Management*. London: Routledge, pp.1–39.

Storey, J. (1992), *Developments in the Management of Human Resources*. Oxford: Blackwell.

Sugimura, Y. (1997), *Yoi Shigoto no Shiso: Atarashii Shigoto no Rinri no Tame ni* (The Philosophy of a Good Job: for a New Work Ethics). Tokyo: Chuo Shinsho.

Suzuki, Y. (2001), 'Switch to Merit-based Pay Takes Some Time Getting Used to', *Nikkei Weekly*, 4 June, p.1.

Tanaka, S. and Asakawa, M. (2001) *Mazu Nihonteki Jinji o Kae yo!* (Let Us First Change the Japanese-style Human Resource Management). Tokyo: Diamondsha.

Tokai Sogo Kenkyujo (Tokai Research Institute) (2001), *Jinji Seido no Genjo to Kongo no Kaizen no Hokosei* (Present Situation of the Human Resource Management System and the Directions of Change). Tokyo: Tokai Sogo Kenkyujo.

Tselichtchev, I. (2000), *The Japanese Company, Towards a New Model*. EAMSA Conference 2000, Singapore: INSEAD.

Ujigawa, M. and Uemura, T. (1970), *Salarymen Kakumei* (The Salaryman's Revolution). Tokyo: Nihon Seisansei Honbu.

United Nations (2000), *Replacement Migration: Is it a Solution to Ageing Populations?* New York: United Nations Department of Economic and Social Affairs, Population Division.

Yashiro, N. (1999), *Koyo Kaikaku no Jidai* (The Time of Employment Reform). Tokyo: Chuo Shinsho.

Yatabe, K. (2000), 'Nenrei-kyu Haishi ni Tomonau Jitsumu Ue no Kadai' (Practical Issues Concerning the Abolishment of the Age Factor in Wages Determination), *Chingin Jitsumu*, No.853, pp.4–12.

Changes and Continuities
in South Korean HRM

JOHNGSEOK BAE and CHRIS ROWLEY

Over the past five years, since we wrote our previous essay on human resource management (HRM) in South Korea (hereafter Korea) in 1997 in the earlier collection, several large events have occurred. These include the 1997 Asian financial crisis, government change, South–North Korean summit talks, labour market turbulence, bankruptcy, restructuring and downsizing, and Korea co-hosting (with Japan) the football World Cup. During this period a climate of 'the only thing unchanged is the fact that everything is changing' prevailed in Korean society. The 'changing is good' mentality also dominated in the process of public and private policy making. Several terminologies have been exposed to, and fixed firmly in the mind of, Korean people, including the IMF, sovereign credit ratings, restructuring, downsizing, early retirement, labour market flexibility, unemployment, workout (that is, a corporate programme for the financial structure improvement), bankruptcy, and so on. All these are closely related to HRM. Up to the 1990s the term *'insamansa'* ('people and personnel affairs are everything') was coined to stress that human resources (HR) were the most critical assets for corporate success. After the 1997 crisis, the term suddenly changed to *'insamangsa'* ('people spoil everything'). Indeed, human resources, once the 'heroes' of Korea's successful economic development, now were criticized as the 'sinners' of the failure. These political, economic and social changes impacted on the HRM system we had previously outlined.

The operating context of Korean HRM has undergone radical shifts since we wrote our first piece in 1997 for a collection similar to this. This has undoubtedly influenced the practice of HRM. Therefore, the research questions and focus of this piece is to compare the current situation with the past and delineate the amount and type of such change vis-à-vis continuity in HRM. The structure of this contribution is as follows. The first section outlines the important contextual factors and issues (political, historical, and economic backgrounds), labour markets, the 1997 crisis and reactions, and the recent economic situation. The next section, on changes in HRM, outlines changes in terms of major ones, in multinational companies (MNC) and future scenarios. This is followed by discussion about the reasons for the changes, their relation to convergence and divergence, and key issues for HRM. Finally, some implications and conclusions complete the picture.

CONTEXTUAL FACTORS AND ISSUES

Political and Historical

Korea is proud of its 5,000-year-old history. This North East Asian country, once known as 'The Hermit Kingdom', occupies almost 100,000 square kilometers of the Southern Korean peninsula. The population has rapidly urbanized and grown, more than doubling since the 1960s, from 20.2 million (1966) to 47.3 million (2001). Of these, 10 million are in the capital Seoul, with a further 3.7 million in Pusan, and 2.5 million each in Taegu and Inch'on. A brief historical overview from the fourteenth century is as follows: Chosun (or Yi) Dynasty (1392–1910); Colonial period (1910–1945); period of US Military Administration (1945–1948); South's independence government (from 1948). This history is characterized by invasions, internal strife within the Korean peninsula, and its division and military governance and a series of misfortunes. There is no way to explain Korean history without mentioning *han* (resentment or frustration), misery or calamity. This historical background made Koreans strong, humble and optimistic. While Koreans usually live in the future, in the hope it will be better than the past, they often have tenacity for the present life as well, on the grounds that there would be no hope otherwise.

There have been important foreign (China, Japan and America) influences on Korea and its management. Before Japanese colonization in 1910, one critical influencer was China. Many systems (political, economic, educational and cultural) were transferred from China. This includes Confucianism and its powerful, early, long and continuing effect on family and social life, society and business (see Rowley and Bae, 2003).

Japanese influences included infrastructure developments, industrial policy imitation; and application of technology and techniques of operations management (Morden and Bowles, 1998) as well as some HRM practices. These include lifetime employment and seniority pay, although with some key differences. For instance, employee loyalty was 'chiefly to an individual, be it the owner or chief executive' (Song, 1997:194), with little to organizations as such, producing a 'quasi-long-term employment ideal' (in contrast to Japanese organizational commitment). While these practices were limited to regular, particularly male, employees in large companies, normative practice extended to smaller firms (Kim and Briscoe, 1997).

After 1945 the country was partitioned, with US military control until the South's independence government while the Soviet Union's military governed North Korea. Then came the Korean War in 1950. US influence came via not only the war, aid and continuing military presence, but also because many Koreans studied the American management system, especially as most overseas students were US-bound. This impacted on managerial, business and academic outlook and views, perspectives and comparisons, and possible sources of practice and examples. The continuing division of the Korean peninsula made armed forces important, and this brought military governments later, to which we now turn.

Another aspect to the historical setting concerns the policy mix of military versus civilian governance. Also, the military influence permeates widely as many executives were ex-officers, and applied their experience to enterprises, while most male employees had been in the military and had had regular military training; companies even maintained reserve army training units. After Korea's first President, Rhee Syngman, resigned in 1960 the army staged a coup the following year with consequent authoritarian and military rule for the next quarter of a century. In October 1987 a new constitution revived direct Presidential elections, and civilian control of the military was re-established under Kim Young-sam in 1992. In the 1997 Presidential elections Kim Dae-jung, head of the opposition, beat the ruling party in the first peaceful transfer of power in Korea's constitutional history. He then had to deal with the economic crisis that enveloped corporate Korea at the start of his term, and also develop his 'Sunshine' policy towards the North to forge links on the reunification issue, resulting in the historic meeting of leaders in 2000 in Pyongyang, North Korea.

Over the 50 post-independence years the three major policy directions and foci were towards: (1) industrialization; (2) democratization; (3) reunification. These were inter-related and inter-mingled and each administration had a different policy mix on them. During military rule the focus was mainly on industrialization at the expense of the others. Presidents Kim Young-sam and Kim Dae-jung were former political leaders of opposition parties and pro-democracy movements. However, both had difficulties with economic issues. Kim Dae-jung's policy direction was more on the recovery of the economy and reunification. All these issues are related to economic, deregulation, and employment policies and institutional infrastructures (for example, capital, product and labour markets). These issues are also connected to the relationships between the 'Three Failures': government, market, organization in Korea (see Rowley and Bae, 1998).

Economic

Korea was known by the beautiful nickname of 'the country of the morning calm'. This image faded with the increasing roar of the hustle and bustle of the changes that transformed post-1960s Korea. The Korean model has been detailed elsewhere (see Rowley and Bae, 1998; Rowley et al., 2002). In short, the route was a developmental, state-sponsored, export-orientated and labour-intensive model of industrialization. Korea speedily moved from a rural backwater with limited natural or energy resources into a world-renowned industrial powerhouse, overseas investor and manufacturer and one of the fastest growing economies in a rapidly growing region, with phenomenal growth rates. Gross domestic product (GDP) real annual growth rates of 9 per cent from the early 1950s to the late 1990s took GDP (in billions) from US$1.4 (1953) to US$437.4 (1994). Per capita GDP grew from a paltry US$87 (1962) to a massive US$10,543 (1996), while gross national product (GNP) (in billions) ballooned from US$3 (1965) to US$376.9 (1994). Korea became the world's eleventh largest economy and joined the OECD in 1996.

Within this picture of overall growth were variegated developments and shifts as Korea moved to a less agricultural and more industrial economy and society (Song, 1997). Between 1960 and 1995, as a percentage of GDP, agriculture's share haemorrhaged, from almost 40 to 6.6 per cent and services grew slightly from 41.5 to 49.9 per cent, while industry boomed, more than doubling its share, from 18.6 to 43.5 per cent. Sectoral employment patterns also changed. Between 1965 and 1995 agriculture's share of employment collapsed, from well over half (58.7 per cent), to just one eighth (12.5 per cent), while services' almost doubled from 28.1 to 54.6 per cent and industry's share more than doubled, from 13.3 to 32.9 per cent. There were differences within this as the composition of manufacturing itself changed. Between 1960 and 1993 the share of employment in food and beverages declined by almost two-thirds, from 36.5 to 12.3 per cent, and in textiles and leather by over two-thirds, from 25.2 to 7.6 per cent. In contrast, metal products and machinery almost quadrupled their employment share, rising from 10.3 to 39.6 per cent of manufacturing.

Within this economic metamorphosis, Korea's large business conglomerates, the *chaebol*, played a crucial role. At their zenith there were more than 60 *chaebol*, although a few dominated. In the 1990s the top 5 (Hyundai, Daewoo, Samsung, LG, SK) alone accounted for some 9 per cent of GDP, the top 30 accounted for 15 per cent of GDP spread across 819 subsidiaries and affiliates. The scope of their influence was reflected in the nickname of one: 'The Republic of Hyundai' (see Rowley and Bae, 2003). Their growth was based on a variety of elements (Rowley and Bae, 1998), and explained as due to organizational efficiency and by a range of theories, from neo-classical economics, Marxist perspectives, culture, network analysis, transaction cost economics, to resource dependence and power theory (see Oh, 1999). Some argue it was the flux and flow of the state–military interactions with the *chaebol* that was the most important external factor, a politico-economic organization that substituted for trust and efficiency and the market (Oh, 1999). The link between the military, government and top executives was often damned as nepotism and 'crony capitalism'. Thus, the one key aspect is the state. The state integrated and strengthened, owning banks creating reliance on government for capital. State policy deliberately promoted *chaebol* as a development strategy post-1960s and directly intervened to maintain a quiescent workforce.

Labour Markets

Throughout Korea's development, being a country with few natural resources, rapid economic growth was aided by abundant, cheap and hardworking labour (Kim, 1997; Rodgers, 1990). This was accompanied by extensive investment in HR development through both formal and informal education (Chung et al., 1997). For instance, in terms of the proportion of education expenditure by central government to GDP, Korea was spending 3.6 per cent in 1982 and 3.2 per cent in 1990, according to the Asia Development Bank, 2001. Thus, a lack of natural resources was turned into a 'blessing' in terms of building capable human capital (Kim, 1997: 60).

Also, from the early stage of industrialization, governments made special efforts to create enough jobs for the new entrants. Unemployment rates declined, from 8.1 (1963) to 4.4 (1970) per cent, and remained lower than 3 per cent during much of the 1990s. The labour force participation rate for males remained over 70 per cent from the 1960s (see Table 1), while that of female workers was greatly expanded from 37 (1963) to 49.5 (1997) per cent.

One feature in the development process was the remarkable growth in real wages from the 1980s. Real wages (nominal wages deflated by

TABLE 1

MAJOR INDICATORS IN THE KOREAN LABOUR MARKET

Year	LFPR1 (%)	LFPR: Male	LFPR: Female	UE2 (%)	HC3 US$	Change in real wages (%)	Working hours4
1963	56.6	78.4	37.0	8.1	NA	NA	NA
1970	57.6	77.9	39.3	4.4	NA	NA	51.6
1975	58.3	77.4	40.4	4.1	NA	3.4	50.0
1980	59.0	76.4	42.8	5.2	NA	−4.1	51.6
1985	56.6	72.3	41.9	4.0	NA	6.6	51.9
1990	60.0	74.0	47.0	2.4	3.71	9.5	48.2
1991	60.6	74.9	47.3	2.3	4.61	7.5	47.9
1992	60.9	75.5	47.3	2.4	5.22	8.4	47.5
1993	61.1	76.0	47.2	2.8	5.64	7.0	47.5
1994	61.7	76.4	47.9	2.4	6.40	6.1	47.4
1995	61.9	76.5	48.3	2.0	7.29	6.4	47.7
1996	62.0	76.1	48.7	2.0	8.22	6.7	47.3
1997	62.2	75.6	49.5	2.6	7.86	2.4	46.7
1998	60.7	75.2	47.0	6.8	5.39	−9.3	45.9
1999	60.5	74.4	47.4	6.3	6.71	11.1	47.9
2000	60.7	74.0	48.3	4.1	NA	5.6	47.5
2001	60.8	73.6	48.8	3.7	NA	1.5	47.0

Key: 1. LFPR: Labour force participation rates.
2. UE: Unemployment rate.
3. HC: Hourly compensation costs for manufacturing workers.
4. Weekly actual working hours (all industries).

Sources: Korea Labor Institute (various years), *KLI Labor Statistics*; Ministry of Labour (1986), *Report on Monthly Labour Survey*; Korea Statistical Office (various years).

the consumer price index), grew at an annual rate of 7.8 per cent during 1986–96, higher than any international standard. The hourly compensation costs for manufacturing workers rose greatly, from US$1.31 (1986) to US$8.22 (1996). Another feature included the long working week and hours and a high incidence of industrial accidents, especially in comparison with Western countries. Although working hours in Korea have continually decreased since the early 1970s, this was slight, from just over 50 hours in the 1960s–1980s to 48 in the 1990s and were still 47 by 2001 (see Table 1) and remain longer than those of countries for which relevant data are reported in the *ILO Yearbook*. In the case of the incidence of industrial accidents, the number injured associated with lost work time fell from 140,400 (1986) to 53,100 (1999) persons. However, the occupational injury rate in Korea, at 3,405 working days lost per 1,000 employees in 1998, is higher than that of any other major economy (see Kim et al., 2000).

1997 Asian Financial Crisis and Reactions

It seemed that the sun would never set on the never-ending economic success story. Yet, it did as the dark shadow of the 1997 Asian crisis was cast over Korea. Economic development came to an abrupt halt and went into reverse. For example, in 1998 the real GDP growth rate was -6.7 per cent, GNP collapsed by two thirds and the currency (won) fell by 54 per cent against the US dollar. The stock market plunged by 65 per cent between June 1997 and June 1998, while the widespread problems and bankruptcy of well known *chaebol* hit the press and smaller banks closed. The number of establishments declined by 14 per cent (68,014) and one million jobs were quickly lost (Korea National Statistical Office). Unemployment exploded, almost quadrupling from the low of 2 per cent in 1996 (420,0000 people) to peak at 8.4 per cent in early 1999 (1,762,000). Nominal wage increase rates were -2.5 per cent in 1998, with real wage rates -9.3 per cent. Partly in response, strikes increased by 65 per cent, from 78 (44,000 workers) to 129 (146,000) in 1997–98. One survey indicated a 12.5 per cent cut in training during 1997–98 with reductions in costs, especially in HR development (Drost et al., 2002).

Current Economic Situation

Unlike some countries in the region, the Korean economy confounded the merchants of doom and gloom, and quickly and strongly recovered from 1999. For instance, GDP grew by 10.9 per cent in 1999. This growth, while lower, has continued. By 2000 GDP was US$461.7 billion, per capita GDP, US$9,823 and GNP, US$459.2. Exports and imports are continually increasing. Post-crisis (in billions) exports rose from US$132.12 (1998) to US$145.16 (1999) and US$195.95 (2000) and imports rose from US$90.49 (1998) to US$116.79 (1999) and US$159.08 (2000). Furthermore, some of the famous *chaebol* seemingly weathered the crisis and survived; some made record profits. Both the Korea Composite Stock Price Index (KOSPI) and the exchange rate to the US dollar have fluctuated (see Figure 1). The rate of the national bond in January 2000 was 9 per cent, then it continually decreased to 5.43 per cent by February 2001. After the sudden rise to 6.8 per cent in two months, it reached the lowest point during the two-year period of 4.45 per cent in September 2001. It then recovered to 6.33 per cent in April 2002. The number and amount of credit-card use is exploding (Moon, 2002). The value of credit-card transactions in 2001 was US$333 billion (almost seven times the 1998 level of US$48 billion). The number of cards is 89.3 million, thus each person over 20 has an average of four cards. Part of this may be due to government policy to discourage tax cheating by small businesses

FIGURE 1

KOREA COMPOSITE STOCK PRICE INDEX AND THE EXCHANGE RATE:
1995 TO 2002

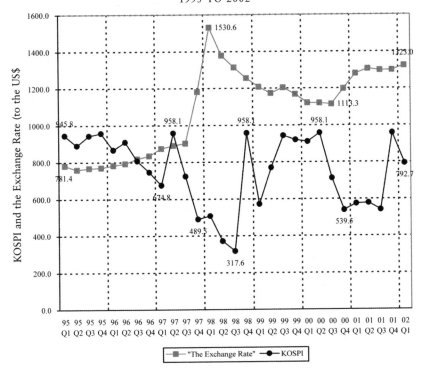

that accepted only cash. The potential downsides to this expansion in terms of exposure to bad debts from a different source, are obvious.

Real wages again rose, by 11.1 (1999) and 5.6 (2000) per cent. Unemployment has been continuously falling. After an initial small decline in female participation rates to 47 per cent (1998), it rose again to almost 49 per cent by 2001, similar to that for Japanese women employees (50.1 per cent in 1998), but much smaller than those of the US and some EU countries. In terms of the proportion of education expenditures by central government to GDP, Korea continued to spend 3.2 per cent in 2000, according to the Asia Development Bank, 2001. The government has continued to endorse training by making it government policy for companies with over 150 employees to establish training centres (Dorst et al., 2002).

However, this recovery may be fragile. Korea remains plagued by reports of poor corporate behaviour and continuing state rescues and strikes. Major, high profile examples include Daewoo's huge debts and accounting fraud, Ford's abandonment of interest in Daewoo Motor in September 2000, which sent shockwaves through Korea and its stock market, while the inordinate length of subsequent negotiations by GM also indicated further problems. Another example was the saga of 'on-off' merger talks between Micron and Hynix Semiconductor.

Skill shortages remain. Also, the 'big dipper' ride in job levels has had an impact on both those that remain in employment and those returning to jobs. Then there remains the 'demographic time bomb'. There is a problem of an ageing workforce. For example, in 1990 the economically active population aged 15–19 was 639,000, by 2002 it was down to 352,000, while over the same period the numbers of workers aged 40–54 increased from 5,616,000 to 8,189,000. Of course, such forces are not restricted to Korea, but the implications are stark given some of the traditional aspects of society, not least its strong family basis and orientation, homogeneity and exclusiveness.

Furthermore, despite this more recent performance, the earlier crisis and economic collapse led to much anxiety and incomprehension among politicians, policy makers, management, workers and the general population and commentators as to how quickly and totally things had gone wrong with the 'Korean miracle'. One set of explanations revolved around HR practices and the perceived need to reform and change them. We now turn our attention to this.

CHANGES IN HRM

The above environmental contexts influenced Korean HRM systems in many ways, as delineated later. Now we focus on commensurate changes here and possible continuities. We detail changes in HRM in general, then another potential source of change, the subsidiaries of MNCs, before outlining some possible future scenarios for HRM.

Major Changes Taking Place

The core ideology of the traditional Korean HRM system has changed from 'organization first', 'collective equality' and 'community oriented' towards 'individual respected', 'individual equity' and 'market principle adopted' (Bae and Rowley, 2001). The main fundamental assumptions of this traditional Korean HRM – lifetime employment and seniority-based remuneration – were key underpinnings of the 'deep structure' of the system. These were crucially interrelated with other HRM functions, including recruitment, remuneration, promotion, training and so on. Surveys (such as Park and Ahn, 1999) showed changes in employment flexibilities. For numerical flexibility, many firms used restriction of overtime, reduction of recruitment, voluntary retirement and outsourcing. For financial flexibility, firms used reduction in basic pay, bonus, and/or fringe benefits, and freezing of wages. To enhance functional flexibility, firms used redeployment policies. To examine HRM changes, we categorize areas of HRM into the '4Rs', the main functions of: (1) Recruiting, (2) Reinforcing, (3) Retaining and (4) Replacing competencies. Their characteristics in 'traditional' and 'emerging' Korean HRM practices are compared in Figure 2.

1st R: Recruiting Competencies – Resourcing and Selection

Patterns have changed from mass recruitment of new graduates to recruitment on demand, and from generalist orientation to specialists with general creativity. Recruitment strategy has also altered (Woo, 2002). This is in terms of directions in four dimensions, as in Table 2.

FIGURE 2

TRADITIONAL AND EMERGING HRM PRACTICES IN KOREA:
THE 4Rs COMPARED

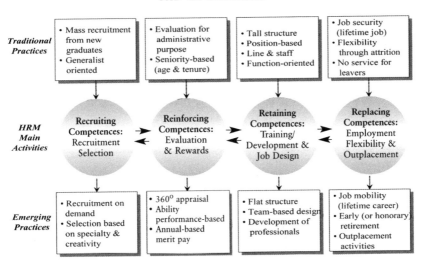

TABLE 2
TRENDS IN RECRUITING

Area	Existing	Trend	New
Resource focus	General purpose	→	Professionally specialized people
Recruitment method	Net casting	→	Fishing/Fish-farm type
Resource scope	Local	→	Global resource pool
Size/Time	Mass/Regular	→	Small/Anytime

These are highlighted in the case of the changed recruitment process at Samsung (Pucik and Lim, 2002; Woo, 2002). Table 3 summarizes the evaluation factors at each stage. Samsung established a new *injaesang* ('ideal image of HR') and core competences as: professionalism (professional ability and motive), creativity (thinking and critical reasoning), leadership (leading the change and challenging the future), and humanity (innate personality and organizational adaptability). Based on this, a new job interview process was developed which evaluated job candidates on their innate personality and ability (both personal competence and adaptability to organize). For the evaluation of these two dimensions, structured tools and methods were used. For evaluating innate personality, Samsung used structured interview questions and observations to examine such factors as personal background, past behaviour, and perception of future situations. Evaluation tools for personal competence include task assignments for problem-solving, case analysis, and simulation. Finally, to examine adaptability to organization, group-based discussion, problem-solving, and behaviour observation were employed.

The so-called 'war for talent' (that is, an attraction strategy to recruit top talent) seems to be the most prominent issue more recently. The term became well known after the McKinsey report on people management strategy was published in 2001. Korean firms have been

TABLE 3

EVALUATION FACTORS AT EACH STAGE OF RECRUITMENT
PROCESS AT SAMSUNG

Stages	Evaluation Factor	Note
1st: Document Screening	• GPA • Foreign language (gaining point) • Certificate (gaining point)	• In the case of GPA, should be above the cut line
2nd: Job Aptitude	• Verbal comprehension, number aptitude, deductive/inductive reasoning • Perceptual speed, sensitivity	• Evaluation on problem solving ability and learning capability
3rd: Personality/Ability Test	• Basic human nature, disposition, talent • Knowledge on specialty, adaptability	• Evaluation on positiveness, creativity, faithfulness, professional knowledge
4th: Physical Examination	• Health examination	• Picking out unqualified
5th: Final Acceptance	• Judging from pass or fail of each stage	• Score at each stage operate independently

Source: Adapted from Woo (2002).

actively involved in recruiting and retaining top talent. Korean *chaebol* that dashed into the war for talent include Samsung, LG, SK, Hyundai Motor, Hanwha, Doosan, and Kumho. They all announced that exceptional people would be recruited regardless of their nationality and ethnic group. For this, firms provided a fast-track system, signing-on bonuses, stock options, and so on. The Samsung group declared that attaining and retaining top talent would account for about 40 per cent in the evaluation of CEOs of affiliates. Importantly, CEOs personally take care of this issue.

2nd R: Reinforcing Competencies – Towards a Performance-Based Approach

The direction of change in remuneration systems has been to de-emphasize seniority while increasing the importance of performance and ability. Financial flexibility rose via wage freezes and reducing bonuses and benefits. Between 1996 and 1998 even basic pay reductions occurred in 41 out of 286 companies (Park and Ahn, 1999). Other data (Choi and Lee, 1998) indicated remuneration flexibility almost quadrupling from 10.7 (1997) to 38.7 (1998) per cent. Cases of change can also be noted. LG Chemical introduced a new system of performance-related pay at its Yochon plant (*Economist*, 1999), while Samsung made pay changes (Pucik and Lim, 2002).

Yet, it is not just a question of either total 'pure' seniority or performance as the basis for remuneration. Bae (1997) presented four scenarios regarding remuneration. These were (using data collected by Park and Ahn, 1999):

1. Traditional seniorityism (42.4 per cent);
2. Seniority-based with performance factor (24.5 per cent);
3. Performance-based with seniority factor (29.1 per cent);
4. Ability/performance-based (4 per cent).

Thus, about one third (33 per cent) of firms had performance-based systems 3 or 4. There seem to be common trends across sectors, although with some greater change in use of system 4 in non-manufacturing vis-à-vis manufacturing. Size did not much affect variation among these options.

One example of a performance-based system is annual pay (annual salary determined in advance based on individual ability or performance which is similar to merit pay). A survey[1] of large firms found 15.1 per cent had already adopted annual pay; 11.2 per cent were preparing for it; and 25 per cent were planning to adopt it (Korea Ministry of Labor, 1999). Hence, just over one quarter (26.3

per cent) of firms had either made, or were preparing to make, changes, while just over half (51.3 per cent) were at some stage of changing pay systems. There seemed to be common trends across organizational size. The operation of annual pay systems can also be seen in cases. These include Samsung, Doosan, Daesang, Hyosung and SK (Rowley and Bae, 2002).

Greater emphasis on performance in remuneration also came via other practices, such as employee shareholding and profit sharing, which have also seemingly spread. There have been government moves to stimulate, as with tax incentives, the introduction of Employee Stock Ownership Plans, which are expected to function in much the same manner as performance-based pay. Thus, in 2000 some 13 per cent of companies listed on the Korean Stock Exchange gave employees share options, more than double the 6 per cent in 1998, while 18 per cent of large companies shared profits in January 2000, compared with just 4 per cent in 1998; another 23 per cent planned to do so by the year end (Labor Ministry survey in *Economist*, 2000). Cases can be seen. Hyundai Electronics in 1999 introduced share options and Samsung Electronics introduced profit sharing (Labor Ministry survey in *Economist*, 2000).

3rd R: Retaining Competencies – Training/Development and Job Design

Under the traditional HRM system retention was not a focus of HR managers. Indeed, strong internal labour markets, career ladders and seniority and limited ports of entry, meant inter-company employment mobility was very limited. Evidence of change was the recent huge outflow of large company core employees to venture firms, whose number dramatically increased more than five-fold, from 2,042 (1998) to 11,392 (2001). There are both push factors (that is, dissatisfaction with rigidity and job insecurity) and some pull factors (that is, the attracting power of high incomes and entrepreneurial cultures) for this outflow. After the 1997 crisis, Korean venture firms started to scout for experienced engineers from large corporations. As a result, labour mobility increased. Younger Korean employees (like their counterparts in other countries), streamed to venture firms and 'dot com' companies in anticipation of 'instant' and 'easy' wealth (Bae and Rowley, 2001). Firms soon realized that retaining HRs was an increasingly critical task.

Large corporations responded to the change in labour markets with multiple strategies. Firms divided employees into three different groups and deployed different employment strategies. For core employees firms chose an attraction strategy (that is, the talent war) and a retention strategy (that is, retention measures for core employees). For full-time employees but poor performers, firms used a replacement strategy (that is, dismissals) and an outplacement strategy[2] (that is, providing information and training for job switching). Finally, for contingent workers, firms employed transactional and outsourcing strategies (that is, a contract-based short-term approach). All these strategies were unfamiliar to most Korean firms before the crisis. Dual (core versus peripheral) or multiple approaches were empirically observed. Bae (2001) found that the scores from the same sample firms for HRM practices (measured by selective staffing, job security, performance-based pay, extensive training and employee involvement) all but one increased in 2000 compared to 1996. This implies that firms used a commitment-maximizing strategy with long-term attachment for core employees, but pursued numerical flexibility through contingent workers.

For core employees, companies at first offered large sums of money to those who wanted to quit. However, HR managers recognized that those who wanted to leave left anyway regardless of their counter offers, and that while they could not compete with venture firms in monetary incentives, these 'deals' actually generated internal disharmony among employees. Even more incompatible was that some employees subsequently returned when the venture bubble burst. One critical barrier to the 'war for talent' in Korean firms is the perception of internal equity. Breaking down the established pay structure, promotion ladders and rigid work structure is a critical task to be resolved.

Beyond this extrinsic motivation strategy, large corporations also used a more intrinsic motivation strategy. For example, for the retention of core employees, Samsung provides a mentoring system, assignment of competent employees to top talents, dual-ladder career paths, succession planning, and fellowship for R&D people. By providing more opportunities for development, mentoring, personal growth, and employability, firms have made efforts to retain top talent. In addition, large corporations (for example, LG CNS, KT, SDS) also adopted internal corporate venturing (CV) programmes, which provide challenging jobs, as in independent ventures. The purpose of launching CV programmes was to retain key talent who would otherwise leave for entrepreneurial opportunities outside, and to build a new mechanism for the creation of new market opportunities (Kim and Bae, 2003). CV programmes can exploit the strength of corporations through resource sharing and, at the same time, appreciate entrepreneurial initiatives, as in independent venture firms. Therefore, core employees can participate in CV programmes and put their entrepreneurial initiatives into internal venture projects. Two different modes of CV programmes are: new venture units (NVU) and corporate venture capital (CVC). Among these, CV programmes using NVUs are directly related to an employee retention strategy. To overcome constraints and inefficiencies of existing units of large firms (such as differences in business models, biases for exploitation, bureaucratic structure, and short-term orientation), LG CNS launched several venture projects. For example, it incubated a venture project through NVUs to develop a new business model reflecting requirements of the target market, and then it was spun-off as Nexerve. Considering the differences in cost structure and decision-making style, it would have been difficult, if not impossible, for existing units at LG CNS to have nurtured the new business targeting medium-sized firms. However, it is still early to judge the efficacy of CV programmes as a mechanism for HR retention.

4th R: Replacing Competencies – Employment Flexibility and Outplacement

The general direction has been away from lifetime employment towards easier and flexible employment adjustments. It is not just a question of total 'pure' lifetime employment versus total flexibility as there are a range of options and degrees. While adjustment can come via reduced hiring, there are difficulties with this in lifetime employment systems. Here HR inflow is young and cheap compared to existing swathes of progressively more expensive HR paid by seniority. Therefore, firms have also used dismissals, with many incidents of redundancies via so-called 'honorary retirement plans'. To enable easier adjustments labour law changes were proposed in 1996, resulting in a general strike, and in March 1997 a more lenient version was approved and implementation postponed. However, a condition of the post-crisis IMF rescue programme was the immediate ending of legal support for lifetime employment, requiring further legislative revision, which followed in 1998. Thus, economic and legal changes were now conducive environments for employment adjustment.

Korea's flexibility, classified as 'low' numerically (Bae et al., 1997), has increased. Numerical flexibility dramatically increased via boosting retirements while reducing working hours, overtime and recruitment. The usage of a contingent labour force (for example, part-timers, temporary workers and leased workers) became widespread after the crisis. Accordingly, the Law on Protecting

Dispatched Workers was enacted in February 1998 to regulate and control the use of contingent workers. The ratio of contingent workers to the total employed population increased from 46 (1997) to 53 (2000) per cent (National Statistical Office, various issues). The extent of change is indicated in another survey.[3] During 1997, one third (32.3 per cent), experienced employment adjustments. By 1998 even this wide coverage had spread, almost doubling (60.3 per cent). In 1997 specific types of employment adjustment were: worker numbers (19.7 per cent), working hours (20 per cent) and functional flexibility (12.7 per cent). In 1998 numbers experiencing employment adjustment hugely increased in all these types: worker numbers more than doubled (43.7 per cent), others almost doubled – working hours (36.7 per cent) and functional flexibility (24.3 per cent). There was a more than doubling in both freezing or reducing recruitment (15 to 38.7 per cent) and dismissal (7 to 17.3 per cent), with a rise in early retirement (5.7 to 8 per cent). These shifts show many firms apparently adopting a variety of means to attain greater numerical flexibility.

Some firms now adopted outplacement programmes. For instance, in Samsung (Life Insurance and Electronics), a Career Transition Center (CTC) was opened to help re-employment or self-employment. People use its facilities, centres (business and job-lead) and rooms (PC, consulting, conference reference and resting). The CTC provides a range of services. These include a 'Candidate Management System', with access to hidden job information data and 'Job-Lead Assistance' to provide job information by region, for both open and hidden jobs.[4] Then there is the 'Self-Diagnosis Programme' which helps elicit competence, values, and occupation orientation to identify career goals and ideal job preferences, while its 'Self-Marketing Strategy' helps prepare a curriculum vitae and a self-introduction statement. Finally, there is 'Self-Employment' which assists in checking core competences and financial conditions and helps to choose a proper business item, market research, and critical procedures, and 'Self-Development Assistance', which provides educational and training programmes to enhance language capabilities and computer skills.

Another area that is expected to change concerns HRM outsourcing. Outsourcing of HRM activities has increased over the past few years. A 1997 survey (Korea Labor Institute) of 107 HR professionals (HR managers and professors or researchers in HRM areas) identified several areas that are expected to be outsourced soon

TABLE 4
HRM ACTIVITIES EXPECTED TO BE OUTSOURCED

Rank	HRM Activities for Outsourcing	Feedback (%)
1	Education and training	85
2	Outplacement	77
3	Building up and utilization of HR information systems	77
4	Job analysis	68
5	Employee recruitment and selection	56
6	Salary pay and operation	53

Source: Park and Yu (2001).

(see Table 4). These top three areas are:

1. Education and training
2. Outplacement
3. Building up and utilizing HR information systems.

Again this mirrors some overseas experience, such as the UK (Hall and Torrington, 1998).

There are, however, some limits to these changes and high profile examples of constraints (see Rowley and Bae, 2002). These include cultural and institutional factors, with examples of restrictive restructuring at companies. Examples include Hyundai Motor and Daewoo, with the need to maintain employment a key constraint.

Changes: MNCs

We now compare HRM over time among MNCs operating in Korea. This is in terms of:

1. Selective Staffing in recruitment and selection,
2. Job Security,
3. Extensive Training and Development,
4. Remuneration based on performance,
5. Participation and Employee Influence.

Nationality and sample sizes for 1996 and 2000 were, respectively, 40 and 33 indigenous; 41 and 25 American; 42 and 27 European; 15 and 10 Japanese (see Bae, 2001). To investigate 'country effects', we compared each HRM factor and the HRM total among country groups. The overall ranking order for the HRM systems in 1996 was: American (4.18 on a 6-point scale), Korean (4.14), European (3.73), Japanese (3.16) firms. This order had not changed by 2000. The results of ANOVA tests among country groups for each HRM factor showed that all but job security were statistically significant at conventional levels. Korean and American firms had higher levels on most of the HRM practices vis-à-vis the other country groups. Japanese firms were lowest on most of the HRM practices, and European firms were in the middle. Korean firms had the highest scores in selective staffing, job security, and training and development; while western firms had higher scores in remuneration, and participation and influence.

The overall picture reveals that most of the values increased between 1996 and 2000. The most prominent change occurred in remuneration, where all country groups showed major increases. Somewhat unexpectedly, the scores of job security of all country groups except Korea (4.85 to 4.67), slightly increased: American (4.60 to 4.92), European (4.30 to 4.93), Japanese (4.30 to 4.90). Some evidence in the West indicates similar patterns despite the popular and media hype surrounding job insecurity. The job security policy of Korean compared with foreign firms had a different change rate. While foreign firms had higher scores in 2000, Korean firms had lower values vis-à-vis 1996. The changes in foreign subsidiaries were unexpected given the strong demand for labour market flexibility and downsizing after the IMF rescue. Why has this happened? Possbly foreign firms were not severely affected by the financial crisis. Rather, some benefited from the different exchange rates. Another explanation is that foreign firms had small numbers of employees which made it easier to stick with job security. Furthermore, foreign firms had formed external labour markets, hence some levels of flexibility already existed.

Why then do all the other HR practices have higher scores in 2000 compared with 1996? One reason may include 'learning effects' (that is, some HR managers remembered the previous survey and so might have responded with more 'desirable' answers) and economic recovery. Another explanation is a dual approach towards employment management by firms. By making a distinction between core and peripheral employees companies pursued flexibility through contingent workers and paid more attention towards core employees. Indeed, contingent workers are increasingly used. Finally, an alternative explanation is related to HR outflow to venture companies. After the IMF bailout the government encouraged people to start new businesses by providing infrastructure and tax benefits. Many firms experienced high HR turnover rates due to the consequent outflow of core employees. As a result firms firstly recognized that people are really important and then they also realized that HR retention was important to create competitive advantage.

We can now summarize these changes in Korean HRM with the situation pertaining at the time of our earlier publication. These are tabulated and scored in Table 5.

TABLE 5

ASSESSMENT OF HRM CHANGES AND CONTINUITIES

Dimensions	Presence	Change
1 Rules – adherence to	✓	+
2 Behaviour– common values and norms	✓	+
3 Key managers – personnel/specialists versus line/general	%	+
4 Personnel selection	✓	+
5 Payment systems	%	+ +
6 Work conditions – harmonized	✓	0
7 Contracts – individual versus standardized	%	+
8 In-house training	✓	0
9 Right to hire and fire	%	+
10 Strategic role for personnel manager	%	+

Key: (*Practice*)
  ✓ present
  % present to some degree
  ✗ not present

  (*Degree of change in past 4 years*)
  + + major change
  + change
  0 none

Source: adapted from Storey (1992).

Possible Changes in the Immediate Future

The main directions of change and future scenarios are shown in Figure 3. Until the mid-1980s, Korean HRM was characterized by seniority-based lifetime employment systems. After 1987 real wages dramatically increased, which then pressurized managers to run companies more efficiently. This high labour cost, along with international competition, encouraged firms to adopt ability/ performance based remuneration systems (see Figure 3). As a result, firms adopted many new HRM practices (Bae, 1997). Then the 1997 crisis pushed firms towards flexible HRM systems. Hence, at this point, it seems that Korean HRM systems can be characterized by a medium-level of numerical flexibility and mixed remuneration systems based on both seniority and ability/performance.

What might occur in the future? All six cells of the nine in Figure 3 are possible future configurations depending on industry, technology, organizational life cycle, strategic choice, culture, company size, external labour market conditions and so on (on constraints to change see Rowley and Benson, 2002; Rowley and Bae, 2003). Five different scenarios are presented in Figure 3. It is unlikely

FIGURE 3
MAJOR CHANGES IN KOREAN HRM

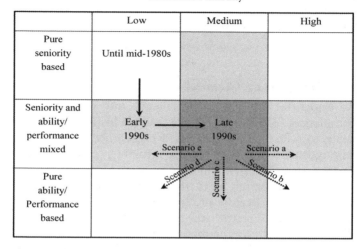

Key:
Areas with light grey represent the positioning of some Korean firms' HRM systems;
heavy grey represents the positions of many Korean firms' HRM systems at this point.

that the reward basis will return to seniority. Then we may assume that the reward basis would remain, but only flexibility could change. This brings three options: 'Scenario a', 'Scenario e', or remaining with the systems of the late 1990s. When we assume the reward basis could change to pure ability/performance, it brings another three options: 'Scenario d', decrease in flexibility; 'Scenario c', staying with existing flexibility; and 'Scenario b', increase in flexibility. For example, LG-CNS (an information process and IT service provider) recently changed its reward system towards pure competence and performance-based annual pay systems, which can, if we assume medium-level flexibility, be 'Scenario c'.

Of relevance here is a questionnaire survey (Lowe et al., 2002) which included Korean respondents (237 managers and engineers, mainly from manufacturing, some services, in a mix of medium and large, private organizations). They used a five point Likert type scale (1 = not at all; 2 = to a small amount; 3 = to a moderate amount; 4 = to a large extent; 5 = to a very great extent) on two dimensions: current state (CS) and desired future state (FS) of HR practices. The questions and scores included: 'Pay incentives' (CS 2.94, FS 3.90) and 'Seniority is important' (CS 2.92, FS 3.50). One of the most interesting results concerned 'Performance as the basis for pay rises', where CS was 1.83, which the authors labelled 'exceptionally low', and FS was 3.27, labelled 'lowest' by the authors. On such evidence, performance in pay practices was not as universally desired for the future as commentatorss often assert.

DISCUSSION

Why Changes Have Occurred

We categorize the reasons for changes into three: (1) Environmental Turbulence; (2) Strategic Choice; and (3) Institutional Influence. These relate to wider convergence and divergence debates that have been reinvigorated by the storms swirling around the impact of globalization. The first and most powerful influence is the 1997 Asian crisis. Several foreign news items were somewhat cynically headlined 'from miracle to crisis' or 'from tiger to beggar' (Rowley and Bae, 1998). The 'IMF factor' was always incorporated into the formula of all activities and programmes of government, firms and all society. All thinking, ways, methods and activities different from the traditional ones were accepted if the password of 'It's an IMF way' was uttered. It seemed that the power of the crisis was stronger than the inertial resistance of people, systems and culture. Under this situation, changes toward labour market and remuneration flexibility were more easily formulated than before. Another critical environmental change was the Korean government policy towards fostering venture firms. This stimulated many employees in large companies, especially who had experience in R&D and management, to leave.

Our second explanation is based on a strategic choice perspective. For some commentators, increased labour costs and restricted right to fire became burdensome to Korean firms. It was argued that securing labour market flexibility would improve competitiveness, echoing similar debates elsewhere, from Australia to Europe. The efficacy of traditional systems was increasingly questioned. Reasons for this include perceived high systemic rigidities and weak individual-level motivational effects. Korean top management were then presented with a golden opportunity to make a strategic choice to resolve these issues.

Third, institutional theory and imitation played another role. DiMaggio and Powell (1983) suggested three mechanisms of institutional isomorphic change: (1) Coercive isomorphism, to gain legitimacy; (2) Mimetic isomorphism, to avoid uncertainty; and (3) Normative isomorphism, stemming primarily from professionalization. It seems that mimetic isomorphism prevailed during the past few years. This paradigm is understandable when there is no sense of direction or no easy way out. Some studies applied this theoretical explanation to explain downsizing (McKinley et al., 1995), adoption of team systems (Lee and Kim, 1999), organizational legitimacy (Hyun, 2001), and management transparency in venture firms (Han and Bae, 2001). Some changes in 4Rs seem to reflect mimetic isomorphism.

Convergence or Divergence

These changes can also be related to the wider debates on HRM convergence. A central proposition is that due to political, economic, social and technological forces, now including globalization, there is a world-wide tendency for all countries, and within them practices such as HRM, to become similar as their copying and transfer, sometimes taken as 'best practice' and linked to ideas of benchmarking, was encouraged. For management an implication was that there were 'universal truths', including in HRM, that could be applied everywhere. In short, HRM systems would converge. Globalization's universalizing tendencies and implications can be located in work of long antecedence (such as, Kerr et al., 1962) and more recent exponents (for example, Peters and Waterman, 1982; Womack et al., 1990). Globalization's impact on HRM may come via the opening up and penetration of economies to external forces and influences. Indicative of this was the attention from the 1980s given to Japan, with attempts to imitate their practices (as in Ford's 'After Japan' and Malaysia's 'Look East' campaigns) and the so-called 'Japanization' of industries.

There is debate on what are 'best practices', the ways HRM affects organizations and if there can be global transference (see Bae and Rowley, 2001). Here benchmarking is seen as useful with its implicit assumption that 'best practice' effects are not company specific, but rather universal and transferable. Without benchmarking, firms may be at a competitive disadvantage. Therefore, imitating 'best practice' may be needed. However, benchmarking is a start rather than a result. Benchmarking 'best practices' becomes a competitive advantage through institutionalization (Kostova, 1999). According to resource-based theorists (Barney and Wright, 1998; Lado and Wilson, 1994), 'unique' (that is, rare, difficult to imitate and supported by the organization) HRM practices cannot be copied easily, hence they result in sustained competitive advantage. The paradox is that imitating 'best practices' may lead to competitive advantage, yet it is hard for these to be imitated when embedded implicitly in the organization. Such scepticism has echoes of earlier contingency-type arguments, which we deal with next.

In contrast to ideas of universal HR practices transferred around the world resulting in converging systems, are contingency approaches. These seek to explain continuing HRM diversity between (and even within) countries, even those grouped together as 'regions', such as Asia (see, *inter alia*, Turner and Auer, 1996; Katz, 1997; Rowley, 1997). This may be because the context is the deciding factor, the impact of practices is dependent on the congruence between HRM and contingent variables and national context (such as institutions and culture). These constrain globalization's encouragement of convergence.

Therefore, HRM differences could result from not just the more obvious variations, such as a country's stage of industrial and economic development or organizational size, but also in operational environments and the spread, impact and way technology is configured and used. There are alternative solutions to common pressures and problems with no single response to market competitiveness. Indeed, management authority and autonomy to introduce and use 'best practices' varies and is not unilateral and unfettered globally. Critically, countries remain distinctive in cultural terms. The term 'country institutional profile' (CIP) reflects this 'distance' (Kostova, 1999). A three-dimensional construct, the CIP is a country's set of: 'regulatory' (i.e. existing laws and rules), 'cognitive' (i.e. schemas, frames, inferential sets, etc.), and 'normative' (i.e. values and norms) institutions. Therefore, CIP and other factors, such as organizational and relational contexts, are important in HR practice transfer.

This sort of perspective is empirically supported. After reviewing employment practices in various countries, Locke and Kochan (1995) concluded that although new practices emerged due to the growing interdependence of national economies, the particular forms and the extent of diffusion varied considerably due to differences in local history and institutions and the strategic choices of actors. Similar observations also can be found in studies of industrial relations system transformation (Erickson and Kuruvilla, 1998; Golden, et al., 1997; Freeman and Katz, 1995). Thus, the manner in which HRM changes are 'introduced, mediated and handled can lead to different outcomes', so even convergence at the global level in terms of economic forces and technologies 'may result in divergence at the national and intranational level, as these forces are mediated by different institutions with their own traditions and cultures' (Bamber and Lansbury, 1998:32). In short, despite globalization, varied national HRM systems remain as distinctive political, economic, institutional and cultural frameworks and features restrict transference, and so convergence, in HRM.

A further issue that requires exploration is that convergence and contingency approaches may operate at different levels of HRM systems (Becker and Gerhart, 1996). Evidence for both growing similarity and distinctiveness may then result from different research foci. Earlier findings indicating tendencies for convergence studies to concentrate on macro-level variables, such as structure and technology, while divergence studies targeted micro-level variables, such as the behaviour of people in organizations (Child, 1981), retain explanatory usefulness. Therefore, a key issue is to move beyond broad brush portrayals, to disaggregate and distinguish aspects of HRM which may be transferred and so converging, from those that may remain resistant, and thus distinctive. Therefore, we need to begin to distinguish possible dimensions of HRM that globalization impacts on. This involves the level, alignment and acceptance of HRM practices (see Bae and Rowley, 2001; Rowley and Bae, 2002).

Key Issues for HRM

Several key issues for HRM emerge from this analysis. First, many Korean HR mangers lost their sense of direction. After the 1997 crisis, a 'change is good' mentality was increasingly formed and promulgated. Then managers were too busy implementing new HR practices to give much thought or reflection. One way to implement a new practice was simply to imitate a competitor or a leading company.

Second, the linkage of HRM to company performance has become ever more important. Firms have paid much more attention to ideas such as the HR scorecard, auditing, and HR performance index in this respect.

Third, the HRM unit itself and HR professionals face challenges. HR managers began to realize their new roles as strategic partners and internal consultants. For this, HR managers need to build up professionalism. Some mechanisms for this include organizing the Korean Society for HRM (KSHRM) and its magazine *HR Professional*, preparation for HR-related exams, and education programmes for HR managers.

Finally, HRM's individual functions, such as evaluation and compensation, on the one hand, and retention and outplacement, on the other hand, contain paradoxes. We note two: 1. emphasizing (short-term) performance and long-term sustainability of the firm at the same time; 2. enhancing flexibility and retaining key talent simultaneously. In addition, executive evaluation is another area recently emphasized.

Implications for Theory Development

All these issues suggest some implications for theory development. First, recent interest in 'best practice' has generated debate on its universal efficacy beyond time and space boundaries. This is directly related to the transfer issue. Marchington and Grugulis (2000) suggested a number of problems with the notion of 'best practice' in relation to the meaning of specific practices, and raised questions about consistency. Bae and Rowley (2001) also argued that the transfer of 'best practices' occurred on multiple levels, suggesting a transfer could be more successful at some levels than others. The notion of 'best practice' may be superficially attractive, but it seems there is still a long way to reach any firm conclusions.

Second, related to the aforementioned paradoxes, one way to manage paradoxes simultaneously is to divide employees into several groups. For example, firms can achieve success for both today and tomorrow through 'multiple architectures' (Tushman and O'Reilly, 1997) or 'hypertext organizations' (Nonaka and Takeuchi, 1995). Employment modes are also becoming multiple types. Lepak and Snell (1999) provided an HR architecture based on two dimensions: 'Value' and 'Uniqueness' of human capital. In this framework, they suggested four employment modes:[5]

1. Internal Development (high value and uniqueness);
2. Acquisition (high value and low uniqueness);
3. Contracting (low value and uniqueness);
4. Alliance (low value and high uniqueness).

Adopting multiple employment modes in a single firm requires greater juggling roles from HR managers. Theorizing this phenomenon is another task to be done.

CONCLUSION

Since the 1997 crisis, changes in Korean HRM have, obviously, occurred. The new Kim Dae-jung government at that time initiated transformation programmes. Most corporations responded to these changes by making restructuring efforts. Restructuring programmes included adjustment in business structure (for example, M&A, management buyout, spin- or split-off, and outsourcing), in financial structure (for example, debt for equity swap, reducing inter-subsidiary loan guarantees, and enhancing transparency), and in ownership and governance structure (for example, reducing family control, adoption of independent external board members, and separation and ownership and management). Along with these, restructuring efforts in employment were also made through downsizing, early retirement systems, performance-based incentives and employing contingent workers. Institutional contexts (that is, labour, product and venture capital markets) also have been changed. With the increase in venture capital firms, it became easier to raise funds for start-up enterprises. As the lifetime employment practice was eroding, labour market flexibility has also been enhanced. In addition, it was unnecessary for large corporations to internalize all business activities as multiple supplier sources were available owing to changed product markets. The development of these external labour/product/venture capital markets promoted the formation of start-up firms. The changes in institutional contexts and organization-wide structural adjustments pushed firms to have more efficiency, flexibility and agility. In addition, large corporations made a dash into the 'war for talent' against start-ups. Firms also usually deployed dual strategies for their core and peripheral HRs.

Yet, simultaneously some levels of continuity are also discernible. The difficulty is in drawing a firm line between them. These include various areas, such as the 4Rs. Several features with regard to these changes can be delineated. First, among several HRM areas, remuneration based on performance is more prevailing, and unlikely to turn back towards traditional seniority-based systems. Another area prevailing is employment flexibility, but which is open to more argument. Second, some paradoxes exist. Firms adopt individual-focused performance-based remuneration while they emphasize knowledge sharing and cooperation (Bae and Rowley, 2001). Other groups of firms simultaneously face a talent war while they pursue numerical flexibility. Such paradoxes, if not impossible to resolve, require expert juggling roles from HR managers. Third, firms are increasingly interested in the linkage of HRM to company performance. Several books recently published have titles reflecting this (for example, *The HR Scorecard* by Becker et al., 2001; *The ROI of Human Capital* by Fitz-enz, 2000). For this, some firms have started to evaluate and audit HRM at several levels: (1) HRM departments for their value-added; (2) business-level HRM units from corporate-level HRM units; and (3) individual HRM practice for its efficacy. Finally, in this line of argument, the transformation of the HRM organization itself, along with new roles for HR managers, is required. Sudden changes in environments, organizations and HRM made HR managers lose their sense of direction. New roles as internal organizational consultants, change agents, strategic partners and employee champions, are unfamiliar to Korean HR managers. To assist in this, many firms started to develop education programmes for the development of HR managers.

It seems that a new era of Korean HRM has arrived, albeit if not fully visible and with traces of past practice and continuity and uncertainty about the future. The 1997 Asian financial crisis had a major impact on Korean HRM. However, to give this event unique and causal status is problematic. The crisis may be *primes inter pares*. Some of the developments were underway prior to this and its effects were varied across Asia. Nevertheless, this has certainly created uncomfortable uncertainties for management, but it could generate new windows of opportunities for both HR managers and academics in the HRM field.

NOTES

1. With over 100 employees, in January 1999 of which 4,303 out of 5,097 business units replied.
2. This strategy is, of course, also used for core talents who want voluntarily to quit. Yet, these core employees usually do not need help from the firm with switching.
3. Of 300 firms in January–November 1997 and December 1997–March 1998 (Choi and Lee, 1998).
4. ' Open jobs' mean those that are revealed; hence you can access information about the jobs. 'Hidden jobs' mean there is no information given to the public. So, some institutions need to search for information and provide this to the job searchers.
5. However, Benson and Zhu (2002) found some problems within this in the Chinese context. One issue is that, unlike the framework Lepak and Snell (1999) suggested, various employment modes did not exist in China due to the underdeveloped external labour market. In addition, the dichotomy between 'buy' and 'make' was not clear because the emerging external labour market mainly consisted of unskilled labour, which would normally be contracted out according to Lepak and Snell (1999).

REFERENCES

Bae, J. (1997), 'Beyond Seniority-Based Systems: A Paradigm Shift in Korean HRM?, *Asia Pacific Business Review*, Vol.3, No.4, pp.82–110.

Bae, J. (2001), 'Changes in Employment Systems in Korea: Transformation or Continuity?', Paper presented at the 4th Asian Regional Congress of the International Industrial Relations Association, *Toward Decency and Fairness: Changing Work and Employment Relations in a Globalizing Asia*. Makati City, Philippines, 20–21 Nov.

Bae, J. and Lawler, J. (2000), 'Organizational and HRM Strategies in Korea: Impact on Firm Performance in an Emerging Economy', *Academy of Management Journal*, Vol.43, No.3, pp.502–17.

Bae, J. and Rowley, C. (2001), 'The Impact of Globalisation on HRM: The Case of South Korea', *Journal of World Business*, Vol.36, No.4, pp.402–28.

Bae, J., Rowley, C., Kim, D. and Lawler, J. (1997), 'Korean Industrial Relations at the Crossroads: The Recent Labour Troubles', *Asia Pacific Business Review*, Vol.3, No.3, pp.148–60.

Bamber, G. and Lansbury, R. (1998), 'An Introduction to International and Comparative Employment Relations' in G. Bamber and R. Lansbury (eds.), *International and Comparative Employment Relations*. London: Sage, pp.1–33.

Barney, J.B. and Wright, P.M. (1998), 'On Becoming a Strategic Partner: The Role of Human Resources in Gaining Competitive Advantage', *Human Resource Management*, Vol.37, No.1, pp.31–46.

Becker, B. and Gerhart, B. (1996), 'The Impact of Human Resource Management on Oganizational Performance: Progress and Prospects', *Academy of Management Journal*, Vol.39, No.4, pp.779–801.

Becker, B.E., Huselid, M.A. and Ulrich, D. (2001), *The HR Scorecard: Linking People, Strategy, and Performance*. Boston, MA: Harvard Business School Press.

Benson, J. and Zhu, Y. (forthcoming) 'Global Competition and State Policy: The Impact on Human Resource Development in the Chinese Enterprise', *Human Resource Development Quarterly*.

Child, J. (1981), 'Culture, Contingency and Capitalism in the Cross-National Study of Organisations' in L.L. Cummings and B.M. Staw (eds.), *Research in Organizational Behaviour*. Greenwich, CT: JAI Publishers.

Choi, K. and Lee, K. (1998), *Employment Adjustment in Korean Firms: Survey of 1998*. Seoul: Korea Labor Institute.

Chung, Kae H., Lee, Hak Chong and Jung, Ku Hyun (1997), *Korean Management: Global Strategy and Cultural Transformation*. Berlin: de Gruyter.

DiMaggio, P. and Powell, W. (1983), 'The Iron Cage Revisited: Institutional Isomorphism and Collective Rationality in Organizational Field', *American Sociological Review*, Vol.48, pp.147–60.

Drost, E.A., Frayne, C.A., Lowe, K.B. and Geringer, J.M. (2002), 'Benchmarking Training and Development Practices: A Multi-Country Comparative Analysis', *Human Resource Management*, Vol.41, No.1, pp.67–86.

Economist, The (1999), 'A Survey of the Koreas', 10 July, pp.1–16.

Economist, The (2000), 'Business in South Korea', 1 April, pp.67–70.

Erickson, C.L. and Kuruvilla, S. (1998), 'Industrial Relations System Transformation', *Industrial and Labor Relations Review*, Vol.52, No.1, pp.3–21.

Fitz-enz, J. (2000), *The ROI of Human Capital: Measuring the Economic Value of Employee Performance*. New York: AMACOM, American Management Association.

Freeman, R. and Katz, L. (1995), *Differences and Changes in Wage Structures*. Chicago: University of Chicago Press for NBER.

Golden, M.A., Wallerstein, M. and Lange, P. (1997), 'Unions, Employer Associations, and Wage-Setting Institutions in Northern and Central Europe, 1950–1992', *Industrial and Labor Relations Review*, Vol.50, No.3, pp.379–401.

Hall, L. and Torrington, D. (1998), *The Human Resource Function: The Dynamics of Change and Development*. London: FT-Pitman.

Han, J. and Bae, J. (2001), 'The Determinants of the Level of Management Transparency in Korean Venture Firms', *Korean Management Review*, Vol.30, No.4, pp.1063–92. (In Korean).

Hyun, S. (2001), 'An Empirical Test of Institutional and Strategic Views on Organizational Legitimacy', *Korean Management Review*, Vol.30, No.4, pp.1291–316 (In Korean).

Katz, H. (1997), 'Introduction' in H.C. Katz (ed.), *Telecommunications: Restructuring Work and Employment Relations Worldwide*. Ithaca, NY: ILR Press.

Kerr, C., Dunlop, J., Harbison, E.H. and Myers, C. (1962), *Industrialism and Industrial Man*. London: Heinemann.

Kim, D. and Park, S. (1997), 'Changing Patterns of Pay Systems in Japan and Korea: From Seniority to Performance', *International Journal of Employment Studies*, Vol.5, No.2, pp.117–34.

Kim, D., Bae, J. and Lee, C. (2000), 'Globalization and Labour Rights: The Case of Korea', *Asia Pacific Business Review*, Vol.6, Nos.3&4, pp.133–53.

Kim, H. and Bae, J. (2003), Revitalizing Big Corporations Through Corporate Venturing: The Korean Experience. Paper presented at the Annual Conference of the Korean Accademic Society of Business Administration, Yong Pyung, 20–22 August 2003.

Kim, Linsu (1997), *Imitation to Innovation: The Dynamics of Korea's Technological Learning*. Boston, MA: Harvard Business School Press.

Kim, S. and Briscoe, D. (1997), 'Globalization and a New Human Resource Policy in Korea: Transformation to a Performance-Based HRM', *Employee Relations*, Vol.19, No.5, pp.298–308.

Korea Ministry of Labor (1999), *A Survey Report on Annual Pay Systems and Gain-Sharing Plans*. Korea Ministry of Labor (In Korean).

Kostova, T. (1999), 'Transnational Transfer of Strategic Organizational Practices: A Contextual Perspective', *Academy of Management Review*, Vol.24, No.2, pp.308–24.

Lado, A.A. and Wilson, M.C. (1994), 'Human Resource Systems and Sustained Competitive Advantage: A Competency-Based Perspective', *Academy of Management Review*, Vol.19, pp.699–727.

Lee, K. and Kim, D. (1999), 'Rationality and Legitimacy as Factors Influencing Adoption of Teams', *Proceedings of the Annual Conference of the Korean Association of Personnel Administration*, Seoul, Korea. (In Korean) pp.25–47.

Lepak, D.P. and Snell, S.A. (1999), 'The Human Resource Architecture: Toward a Theory of Human Capital Allocation and Development', *Academy of Management Review*, Vol.24, pp.31–48.

Locke, R. and Kochan, T. (1995), 'Conclusion: The Transformation of Industrial Relations? A Cross-National Review of the Evidence' in R. Locke, T. Kochan, and M. Piore (eds.), *Employment Relations in a Changing World Economy*. Cambridge: MIT Press, pp.359–84.

Lowe, K.B., Milliman, J., De Cieri, H. and Dowling, P.J. (2002), 'International Compensation Practices: A Ten-Country Comparative Analysis', *Human Resource Management*, Vol.41, No.1, pp.45–66.

Marchington, M. and Grugulis, I. (2000), '"Best Practice" Human Resource Management: Perfect Opportunity or Dangerous Illusion?', *International Journal of Human Resource Management*, Vol.11, No.6, pp.1104–24.

McKinley, W., Sanchez, C.M. and Schick, A.G. (1995), 'Organizational Downsizing: Constraining, Cloning, Learning', *Academy of Management Executive*, Vol.9, No.3, pp.32–44.

Meyer, J. and Rowan, B. (1977), 'Institutionalized Organizations: Formal Structure as Myth and Ceremony', *American Journal of Sociology*, Vol.83, No.2, pp.340–63.

Moon, I. (2002), 'Falling Madly in Love with Plastic', *Business Week* (Asian edn), 13 May, p.57.

Morden, T. and Bowles, D. (1998), 'Management in South Korea: A Review', *Management Decision*, Vol.36, No.5.

Nonaka, I. and Takeuchi, H. (1995), *The Knowledge-Creating Company: How Japanese Companies Create the Dynamics of Innovation*. New York: Oxford University Press.

Oh, Ingyu (1999), *Mafioso, Big Business and the Financial Crisis: The State–Business Relations in South Korea and Japan*. Aldershot: Ashgate.

Park, J. and Ahn, H. (1999), *The Changes and Future Direction of Korean Employment Practices*. Seoul: The Korea Employers' Federation (In Korean).

Peters, T. and Waterman, R. (1982), *In Search of Excellence: Lessons from America's Best Run Companies*. London: Harper and Row.

Pucik, V. and Lim, J.C. (2002), 'Transforming HRM in a Korean *Chaebol*: A Case Study of Samsumg', in C. Rowley, T.W. Sohn and J. Bae (eds.), *Managing Korean Businesses: Organization, Culture, Human Resources and Change*, London & Portland, OR: Frank Cass, pp.137–60.

Rodgers, Ronald A. (1990), 'An Exclusive Labor Regime under Pressure: The Changes in Labor Relations in the Republic of Korea since Mid-1987', *UCLA Pacific Basin Law Journal*, Vol.8, pp.91–161.

Rowley, C. (Ed.) (1999). HRM in Services. *Personnel Review*, 28(5/6).

Rowley, C. (1997), 'Conclusion: Reassessing HRM's Convergence', *Asia Pacific Business Review*, Vol.3, No.4, pp.197–210.

Rowley, C. and Bae, J. (eds.) (1998), *Korean Businesses: Internal and External Industrialization*. London & Portland, OR: Frank Cass.

Rowley, C. and Bae, J. (2002), 'Globalisation and Transformation of HRM in South Korea', *International Journal of Human Resource Management*, Vol.13, No.3, pp.522–49.

Rowley, C. and Bae, J. (2003), 'Management and Culture in South Korea' in M. Warner (ed.), *Management and Culture in Asia*. London: Curzon.

Rowley, C. and Benson, J. (2002), 'Convergence and Divergence in Asian HRM', *California Management Review*, Vol.44, No.2, pp.90–109.

Rowley, C., Sohn, T.W. and Bae, J. (eds.) (2002), *Managing Korean Businesses: Organization, Culture, Human Resources and Change*, London & Portland, OR: Frank Cass.

Song, Byung-Nak (1997), *The Rise of the Korean Economy*, Oxford: Oxford University Press.

Storey, J. (1992), *Developments in the Management of Human Resources*. London: Routledge.

Turner, L. and Auer, P. (1996), 'A Diversity of New Work Organization: Human-Centred, Lean and In-Between' in F.C. Deyo (ed.), *Social Reconstructions of the World Automobile Industry*. London: Macmillan, pp.233–57.

Tushman, M.L. and O'Reilly, III, C.A. (1997), *Winning Through Innovation: A Practical Guide to Leading Organizational Change and Renewal*. Boston, MA: Harvard Business School Press.

Womack, J., Jones, D. and Roos, D. (1990), *The Machine that Changed the World*. New York: Rawson Associates.

Woo, J. (2002), 'A Case on Recruitment Strategy and Selection Technique for Core Talents' in *Proceedings of the Annual Conference of the Korean Association of Personnel Administration*, Seoul, Korea (in Korean), pp.151–63.

Change and Continuity:
Recent Developments in HRM
in the Philippines

CHRISTOPHER SKENE

Studies of Philippine industrial relations (IR) and human resource management (HRM) practices tend to take on different tones depending on whether the focus of the study is on the older import substitution sector of the economy or the newer export oriented sector. This study takes the position that, over the past few decades there has been a substantial amount of divergence between HRM practices in firms engaged in the import substitution industrialization (ISI) sector and those in the export-oriented industrialization (EOI) sector. The former has traditionally been characterized by fairly rigid workplace structures and rules, while most firms in the latter sector, by virtue of being much more exposed to global competition have, for some time, employed practices to promote flexibility in the workplace. Recently, as a consequence of increasing exposure to global competition resulting from the persistent drive towards economic liberalization, managers in the former sector are now adopting practices more characteristic of the latter sector.

Maragtas Amante (1997) conducted the earlier thorough examination of HRM practices in seven major Philippine corporations. Amante organized his study around three major practices, including, skills development, compensation and the determination of work rules. According to Amante, HRM practices that have been well entrenched in the country include job positions with rigid descriptions of duties and responsibilities, the dominance of supervisors, collective bargaining focusing on pay increases, and a focus on minimizing payroll costs (Amante, 1997: 116–17). Yet Amante also suggests that there have been definite trends towards the adoption of more modern and Western HRM practices. Amante concluded that Philippine HRM practices could best be described as a *halo-halo* (or mixed) approach; a pragmatic blend of Western practices with those that are specific to Philippine culture. As the seven corporations used as case studies are among the largest Philippine-owned firms in the country, and are considered industry leaders, Amante implies the practices employed by these firms constitute, in the context of the Philippines, examples of the 'best practice' approach (Amante, 1997: 129).

One question that should arise from such a study is whether or not HRM practices are similar in different sectors of the economy. While Amante notes that 13 per cent of San Miguel's sales and 40 per cent of Ramcar's sales are in international markets, all seven of his cases are firms primarily geared to servicing the domestic market and none can be thought of as being engaged in the export sector per se. As current efforts in the area of economic development have been based on EOI (Broad and Cavanagh, 1988; Kuruvilla, 1996a; Kuruvilla et al., 2000), overlooking the export sector may prevent one from getting a true picture of HRM practices in the Philippines. EOI is built on a very different set of assumptions than production geared towards producing for the domestic market and it is reasonable to believe that different industrialization strategies can influence both IR and HRM practices (Kuruvilla, 1996a). What is needed, therefore, is a step backwards to view HRM in the Philippines from a broader perspective. This will allow one to determine whether HRM systems differ in different sectors of the economy and why this may be so.

The purpose of this essay is three-fold: to build on Maragtas Amante's 1997 study on HRM practices in the Philippines, to demonstrate differences in HRM practices in the ISI and EOI sectors and to highlight the changes that have taken place over the past few years. Overall, this essay makes two main assertions. First, Amante was correct in noting that there is a trend in the Philippines towards the adoption of more modern and more Western HRM practices, and second, the changes that are occurring are largely confined to firms in the ISI sector of the economy. The reason for the movement is that the regulatory protection that was once afforded the ISI sector has now been systematically removed, consequently, firms have had to adjust to the realities of competition. By contrast the EOI sector has demonstrated relatively little change because this sector has always been geared towards competing in the global economy. The net result of these developments is that the ISI firms have been adopting practices more characteristic of those employed in the EOI sector. The balance of this essay is divided into three main sections. First, the context in which Philippine HRM systems operate is highlighted. The second section details some of the major changes taking place. This section will illustrate that the majority of the changes have taken place in the ISI sector and many of the practices being adopted here are those employed in the EOI sector. The final section will explain why changes are occurring and outline a couple of the current issues in Philippine HRM.

CONTEXTUAL FACTORS AND ISSUES

Political and Historical

In a region that has been famous for economic dynamism, the Philippines have often stood out as an exception. Although the country has often been regarded as one of the oldest democracies in East Asia, the Philippines have seen more that their share of political turmoil. Over the past few decades, the country has survived a 14-year dictatorship, guerrilla war, several coup attempts, repeated natural disasters and economic crises. By the mid-1990s, the Philippines appeared to show promise as political stability returned and economic growth appeared to be accelerating to levels similar to those achieved by their more dynamic neighbours. But, as this section will reveal, the euphoria of the mid-1990s proved to be short lived as the country went through the Asian financial crisis and further political turmoil.

Economic

Today, the Philippine economy is largely configured along the lines of the EOI model. This has been the result of a long transformation from the ISI model that was instituted in the early 1950s and actively developed into the 1960s. That era has often been referred to as the golden age of Philippine industrialization as growth rates were in excess of 10 per cent per annum throughout the 1950s. The ISI sector is generally considered to consist of large state and privately owned firms operating in the areas of manufacturing, utilities, communications and transportation.[1] The common thread between them is that all were established primarily to service the domestic market and all had traditionally been protected from foreign competition. In some cases competition was encouraged at the domestic level, while in other cases, state-owned monopolies were set up in key sectors (Kuruvilla, 1996b). During the ISI era, higher wages and unionism were acceptable to managers because, under ISI, workers were also considered to be consumers of the goods that were manufactured. In fact, the Philippine government encouraged the formation of trade unions as a vehicle for creating demand, which, in turn, benefited the firms as well as the workers (Lloyd and Salter, 1999: 3).

EOI in the Philippines can be traced back to around 1970. Much of the impetus for EOI has been pressure from the international financial institutions (IFI), particularly the International Monetary Fund (IMF) and the World Bank. Chronic problems in the country's national finances have made the Philippines a regular client of the IFIs. From 1973 to 1999, the Philippines signed 14 IMF agreements as well as at least 10 World Bank Structural Adjustment Loans (Skene, 2002: 491). The Philippines' debt problems have given the IFIs an enormous amount of influence over the country's economic policies. In the 1980s, the Philippines became one of the first countries to receive a World Bank Structural Adjustment Loan. At that time, the World Bank targeted the Philippines as one of 30 countries that it believed could replicate the success of the East Asian Newly Industrialized Countries (NIC).[2] The Bank pushed the Philippines to liberalize its economy and adopt EOI because it believed that the country was in a position to compete as a supplier of low cost labour (Broad and Cavanagh, 1988: 86).

As a result of the near continuous relationship with the IFIs, the Philippines has been under constant pressure to liberalize its economy, to remove regulatory barriers to foreign investment and products and to privatize state-owned firms. Compliance with IFI loan conditions has led to the removal of much of the regulatory protection that once characterized the ISI sector (Kuruvilla, 1996b), leaving firms scrambling to adapt to their new environment. In the mid-1990s, the then President Fidel Ramos incorporated much of the wisdom of liberalization, privatization and structural adjustment in his Medium Term Philippine Development Plan, commonly referred to as 'Philippines 2000'. Explicitly friendly to foreign capital in content and philosophy, 'Philippines 2000', combined with the return of political stability, generated a great deal of enthusiasm among foreign investors who began to invest heavily in the country. The resulting influx of foreign investment into the country led to growth rates of 5–7 per cent in the mid-1990s, leading many to believe that NIC status was in sight.

Today, reliance on foreign investment constitutes the sine qua non of the Philippine economic development strategy (Kelly, 1997: 159). As the domestic savings rate has normally been fairly low and consistently below the investment rate, the Philippines always needs foreign capital to make up for the lack of domestic capital. Overall, foreign equity accounts for 65 per cent of all investment in manufacturing and 21 per cent of all employment in the country (Kuruvilla et al., 2000: 12). However, EOI production in the Philippines has been, and remains, primary level EOI – that is, low cost, labour intensive assembly and testing of goods for export (Kuruvilla, 1996b; Kuruvilla et al., 2000: 15). This has meant that EOI production has, thus far, not enabled the Philippines to climb the technological ladder and engage in more advanced processes to any significant degree. Nevertheless, like many developing countries, the

Philippines looks to foreign investment not only to provide needed technology, managerial skills, and knowledge of foreign markets, but also to provide the very impetus for economic growth.[3]

Labour Markets

With respect to the labour market, the Philippines has a very large and reasonably well-educated workforce. In 2001, the Philippine labour force stood at 32,808,000, up from 30,911,000 the year before (Pacific Bridge, 2002: 2). And, despite the focus on the industrial sectors in this and other HRM studies, agriculture still remains the single largest occupation group in the country, accounting for around 37 per cent of the workforce (Pacific Bridge, 2002: 3). Unemployment and under-employment remain stubborn problems in the country. Currently, unemployment stands at around 11.2 per cent (Pacific Bridge, 2002: 2), up from 9.6 per cent during the crisis year of 1998 (Aldaba, 2000: 11). Under-employment, while down from 2001, remains stubbornly high at 17.2 per cent (Pacific Bridge, 2002: 2). Hence, there is constant pressure on the Philippine economy to produce jobs for the large number of participants in the labour force. Whereas between 2000 and 2001 the labour force increased by 1,897,000, the number of employed persons only grew by 1,702,000 (Pacific Bridge, 2002: 2). Thus, while the economy grew by 3.7 per cent over the same period, it appears that much more dynamic growth will be necessary if enough employment opportunities for the country's workers are to be generated. Finally, as high as the unemployment and under-employment figures are, it must also be remembered that these figures have been significantly mitigated by the large numbers of Filipinos who have secured employment overseas. In 1998, for example, over 756,000 Filipino workers were deployed in overseas jobs and this figure has been increasing (Aldaba, 2000: 13).

Labour relations in the Philippines are governed by the Labour Code of the Philippines. The code was first drafted by the Marcos government during the martial law era, and its major thrust was the promotion of labour peace. At that time strikes were proscribed and union activity was severely restricted. After assuming power in 1986, President Corazon Aquino lifted a number of the more blatant restrictions in the code, yet, by 1989, her government had implemented Republic Act 6715, which created a relatively restrictive atmosphere for union activity and provided the state broad powers to intervene in industrial disputes. Thus, despite the return to democracy, there have been no fundamental changes to Philippine labour law since the early 1970s (Frenkel and Kuruvilla, 2002: 402). On the other hand, the labour code does contain a wide range of safeguards for workers with rules governing everything from annual leave to unionization (see Ofreneo, 1996), most of which have been framed in relatively liberal terms. The 1987 Philippine Constitution, drafted after the country returned to democratic governance, also contains a number of specific provisions for workers, including the entrenchment of the right to organize into unions, the right to strike, the right to a living wage, and the like. In this respect, some have claimed that the Philippines has one of the more liberal labour law regimes in South East Asia (Kelly, 2001). Yet, at the same time, there is considerable evidence that many of these provisions for workers often go unenforced.[4]

Overall, the primary focus in HRM in the Philippines is on flexibility (Kuruvilla and Erickson, 2002). In the EOI sector, this concern for flexibility is accompanied by a similar concern for union avoidance. A few leading – primarily American-owned – transnational corporations (TNC) have sought increased competitiveness through the use of functional flexibility. This refers to methods firms use to enhance the productivity of their existing workforces. Measures such as reorganizing the structure of the firm, promoting teamwork, multi-skilling, job rotation, investing in training and the like, allow firms to enhance the skills of their workers, enabling them to do more work and work of better quality (Kuruvilla and Erickson, 2002: 178). This raises the productivity of the firm without the need for significantly enlarging the size of the workforce. However, most firms in the Philippines have sought flexibility through numerical flexibility (Kuruvilla and Erickson, 2002: 198); which refers to the ability of managers to adjust the size of their workforces in a manner that reflects current demand for the goods that are being produced. The two most pervasive avenues by which employers have sought to promote this sort of flexibility are through the use of job subcontracting and labour contracting (or service contracting) (Barranco-Fernando; Ofreneo and Wallace, 1997).

The Labour Code of the Philippines recognizes both subcontracting and labour contracting as legitimate forms of employment and has rules for each in order to provide protection for workers. For job subcontracting, the labour code stipulates that both the principle and the subcontractor are jointly and severally liable for unpaid wages owed to the employees of the subcontractor (Ofreneo and Wallace, 1997). Job subcontracting has been particularly prevalent in the garment industry where numerous firms have sought to lower costs by farming out the labour-intensive portions of the process such as cutting and sewing to subcontractors (Ofreneo and Wallace, 1997).

For the purposes of this study, 'labour contracting' specifically refers to the use of contract workers, labour-only contracting, and other temporary arrangements as alternatives to hiring regular workers. Labour contracting is legal provided that only one of the following conditions holds: either a) the person supplying workers does not have substantial capital or investment to actually perform the job, work or service on his/her own account; or b) workers recruited are performing duties directly related to the main business of the principal (Ofreneo and Wallace, 1997). If both conditions are present, then the arrangement becomes categorized as 'labour-only contracting' which is strictly prohibited by law. Increasingly, employers are hiring workers through independent employment agencies, which often saves employers a great deal of time and money otherwise spent on advertising, screening and selecting new workers. Employment agencies have existed for some time providing employers with workers to perform ancillary services such as cleaning and catering. But recently, such services have expanded to provide workers to do many essential jobs for employers, including equipment maintenance, office management, packaging and bottling, marketing, transportation and the like (Ofreneo and Wallace, 1997). Yet, the agencies do not have the means to perform the jobs and services themselves, hence, both conditions governing labour contracting are present which, under Philippine law, is illegal.

It is very difficult to say how many workers are employed through various forms of labour contracting, but all the indications suggest that the number of workers employed through these types of arrangement is growing. In 1990, the International Labour Organization calculated that about 36 per cent of all employers hire temporary labour as an alternative to regular workers (Kuruvilla et al., 2000: 45). Between 1994 and 1998, the Department of Labour and Employment reported that the number of firms using contractual labour increased by 51 per cent, most of them large employers (ICFTU, 1999). As of 1995 there were 252 registered employment agencies which placed 49,055 workers, while the number of unlicensed agencies operating in the country was believed to be double this figure (Tujan, 1998). Currently, the Kilusang Mayo Uno (KMU), one of the major union federations in the Philippines, maintains that only one in seven workers in the Philippines today can be considered to be a regular worker under the law.[5] If the KMU is correct, this would mean that six out of every seven workers, about 85 per cent, are engaged on a non-regular basis and do not enjoy the full protection provided by the labour code.

The significant movement towards adopting flexible practices, including the use of subcontracting, labour contracting as well as more legally questionable practices has been possible, in part, because of union weakness. Most unions in the Philippines are enterprise-based unions and have never been very strong,[6] but as a result of globalization and the Asian crisis, they have never been weaker. Today, out of a workforce of nearly 33 million, only 3.85 million workers belong to one of 10,924 unions. More significantly, of the 3.85 million union members, only 462,000 are covered by a collective bargaining agreement, and this number has been falling (BusinessWorld, 2002a). Union strength is further weakened by the fact the 10,924 unions are scattered among 174 different labour federations, many of which often see each other as rivals. As a result of low union membership and the high degree of fragmentation in the union movement, unions have not been able to act as an effective counterbalance to employer power (Frenkel and Kuruvilla, 2002: 401–2).

Today, the old ISI sector is the most heavily unionized sector of the economy,[7] and, while there are some notable exceptions such as the San Miguel Corporation, which is an industry leader in virtually every facet of its operations (Kuruvilla et al., 2000: 78), many of the firms in this sector are facing difficulties, even collapse. The steel, petrochemicals, cement and paper industries are among those that have been hard hit by the increased foreign competition that economic liberalization and structural adjustment have brought (BusinessWorld, 2002b). As a result of these problems, many Filipinos have concluded that 'local industries are in their last two minutes'.[8]

1997 Asian Financial Crisis and Reactions

Prior to the Asian financial crisis, the Philippine peso was pegged at around 26 pesos to the US dollar, but many economists felt that it was overvalued. Once the Thai baht was devalued in 1997, the Philippines became the next target of the financial markets (Aldaba, 2000: 8). Whilst some observers have argued that the Philippines did not suffer as badly as many of its counterparts in the region (Pacific Bridge 2001: 1), the country was still battered by rising prices, increased unemployment and falling investor confidence. GDP growth fell from 5.1 per cent in 1997 to -0.5 per cent in 1998 and interest rates peaked at 30 per cent on bank loans and over 20 per cent for Treasury Bills, leading to a credit crunch (Aldaba, 2000: 8–9).

The initial response of the Philippine government to the crisis was to defend the peso. The Bangko Sentral ng Pilipinas (Philippine Central Bank) spent US$2 billion in an unsuccessful effort to defend the peg, after which the peso was allowed to float (Aldaba, 2000: 8). The response of the Philippine government to broader social concerns was both belated and modest, given the lack of available funds. In February 1998, a deal was struck between labour groups, employer confederations and the government in which employers promised to use lay-offs as a last resort and workers promised to refrain from industrial action (Aldaba, 2000: 15). However, this has not prevented employers from using other types of schemes to reduce payroll costs. After President Joseph Estrada assumed power in 1998, his administration alleviated some of the pressures of the crisis by negotiating a deal with the IMF to allow the government to use deficit spending to 'pump prime' the economy (Aldaba, 2000: 14).

Current Economic Situation

Today, two major events have had a profound effect on the Philippines. First, the impeachment and removal of president Joseph Estrada had a decidedly negative impact on both the political and economic landscape. In early 2001, as the impeachment proceedings came to an abrupt halt and the people took to the streets in a mass rally that became known as EDSA II, the Philippine peso plummeted to an all-time low of around P55 to the US dollar. The cumulative effect of both the Asian crisis and the overthrow of Estrada has been the evaporation of the bullishness present in the mid-1990s, and reflected in Amante (1997). A second factor that has undermined confidence in the country has been the partial resurgence of guerrilla activity in the South, particularly the Abu Sayyef group which has not confined its operations to the island of Mindanao. Abu Sayyef has drawn a great deal of attention to itself through the kidnapping of foreign nationals and the occasional bombings in Manila. The Philippine government has responded by stepping up military operations against the insurgents and has welcomed US assistance in its fight against the Muslim guerrillas. Yet foreign investors remained very uneasy about the Philippines throughout 2001, signalling that President Gloria Arroyo must continue economic reforms to demonstrate that the country remains friendly to investment (BusinessWorld, 2001). Even today investors remain somewhat skittish about investing in the Philippines (FEER, 2003: 24–35).

CHANGES IN HRM

In order to demonstrate to what extent there has been convergence in the area of HRM practices in the Philippines, one should look at practices in both the ISI and the EOI sectors. This study maintains that the major changes in HRM practices that have been occurring are located in the ISI sector. As numerous ISI firms have been hit hard by the pressures of global competition and the Asian financial crisis, many of these firms have sought to restructure their operations in order to better compete. Table 1 provides a brief synopsis of the changes that have taken place over the past five or so years. The balance of this section will discuss some of changes in HRM practices that have been taking place.

Major Changes Taking Place

To a great extent personnel recruitment is more or less the same throughout the Philippines. With high unemployment, employers usually have an ample number of applicants to choose from. Although a number of firms have recruitment tests, the jobs can just as easily go to a friend, a relative or some other close acquaintance from the manager's home province (Selmer and De Leon, 2001: 139). It is also common for existing workers to recommend a friend or relative for a vacant position. While this practice is not unique to the Philippines, here it is understood that the 'backer' who recommends the prospective employee also puts his/her reputation on the line as a type of guarantor ensuring that the new worker will be productive and will not cause trouble (Chant and McIlwaine, 1995; Selmer and De Leon, 2001: 137).

It is worth noting that a significant number of EOI firms, particularly those in the electronics sector, have developed some interesting practices for screening and hiring workers. In most cases, the requirements for employment in EOI firms are a birth certificate, a curriculum vitae, diploma and/or transcripts, medical certificate or

TABLE 1

ASSESSMENT OF HRM CHANGES AND CONTINUITIES

Dimension	Presence	Change
Rules: Adherence to	✓	0
Behaviour: use of values and missions	✗	0
Key managers: HRM specialists	✗	0
Personnel selection	✓	0
Payment systems (rewarding performance)	%	+
Work conditions: harmonized	%	0
Use of contractual arrangements	✓	+
In-house training	✓	+
Right to hire and fire	✓	0
Strategic role for personnel managers	%	+

Key: (*Practice*)
  ✓ present
  % present to some degree
  ✗ not present

  (*Degree of change in past 4 years*)
  ++ major change
  + change
  0 none
Source: adapted from Storey (1992).

medical examination by a company doctor, social security number, police clearance and/or National Bureau of Investigation (NBI) clearance, and a letter of recommendation from one's mayor and/or *barangay* captain.[9] Employers require letters of recommendations from local officials because they provide connections they can use in the event of labour disputes. In short, this is an extension of the guarantor system. By offering their recommendations to prospective workers, it is understood that, if trouble arises, the company and/or export processing zone (EPZ) authority can contact the mayors and *barangay* captains and ask them to help pacify the workers (McKay, 1999: 7–8; Kelly, 2001). Unlike the ISI sector, most EOI firms are not unionized, hence one of the primary goals of HRM in the EOI sector is to help prevent unionization. To achieve this goal, firms, particularly electronics firms, now employ elaborate hiring and screening procedures to weed out anyone who might be considered undesirable, uncooperative and pro-union before they are hired (McKay, 1999: 7).

While a increasing amount of effort is now being put into recruiting workers who will be generally cooperative, a much more significant issue is the terms on which employees are engaged. Here, one the most significant trends in the Philippines has been the aforementioned movement towards the use of various forms of labour contracting. The use of labour contracting has become a very contentious issue because the situation has arisen whereby a significant number of those hired on a contractual basis are becoming 'permanent contractual' workers instead of regular workers (Barranco-Fernando; Ofreneo and Wallace, 1997). This situation has arisen as a result of a provision in the labour code that permits a probationary period of up to six months for all newly hired workers, after which the new employees are to become regular workers. In practice, however, what actually happens is that many workers are intentionally hired for periods less than six months and then dismissed, after which new workers are hired to replace them, again, for a period of less than six months. In fact, it is not uncommon for the same workers to be rehired by the same employer on a new contract for the same job on the same terms and conditions as before (Barranco-Fernando; Ofreneo and Wallace, 1997).

Today, the use of labour contracting can be found in most sectors of the Philippine economy, including, the EOI sector, the mining sector and, now, the ISI sector and even retailing. For example, one of the largest department store chains in the Philippines, Shoe Mart (or SM) has around 20,000 employees, of which only 1,731 of them are regular employees covered by a collective bargaining agreement.[10] The majority of the remaining employees – 63 per cent – are retained through some form of labour contracting (IBON, 2000: 10). Likewise,

Philippine Long Distance Telephone has around 5,000 casual workers and has been expanding the number of jobs done by contractual workers (Amante, 1997: 126).

The extensive use of labour contracting and subcontracting arose out of the pressures of the EOI strategy as a means to enhance competitiveness through boosting numerical flexibility and reducing labour costs. Particularly in industries that employ relatively low levels of technology, such as garments and textiles, competition between firms is very intense and this puts pressure on managers to cut costs whenever possible. Hence, firms have been reducing the number of regular workers in their employ by replacing them with contractual workers. For example, a firm identified as Chosen Wear employs nearly half of its staff (387 out of 844) on contractual bases (EILR, 2001: 46), of which the majority receive only 75 per cent of the legal minimum wage (EILR, 2001: 55). On an aggregate level, it is difficult to ascertain how many are actually employed through labour contracting. However, a recent study revealed that the average wage paid in the garment and textile industry was about 90 per cent of the legal minimum wage, suggesting the practice is quite widespread (IBON, 2001: 44–5). In addition, Chosen Wear, like a large number of garment firms, supplements its factory work force with subcontracting arrangements (EILR, 2001: 46). Subcontractors are normally engaged on a piece-rate basis, consequently, firms only need to engage subcontractors as and when demand levels require the addition capacity.

By contrast, labour contracting and sub-contracting arrangements have not been as prevalent in the electronics industry because the nature of the work requires workers to become quite well skilled. As these skills are often firm specific, employers prefer a stable and committed workforce, and this stability cannot be achieved if employees are retained for only short periods of time. For example, the Japanese firm Uniden, a low-cost producer of electronic goods, retains its production workers on a permanent basis, but also cuts costs and enhances numerical flexibility through hiring ancillary workers such as canteen staff and security personnel on contractual bases (Kuruvilla et al., 2000: 77). Overall, roughly 73 per cent of the workers in the electronics industry are regular employees while 16 per cent are contractual and 11 per cent are probationary (EILR, 2001: 54). However, a workforce with a full complement of skilled regular workers is fertile ground for unionization (McKay, 1999: 7). It is for this reason that firms devote so much time and effort to recruit workers that are unsympathetic to and/or uninformed about union activity.

In addition to the use of non-regular employment practices, many workers hired to be regular workers are now engaged for a considerable period of time in one or more non-regular schemes before they are regularized. This is happening even in firms that are producing for the Philippine domestic market. For example, at a Japanese car manufacturer identified as Topcar, all employees are required to undergo on-the-job training for one month. After the training period, employees are hired as contractuals for five months and then as probationary workers for six months before they are finally made regular and permanent workers (EILR, 2001: 55). Here Topcar is exploiting the provision of a six-month probationary period and effectively extending it to 12 months by adding a short-term contract to the hiring process. The reasons for doing this stem from the fact that probationary workers can be paid only 75 per cent of the minimum wage, and because employers do not have to provide all of the benefits due to regular employees stipulated in the labour code until employees are regularized (Lloyd and Salter, 1999).

ISI firms are also seeking to restructure their operations and enhance competitiveness by downsizing their workforces. This is a tactic that has often been used by garment firms in the EOI sector to remain afloat during periods of low demand (IBON, 2001: 49). Since privatization in 1994, Petron, the former state-owned oil company, has been attempting to adjust to its new reality as a private corporation, albeit slowly. Its biggest accomplishments thus far have been to link pay with performance and to cut the size of its workforce. After privatization, Petron regarded itself as heavily overstaffed. In the wake of the Asian crisis, it has been able to reduce its staff from 1,700 to 1,300 employees, and both professional and managerial staff were among those cut (Kuruvilla et al., 2000: 79). Likewise, the Philippine National Bank is seeking to reduce its workforce by around 20 per cent and has initiated a voluntary retirement programme as a first step towards this goal (Kuruvilla et al., 2000: 57). Out of a total workforce of 1,500, Philacor, the leading manufacturer of refrigerators and freezers in the Philippines, cut 378 workers in 1997 and another 325 in 1998. The Philacor example is a particularly noteworthy achievement because the union representing the company's employees was militant and had strongly resisted previous restructuring efforts – walking off the job in 1992 and again in 1994 in protest of company plans for laying-off workers and contracting out, respectfully. The union went so far as to make it clear that any further attempts at restructuring would be resisted with both strikes and violence (Kuruvilla et al., 2000: 51) – until the Asian financial crisis changed everything.

One of the most interesting consequences of the Asian crisis was the breakdown of union resistance to company restructuring efforts. Compared with the pre-crisis era where unions actively resisted such efforts, this breakdown has proved to be an important development and has quickly led to noticeable changes in the ISI sector. Seeing that the crisis was having a profound effect on the entire Philippine economy, the union at Philacor found itself unable to justify further resistance to management initiatives. Instead, the union found it more productive to negotiate severance pay for redundant workers and following this path it was able to secure an agreement whereby 200 of the most senior employees were transferred to Philacor's newly built second plant and trained on the new equipment. Furthermore, because of the disappearance of union resistance, Philacor has been able to implement a wide range of new HRM practices at its new plant (see below) (Kuruvilla et al., 2000: 51).

In the ISI sector, and to a large extent, the EOI sector, training normally takes place on the job. Traditionally, firms train employees to do the jobs they were hired to do. ISI firms have traditionally been very rigid in this respect (Kuruvilla, 1996b). This has meant that retraining and upgrading programmes (not to mention practices such as multi-skilling) for rank-and-file workers have been rare (Ofreneo, 1995: 40). Recently, there has been some evidence that things are changing. For example, San Miguel and Philippine Airlines have invested in their own training centres (Amante, 1997:119). In addition to training its own employees, the Philippine National Bank is now sending some of its employees on training programmes outside the firm. Although a step forward, this programme is relatively modest as the Bank cannot afford to send large numbers of employees to such programmes. Employees who do attend are required to conduct 'echo sessions' in which they share what they have learned with their colleagues (Kuruvilla et al., 2000: 57).

One reason for the increased attention that training is receiving from Philippine firms is connected to efforts on the part of, at least, some firms to enhance competitiveness through functional flexibility. In this respect, Philacor is a case in point. Prior to the Asian crisis, Philacor had been operating a production facility with fairly rigid workplace structures and work rules. But since the early 1990s, Philacor has been feeling the pressure of competition from Thailand where, despite the fact that labour costs are 30 per cent higher than they are in the Philippines, Thai produced refrigerators sell for about 30 per cent less (Kuruvilla et al., 2000: 50). In addition, the Montreal Protocol Agreement, signed in the early 1990s, demanded that CFCs no longer be used in the production of refrigerators and freezers. This meant that new manufacturing equipment and techniques would have to be employed in the future. Philacor's solution to these problems was to build a new state of the art plant and employ new production methods and HRM practices. At the new facility, Philacor has adopted practices to enhance both numerical flexibility, through the use of subcontracting, and functional flexibility, through increased training, requiring every worker to be multi-skilled and employing frequent job rotations (Kuruvilla et al., 2000: 52). However, in the Philippines, this is somewhat unique as efforts towards functional flexibility have been, thus far, sporadic.

In the EOI sector, electronics firms generally invest a fair amount in training. Motorola, for example, has invested a great deal in training in order to achieve functional flexibility. As a leading firm in the electronics industry, Motorola runs its Philippine operations in essentially the same way as its entire worldwide operations. Employees receive at least 40 hours of training per year and are expected to learn one new skill every six months. Training is very comprehensive and includes skills training, production, quality, maintenance, trouble-shooting, and the like. As Motorola uses fully automated production lines, operators are generally responsible for monitoring the lines through the use of computer terminals. All operators are trained to maintain the lines and, on their own, fix problems should they arise (Kuruvilla et al., 2000: 73–74). All of this is directed towards developing multi-skilled workers who can both operate the production lines and attend to breakdowns in the system.

Leading TNCs such as Motorola have essentially transplanted their entire HRM systems into their subsidiary plants. However, they tend not to be very representative of the Philippine electronics industry as a whole. By contrast, Uniden is, perhaps, more representative of the practices used by electronics firms operating in the Philippines (Kuruvilla, 1996b). At Uniden work is organized along more Tayloristic principles. Training is on the job and is job specific. Workers are generally expected to learn how to operate a number of different machines, but workers are not permitted to attend to machine breakdowns. Nor are they trained to do so, as maintenance is left to an engineering staff. Material supply and inspection are the responsibility of line leaders and assistant line leaders (Kuruvilla et al., 2000: 76–7).

As most firms in the ISI sector are unionized, compensation levels in ISI firms are normally negotiated with the unions in the formulation of collective bargaining agreements. In his study, Amante noted that all seven of the firms studied were unionized and all paid wages significantly more than the minimum wage and had benefit packages ranging from 50 to 100 per cent of basic pay. Generally speaking, compensation systems in ISI firms have not linked pay to productivity or skill acquisition. While the Philippine government has encouraged the incorporation of productivity incentives into worker compensation packages (Ofreneo and Wallace, 1997), unions have generally opposed it. In addition, firms are compelled to increase wages in response to government mandated increases in the minimum wage. This sometimes creates 'distortions' when the new mandated wage overtakes the wages of regular employees (i.e. those at the bottom of the pay scale) (Amante, 1997: 122).

Recently there have been some changes in compensation systems. Petron, for example, has now developed a mechanism to link pay to performance. The company bases its performance-related salary increases on what degree the company achieves its key performance targets. Employees are paid on the basis of the average performance level of their particular line functions; i.e. refining, marketing, supplies, and so on. (Kuruvilla et al., 2000: 79). Petron's motivation for adopting new pay systems and streamlining its workforce stems from having to compete with Shell, a recognized industry leader, without the security of being a state-owned firm (Kuruvilla et al., 2000: 80). Likewise, the Philippine National Bank has now established three pay levels for every job category: a minimum, a mid-range, and a maximum. Moving from one level to the next is based on merit rather than seniority (Kuruvilla et al., 2000: 57). This scheme is also a response to the pressures of competition as the Bank, like Petron, is a newly privatized state-owned corporation.

In the EOI sector, which has very few unionized firms, the majority of those who are employed as regular workers receive the relevant minimum wage. A few of the big foreign TNCs, such as Motorola which pays around 25–40 per cent above the minimum wage and has geared its compensation system to performance and productivity (Kuruvilla, 1996b), have very generous compensation packages. On the other hand, Uniden, which tends to be more representative of Philippine electronics firms, compensates operators with two years of experience a mere 7 per cent above the minimum wage. Uniden's compensation system is based on fixed wage scales with guaranteed increments and does not contain any production or merit-based incentives (Kuruvilla et al., 2000:77). In this respect, it may be possible that the ISI sector might actually be moving ahead of much of the EOI sector. While ISI firms are now starting to offer incentives for productivity in a manner similar to firms like Motorola, in most EOI firms there is often little relationship between higher skills and better pay. One company paid operators certified on ten different machines

P12 (or US$0.24) per day more than standard operators with only three certifications (McKay, 1999: 8).

DISCUSSION

Why Changes Have Occurred

Over the past five years, two basic trends can be discerned. First, in the ISI sector, there has been a movement towards the use of HRM practices designed to promote flexibility and competitiveness. For example, both Philacor and Petron have been pursuing numerical flexibility by cutting their workforces. Other firms like Philippine Long Distance Telephone and SM have made extensive use of contractual labour. Conversely, firms such as Philippine National Bank and Philacor are putting greater emphasis on training. For Philacor, training is an important ingredient to achieving functional flexibility. Like some of the leading TNCs, Philacor is now requiring workers to be multi-skilled and versatile. In short, ISI firms are attempting to make themselves leaner, more flexible and more competitive by adopting practices that many EOI firms have used for some time. Table 2 offers a quick summary of the changes that have taken place over the past five or so years.

The reason for the changes in the ISI sector directly stem from successive efforts to liberalize the Philippine economy. With the removal of trade and investment barriers and the privatization of state-owned firms brought about by numerous structural adjustment programmes, ISI firms have lost much of the regulatory protection they once enjoyed. The pressures of competing in the global economy are forcing firms to adapt to the new environment or collapse. As a result, HRM has become increasingly important as managers are in the midst of restructuring their companies. The specific HRM measures adopted by Petron, Philacor and the Philippine National Bank, for example, are all strategies designed to help the firms survive in a new competitive environment. The Philacor example is particularly noteworthy as it demonstrates that the changes the firm made – building a new factory and instituting new HRM practices – were a direct result of the pressure arising from foreign competition. Similarly, the changes instituted by Petron were a response to the necessity of having to compete and survive as a private firm against Shell. In general, many of the changes in the ISI sector have been instituted only in the past five years because, prior to the Asian crisis, unions actively resisted any measures that threatened worker security. As the crisis decimated what strength Philippine unions had prior to 1997, nearly all of the changes in HRM practices initiated in the past

TABLE 2

SUMMARY OF THE RECENT DEVELOPMENTS IN PHILIPPINE HRM PRACTICES

	Pre-1997 Practices	Current Practices
ISI ERA sector	Fairly rigid workplace structures	Fairly rigid workplace structures
	Adherence to work rules	Adherence to work rules
	Rigid compensation systems with no linkages to skill acquisition or merit	Some efforts to link pay to merit
		Increasing emphasis on training and skill upgrading
	Virtually all workers employed on a regular basis	Efforts towards greater numerical flexibility through layoffs, labour contracting and some sub-contracting
	Little emphasis on training beyond initial recruitment stage	
	Passive attitude towards flexibility.	Efforts towards functional flexibility in some firms
	Restructuring efforts hampered by union resistance	Employers largely free to implement restructuring as a result of union weakness
EOI sector	Fairly rigid workplace structures in most firms	Fairly rigid workplace structures in most firms
	Strong focus on numerical flexibility via labour contracting and subcontracting	Increasing concern over cost containment
	Efforts to de-link pay from skill acquisition	Widespread use of practices to enhance numerical flexibility including labour contracting, sub-contracting and layoffs
	Use of layoffs particularly in garment industry	Efforts to de-link pay from skill acquisition
	Low levels of unionization particularly in the electronics industry	Low levels of unionization particularly in the electronics industry
	Significant use of anti-union practices	Significant use of anti-union practices
	Some effort towards functional flexibility in foreign owed electronics firms	Some effort towards functional flexibility in foreign owed electronics firms
	Involvement of EPZ authorities and local government in HRM	Involvement of EPZ authorities and local government in HRM

Sources: Kuruvilla 1996b; Frenkel and Kuruvilla (2002); Kuruvilla and Erickson (2002); Kelly (2001).

five years have been solely employer-driven initiatives (Kuruvilla et al., 2000: 86).

Second, firms in the EOI sector do not appear to have changed much. The reason for this lack of dramatic change is the fact that nothing has happened in the past five years to significantly alter the course of the EOI sector. Rather, recent events have, if anything, strengthened the tendencies to focus on numerical flexibility and union avoidance (Kuruvilla and Erickson, 2002: 199). This stems from the fact that since EOI was initiated in the Philippines, it has not progressed beyond the primary stage of labour intensive production (Kuruvilla et al., 2000: 15). Since one of key sources of competitiveness in primary EOI is cheap labour, both individual firms and the Philippine government have an interest in keeping labour costs down. This explains the lack of a relationship between greater skill levels and higher pay in much of the EOI sector. Except for a handful of – mostly American – firms that have invested heavily in promoting functional flexibility, most firms have sought to enhance competitiveness through numerical flexibility, and it is unlikely that there will be a significant amount of change in this regard in the near term.

Convergence or Divergence

The evidence presented here should indicate that, at the national level, there has been a convergence in HRM practices as a result of the changes taking place within the ISI sector. Yet, as most of the changes are very recent, it is still too early to predict how much the HRM practices in the two sectors will ultimately converge. That said, it can be predicted with some certainty that convergence will not be complete. This is because, despite deregulation in the ISI sector, the environment in which firms operate is not identical to that of the EOI sector. Generally speaking, the EOI sector is still operating on a model of development in which competitive advantage is based on maintaining low costs. Firms that seek to capitalize on low costs have little incentive to invest heavily in the training, upskilling, etc. associated with functional flexibility (Kuruvilla and Erickson, 2002: 216). Competition from firms in countries such as China and Vietnam, both of which have much lower costs, further reinforces the focus on numerical flexibility (Kuruvilla and Erickson, 2002: 199). While ISI firms are now far more exposed to competition, by virtue of the fact that most firms are not producing for export per se, competitive advantage can be secured through means other than containing labour costs. As a result of this difference, the situation may arise in the future whereby ISI firms are employing more innovative HRM practices than EOI firms.

Key Issues for HRM

Today, in the Philippines there are at least two major issues that are of interest to HRM researchers. One issue relates to the growing need for firms to adopt practices to promote functional flexibility rather than continuing to rely on numerical flexibility. The reason this is becoming an issue stems from the fact that while the use of practices such as labour contracting, sub-contracting and worker retrenchments have helped firms to become leaner and more competitive, they have also created fear and apprehension among workers, which has had a decidedly negative effect on worker motivation. Hence, it is now being suggested within the Philippines that only by investing in people, making workers multi-skilled and versatile, can firms adjust to changes in the global economy without contributing to the erosion of job and income security (*Philexport*, 2001). Globally competitive TNCs such as Motorola have demonstrated that it is possible to compensate workers well, adopt advanced HRM practices and still successfully compete in the global economy.

A second concern for HRM in the Philippines may well be how to retain good workers. Every day 2,700 Filipinos leave the country to take overseas jobs (*BusinessWorld*, 2002c) and the Philippines is now the largest supplier of commercial seafarers in the world, providing 16 per cent of the world's seamen (Tyner, 2000: 71). This level of international migration must have serious implications. For highly skilled workers such as those in information technology, the modest levels of compensation offered in the Philippines often prompts employees to look for better positions overseas. Philippine firms have responded by offering generous benefit packages to professional workers, but this is often not enough. One observer noted that he would consider a company lucky 'if they didn't have one employee ... working hard to get out of the country' (*Computerworld Philippines*, 2001).

Implications for Theory Development

Given that many of the changes taking place in the Philippines are recent developments, the overall contribution this case can make to HRM theory building is relatively modest. Nevertheless, the findings presented here may suggest two points. First, while there has been convergence between the ISI and EOI sectors, it is unlikely that the two sectors will become identical. The emergence of merit-based pay schemes in the ISI sector and their relative absence in the EOI sector suggest that there will still be some diversity in the future. Further, change in one sector and continuity in the other suggests that the two should still be regarded as different by theorists. Second, at the international level, the findings here caution against the development of an Asia-Pacific theory of HRM. Rather, to the extent that this essay suggests that changes in HRM practices reflect efforts by firms to cope with changes to their environment, it would suggest that the amount of convergence between countries at different levels of development, employing different industrialization strategies and with different attitudes towards unionization will necessarily be limited. Rather, if one were to compare the Philippines with other developing countries with similar environments and development strategies, there may well be a greater degree of convergence in HRM practices. But further research will be necessary to test this thesis.

CONCLUSION

This study was intended to expand on the arguments initiated in the 1997 study. This study has argued that to have a better understanding of developments in Philippine HRM practices, a broader and more nuanced approach is necessary. It has been demonstrated that, over the recent past, the ISI sector has responded to the increased pressures of competition by adopting practices that have traditionally been more characteristic of the EOI sector, including the increased use of subcontracting, labour contracting, retrenchment, and the like. Without the regulatory protection that has traditionally characterized the ISI sector, firms have had to become leaner, more flexible and more competitive in order to survive. However, the fact that some diversity still exists suggests that country studies which focus on one sector and hint, implicitly or explicitly, that the findings can be generalized for the economy as a whole, will probably fail to capture the true situation.

NOTES

1. Kuruvilla (1996b). ISI is normally defined as local industrial production of goods to replace the need to import finished products. However, recent treatments of the ISI sector in the Philippines often include large domestically owned firms in the services sector as well. This study follows this trend of including domestic service oriented corporations.
2. The reference to NICs here specifically refers to South Korea, Taiwan, Hong Kong and Singapore. For more on the influence of the IFIs on the Philippines see Broad (1988) and Broad and Cavanagh (1988).
3. Interview with Danilo Arao, Manila, 15 Jan. 2001.
4. Ofreneo, 1996; Mendoza, 1998; Tujan, 1998; ICFTU, 1999. For more information on violations of labour rights and why they occur in the Philippines, see Skene (2002).
5. Interview with Crispen Beltran.
6. Most unions in the Philippines can be considered to be enterprise unions. However, some local unions are not legal entities themselves but chapters of larger union federations (Dejillas, 1994: 4fn).

7. Interview with Rene Ofreneo, Quezon City, 16 Jan. 2001.
8. *Philippine Daily Inquirer*, 1999. The article used a sports metaphor: The last two minutes of a basketball game is likened to the end game for Philippine industry.
9. Chant and McIlwaine, 1995; EILR, 2001: 52. A *barangay*, or *barrio*, is the smallest political unit in the Philippines. A *barangay* is best thought of as a sub-unit of a municipality. A *barangay* captain is the elected leader of a *barangay*.
10. Interview with Crispen Beltran.

REFERENCES

Aldaba, F. (2000), 'Globalisation and Social Development in the Philippines: Socio-economic impact of the East Asian Crisis', Center for ASEAN Studies Discussion Paper No. 27.

Amante, M. (1997), 'Converging and Diverging Trends in HRM: The Philippine "Halo-Halo"Approach', *Asia Pacific Business Review*, Vol.3, No.4, pp.111–31.

Barranco-Fernando, N. (no date), 'Globalization and its Impact on the Philippine Labor Market', Unpublished paper of the School of Labor and Industrial Relations, University of the Philippines.

Broad, R. (1988), *Unequal Alliance: The World Bank, the International Monetary Fund and the Philippines.* Berkeley: University of California Press.

Broad, R. and Cavanagh, J. (1988), 'No More NICs', *Foreign Policy*, Vol.72, pp.81–103.

BusinessWorld (2001), 'Luring Back Investor Confidence Not Easy', 23 May, p.1.

BusinessWorld (2002a), 'Long Way to go Before Full Labor–Management Partnership', 12 June.

BusinessWorld (2002b), 'Traders, Labor Protest Death of Local Industry', 6 Aug.

BusinessWorld (2002c), 'Weekender: Labor and Management', 22 Nov. p.1.

Chant, S. and McIlwaine, C. (1995), 'Gender and Export Manufacturing in the Philippines: Continuity or Change in Female Employment? The Case of the Mactan Export Processing Zone', *Gender Place and Culture: A Journal of Feminist Geography*, Vol.2, No.2, pp.147–76.

Computerworld Philippines (2001), 'No End Seen to IT Manpower Exodus', 9 July, p.1.

Dejillas, L. J. (1994), *Trade Union Behavior in the Phillippines 1946–1990.* Manila: Ateneo de Manila University Press.

Ecumenical Institute for Labor and Research [EILR] (2001), 'Managing Discontent: Labor Control Strategies of Export-Zone TNCs in the Philippines', *Asia-Pacific Journal*, Vol.4, pp.43–71.

Far Eastern Economic Review [FEER] (2003), 'Now the Real Work Begins', 16 Jan., pp.24–5.

Frenkel, S. and Kuruvilla, S. (2002), 'Logics of Action, Globalization, and Changing Employment Relations in China, India, Malaysia, and the Philippines', *Industrial and Labor Relations Review*, Vol.55, No.3, pp.387–412.

IBON Foundation Inc. (2000), 'Globalization's Scourge', *IBON Facts and Figures*, Vol.23, Nos 6–7, pp.9–10.

IBON Workers Desk (2001), *The Philippine Garment and Textile Industries.* Manila: Foundation Inc.

International Confederation of Free Trade Unions [ICFTU] (1999), 'Internationally Recognized Core Labour Standards in the Philippines', A report prepared for the WTO General Council Review of the Trade Policies of the Philippines.

Kelly, P. F. (1997), 'Globalization, Power and the Politics of Scale in the Philippines', *Geoforum*, Vol.28, No.2, pp.151–71.

Kelly, P. F. (2001), 'The Political Economy of Local Labor Control on the Philippines', *Economic Geography*, Vol.77, No.1, pp.1–22.

Kuruvilla, S. (1996a), 'Linkages Between Industrialization Strategies and Industrial Relations/Human Resource Policies: Singapore, Malaysia, Philippines and India', *Industrial and Labor Relations Review*, Vol.49, No.4, pp.635–57.

Kuruvilla, S. (1996b), 'National Industrialisation Strategies and their Influence on Patterns of HR Practices', *Human Resource Management Journal*, Vol.6, No.3, pp.22–41.

Kuruvilla, S., and Erickson, C. (2002), 'Change and Transformation in Asian Industrial

Relations', *Industrial Relations,* Vol.41, No.2, pp.171–227.

Kuruvilla, S., Erickson, C., Anner, M., Amante, M. and Ortiz, I. (2000), *Globalization and Industrial Relations in the Philippines.* Bangkok: International Labour Organization.

Lloyd, D. and Salter, W. (1999), *Philippines: Corporate Social Responsibility and Working Conditions.* Manila: ILO, South-east Asia and the Pacific Multi Disciplinary Advisory Team.

McKay, S. (1999), 'Total Quality and the Control of Workers: HRM in the Philippine Electronics and Semiconductor Industries', *Asian Labour Update* No.31, pp.7–9.

Mendoza, D. (1998), 'Prospects for Filipino Workers in a Globalized Economy and the Role of ILO', in Proceedings of the Tripartite Round Table Discussion on *The Social Dimension of Globalization and the Role of the ILO in the Next Century.* Manila: Department of Labor and Employment, pp.74–7.

Ofreneo, R. (1995), *Philippine Industrialization and Industrial Relations.* Quezon City: University of the Philippines Center for Integrative and Development Studies.

Ofreneo, R. (1996), 'Labor Standards and Philippine Economic Development' in Lee, J. (ed.), *Labor Standards and Economic Development.* Taipei: Chung-Hua Institution for Economic Research.

Ofreneo, R. and Wallace, P. (1997), 'Identifying Strategic Industrial Relations/Human Resource

Adjustments and Policy Responses to the Challenge of Global Competitiveness', *Policy.com.ph,* accessed at http://www.policy.com.ph.

Pacific Bridge (2001), 'Human Resources in the Philippines: Spring 1999', Pacific Bridge Incorporated internal publication, accessed at www.pacificbridge.com/pdf/Philippines_HR_1999.pdf

Pacific Bridge (2002), 'The Philippines HR update: Winter 2002', Pacific Bridge Incorporated internal publication, accessed at www.pacificbridge.com/pdf/Philippines_HR_2002.pdf

Philexport (2001), 'Race to the Top: Key to the Competitiveness', 8 June, accessed at www.philexport.ph.

Philippine Daily Inquirer (1999), 'Incentives Not Enough to Lure Foreign Firms', 27 March, accessed at http://www.inquirer.net

Selmer, J. and De Leon, C. (2001), '*Pinoy*-style HRM: Human Resource Management in the Philippines', *Asia Pacific Business Review,* Vol.8, No.1, pp.127–44.

Skene, C. (2002), 'The Impact of External Constraints on Labour Rights: The Case of the Philippines', *International Journal of Human Resource Management,* Vol.13, No.3, pp.484–500.

Storey, J. (1992) *Developments in the Management of Human Resources.* London: Routledge.

Tan, A. (1996), 'Growth of 7%, But Inflation Worries', *Asia Today,* Oct.

Tyner, J. (2000), 'Global Cities and Circuits of Global Labor: The Case of Manila, Philippines', *Professional Geographer,* Vol.52, No.1, pp.62–74.

Tujan Jr., A. (1998), 'Globalization and Labor: The Philippine Case', *Institute of Political Economy Journals,* Vol.15.

Interviews

Arao, D., Head of the Research and Databank Department, IBON Foundation, Inc., conducted on 15 Jan. 2001, Manila, Philippines.

Beltran, C., Chairman, Kilusang Mayo Uno, conducted on 27 Jan. 2001, Quezon City, Philippines.

Ferrer, M., Professor and Director of the Third World Center, University of the Philippines, conducted on 22 Jan. 2001, Quezon City, Philippines.

Ofreneo, R. E., Professor, School of Labor and Industrial Relations, University of the Philippines, conducted on 16 Jan. 2001, Quezon City, Philippines.

Villanueva, E., Secretary-General, United Filipinos in Hong Kong, conducted on 19 Dec. 2000, Hong Kong.

HRM in Singapore:
Change and Continuity

DAVID WAN

Since Singapore embarked on its 'second industrial revolution' in 1979, the strategic development of human resources (HRs) has gained added significance in the country's national development effort. Singapore is a very small country with a total land area of 683 sq km, about half the size of Hong Kong. The total population in 2001 was 4 million while the total labour force was 2.12 million. With neither land nor mineral resources to exploit, people are the country's only natural resource.

In the early days, Singapore was (and still is) a major entrepôt for the Asia Pacific region. In its search for high technology and high value-added industries, it has increasingly used Japan as the model for development since the early 1980s. Singapore is now a major regional financial, business and service hub. It also has a significant manufacturing centre, which employed 18.8 per cent of the employed persons in 2001. The biggest sector by employment is community and personal services (24.7 per cent), followed by commerce (21.1 per cent), manufacturing (18.8 per cent) and financial and business services (17.2 per cent).

Singapore has a long history of government involvement in economic and manpower planning (Yuen, 1997). Since the early days of industrialization, it has been dependent on multinational companies (MNCs) to generate jobs and economic growth – a deliberate government policy to jumpstart its economy. Due to the pro-business government policy (for example, favourable tax and investment conditions), strategic geographic position, social and political stability, an English-speaking workforce, many foreign companies have set up their businesses (and increasingly, regional headquarters) in Singapore over the years. The country has always had a problem of chronic shortage of labour. Due to the tight labour market in most of the years, recruitment and retention were the biggest challenges facing companies.

This essay traces the development of human resource management (HRM) in Singapore from the mid-1990s until the present day, with particular reference to the HRM scene since the publication of Yuen's work (1997) and the 1997 Asian financial crisis. National HRM concerns and strategies of particular relevance to the management of human capital in an increasingly knowledge-based economy are highlighted. The issue of convergence versus divergence in the development of HRs will also be addressed. Current and future challenges that are most likely to impact on the country's competitiveness and economic performance are explored.

CONTEXTUAL FACTORS AND ISSUES

Political and Historical

In the years immediately after becoming an independent nation in 1965, one of the most critical problems facing the government was job creation. At that time, although the country had already become a key shipping port, reliance on entrepôt trade alone could not generate enough employment for the growing population. Extensive industrialization and investment in both hardware and manpower were needed to overcome high unemployment.

Moving from an entrepôt-based economy to an industrial one was far from easy. More workers were needed to take up manual employment. As a result, the Employment Act was introduced in 1968 to streamline and standardize the minimum terms and conditions of work of all employees (Tan, 1999). To attract foreign investment, the relative power of unions and employers was altered with the passage of the Industrial Relations (Amendment) Act in the same year. It specified that highly sensitive issues like recruitment, promotion, transfer, dismissal, reinstatement, retrenchment and allocation of duties, were non-negotiable. The act also introduced the principles of conciliation by the Ministry of Labour if there were a breakdown in collective bargaining and compulsory arbitration by an industrial arbitration court where necessary (Anantaraman, 1990).

Full employment was achieved by the early 1970s. The National Wages Council (NWC) was established in 1972 to ensure orderly wage increases. Apart from producing annual wage guidelines, the Council also provided the opportunity to promote cooperation between the Government, labour and employers. In 1981, a National Productivity Board (NPB) was set up to launch the national productivity movement. Quality control circles, work improvement teams, labour–management consultation committees, house unions and other proactive HR policies and practices were promoted.

Economic

By 1985, Singapore's relative unit labour cost was about 50 per cent higher than its neighbouring competitors. The 1985–86 economic recession called for drastic action to reduce wage costs. A national wage restraint policy, though painful, was successfully implemented with the support of the labour movement. In addition, wage reform was identified as a prerequisite for continued economic growth. The basic idea of having a more flexible wage system at the workplace was to ensure the cost-competitiveness of companies and to enhance the crucial link between financial rewards and employee performance.

In view of its limited natural resources and domestic market, the government in the early 1990s encouraged Singaporeans to look for opportunities beyond the country and 'go regional'. Singapore firms were urged to set up businesses in the region (namely, India, China, Malaysia, Indonesia, the Philippines, Vietnam and Thailand) or to form strategic alliances with overseas players. The government itself also took an active lead in direct investments in the region.

Over the years, Singapore has successfully transformed itself into one of the world's most competitive economies. To a large extent this was made possible by the level of political stability due to the longevity of the ruling People's Action Party, and the low level of industrial conflict that resulted from a unified labour movement and the effective tripartite consensus-building at national level.

Labour Markets

In 2001 Singapore had a labour force of 2.12 million, of which 56.2 per cent were males and 43.8 per cent were females. The labour force participation rate was 77.8 per cent and 54.3 per cent for males and females respectively. At present, the age profile of the Singapore workforce is still relatively young. In 2001, 27.4 per cent of workers were aged between 15 and 29, 55.6 per cent were aged between 30 and 49, while another 13.0 per cent were aged between 50 and 59. However, as in many countries in the developed world, the population is ageing.

Unemployment in 2001 was 3.3 per cent compared with 2.4 per cent in 1997 (Ministry of Manpower, 1999). Since 1998, the figure has been over 3 per cent. The job vacancy rate fell from 4.4 per cent in 1997 to 1.5 per cent in 2001 while the monthly resignation rate remained low at 2.2 per cent. In general, the years 1998 to the present were difficult for workers because of the 1997–98 recession followed by the 11 September 2001 tragedy in the US. The fallout from the attack affected the profitability of the local carrier, Singapore Airlines, and the local tourism industry.

The educational profile of Singapore's workers reveals that there is still room for improvement. In 2001, only 16.9 per cent had a degree, while 21.0 per cent had a diploma or post secondary qualification. About one in five of the workforce had primary education or less. Those who had lower secondary education constituted another 14.2 per cent.

Singaporeans generally place a heavy emphasis on hard work, self-discipline, honesty and excellence. Literacy rate in the country is high; 97 per cent for males and 90 per cent for females. The government considers quality education and life-long learning crucial for national competitiveness. Because of the emphasis on competition and excellence, the country is slowly transforming itself from a society that endorses traditional Asian values (in particular, group well-being) to one that places more on individual success.

Hofstede (1980) found that the national culture of Singapore was high in power distance, low in uncertainty avoidance, high in long-term orientation, collective by nature and displayed neither prominent masculine nor feminine features. Interestingly, in a survey of 870 employees (90 per cent of them were Singaporeans) in five firms (one American, two Japanese and two local firms from the electronics industry), Chew (2000) revealed that Singaporeans were low in power distance and masculinity but high in uncertainty avoidance. Only Hofstede's prediction that Singaporeans would score low on individualism and high on long-term orientation was supported.

The implication of Chew's findings is that with a lower power distance recorded, workers nowadays should be more receptive towards the introduction of high performance work systems (HPWS). Nonetheless, greater uncertainty avoidance may imply greater risk avoidance and hence may not be a desirable attribute for an employee working under HPWS (Bae et al., 2001).

There are three main employer organizations in Singapore. They are the Singapore National Employers Federation (SNEF), the Singapore Confederation of Industries (SCI) and the Singapore International Chamber of Commerce (SICC). They assist employers in matters related to employment relations. There were also 72 employees' trade unions in 2000. The number has been dropping steadily since 1997, mainly due to the restructuring of the economy. On the other hand, union membership increased over the same period from 260,130 in 1997 to 314,478 in 2000. This was primarily due to the aggressive recruitment effort by the National Trades Union Congress (NTUC), the only federation of trade unions in Singapore, and its affiliated unions (including general, industrial, enterprise and craft unions). In view of the generally cordial labour–management relations in the country, there has been no strike since 1987.

1997 Asian Financial Crisis and Reactions

The regional economic crisis began as a currency crisis in Thailand, followed by the Philippines, Indonesia and Thailand. By October 1997 the turmoil had spread to Hong Kong, Taiwan, South Korea and Japan. Singapore was also affected because of the country's inescapable links to the Asian region. Any sharp fall in external demand affects its economic destiny.

Before the crisis, there were on average 25 job openings for every ten job seekers. By the middle of 1998, there were only eight job openings per ten job seekers. The huge drop in the value of regional currencies against the US dollar since the crisis meant that countries such as South Korea, Thailand and Malaysia were, in terms of cost of production, more competitive relative to Singapore. The costs of doing business in Singapore had to be slashed quickly and decisively. Bonuses and salary increases were reduced and/or frozen. Employers' contributions to the Central Provident Fund (CPF) were cut, from 20 per cent to 10 per cent. However, even with wage restraint, reduction of variable pay and a cut in employers' CPF contributions, retrenchment among workers and executives was still inevitable.

The labour movement under the leadership of the NTUC urged employers not to rely solely on cost-cutting measures but also to exploring other ways of enhancing competitiveness (for example, introducing new products and services, exploring new markets and retrain excess workers). The SNEF welcomed the union centre's support for cost-cutting measures and suggested that companies took the opportunity to restructure their operations, retrain workers, invest more in R&D and look for new markets (*The Straits Times*, 3 Nov. 1998).

The crisis provided a golden opportunity for the country to reinforce and sharpen its competitive edge. The Committee on Singapore's Competitiveness (CSC) convened its first meeting in May 1997. In addition to addressing the many immediate issues that led to the country's loss of competitiveness, it also articulated the vision for Singapore – to be an advanced and globally competitive knowledge economy within the next ten years. The 1997–99 crisis did not drag on for a long time. By the second quarter of 1999, Singapore's economy grew by a robust 6.7 per cent (Chow, 1999).

Current Economic Situation

Rapid technological change, deregulation, globalization and the emergence of a knowledge-based economy explain the continuous need for re-engineering Singapore's workforce capabilities (Low, 2000). This is especially so since the Asian crisis as many of the new jobs created require increased skills and knowledge. These include R&D, product design, product development, life sciences, e-commerce, process engineering, pharmaceuticals, bio-tech and logistics.

Even in early 1999, there was still a relatively large proportion of the Singapore workforce (38 per cent) with lower than secondary education qualifications. Furthermore, six in ten of these workers were aged 40 or above (*The Straits Times*, 31 Aug. 1999). The growing mismatch between new job requirements and labour skills requires concerted action by the government, the employers and the unions. Workers need to be highly skilled, innovative and flexible in view of the rapidly changing market forces (Arun and Lee, 1998). The government realized this importance and formulated the Manpower 21 Plan in 1998.

The Manpower 21 Steering Committee was charged with developing and coordinating a blueprint for national HR planning called 'Manpower 21' (M21). The terms of reference of the Committee were to identify and address Singapore's HR needs and challenges as the country moves towards a knowledge-based economy. The M21 vision is for Singapore to be 'a talent capital, a centre of ideas, innovation, knowledge and exchange'. Six core strategies were formulated to address critical aspects of the 'manpower value chain'. They covered integrated HR planning, lifelong learning for lifelong employability, augmenting the country's talent pool, transforming the work environment, developing a vibrant manpower industry and redefining partnerships between key players and institutions (*Manpower 21: Vision of a Talent Capital*).

In terms of competitiveness ranking, the Global Competitiveness Report (compiled by the World Economic Forum in association with Harvard University) revealed that Singapore ranked fourth in 2001, after Finland, US and Canada. The country was ranked as number 1 from 1997 to 1999 before it dropped to number 2 in 2000 (*The Straits Times*, 19 Oct. 2001). While this apparent slide is not alarming since Singapore is still among the top five most competitive economies in the world, a high-powered new Economic Review Committee (ERC) was formed in December 2001 to undertake a fundamental review of the country's development strategy. The need for such a re-examination is not so much affected by the drop in competitive ranking but more because of the ever changing global economic environment. The Chairman of this review committee is the Deputy

Prime Minister, BG Lee, who was also the Chairman of the 1985 ERC. The main committee will oversee seven sub-committees:

1. Manufacturing
2. Service industries
3. Domestic enterprises
4. Human capital
5. Impact of economic restructuring
6. Taxation, CPF, wages and land
7. Entrepreneurship, growth and internationalization of Singapore-based companies.

The Human Capital sub-committee is headed by the Minister of State for Education and Manpower. Its responsibility is to 'recommend measures to enhance human capital to support all sectors of the economy, including foreign talent issues'. One of the immediate tasks is to review the current Employment Act and see if it is adequate enough to cope with the changing employment patterns in Singapore. These include, for example, the employment of more contract and part-timers given the trend towards organizational restructuring.

CHANGES IN HUMAN RESOURCE MANAGEMENT

Major Changes Taking Place

To fully understand the various changes taking place in the area of HRM, it is important to examine some of the key developments in the wider economic and global environments. This is especially so since Singapore is a small and open economy.

With the successful conclusion of the Uruguay Round Agreement by GATT members in 1995, trade liberalization has since flourished. The admission of China into the World Trade Organization (WTO) will further enhance international trade and investments. Singapore has also been keen to establish free trade agreements with different countries, including, for example, US, Australia, New Zealand, Europe, China and Japan. This will mean greater market access for all parties involved. At the same time, with the rapid advancements in information technology (IT) and telecommunications, Singapore can benefit from the increase in global exports of commercial services by offering its experience in logistics management, IT consultancy and e-commerce.

While globalization provides ample opportunities for the country, the increasing compression of product life cycles, rapid technological breakthrough and strong competition from both developed and developing countries also imply that Singapore has to continuously sharpen its niches (Committee on Singapore's Competitiveness, 1998). To start with, transition to a knowledge-based economy requires a capable, cost-effective and innovative workforce. The country also needs to increase its pool of talent (professionals, skilled workers) and nurture an entrepreneurial spirit. For a long time, Singaporeans have been too dependent on the government to provide directions and handle economic/social problems. This mentality has to change if Singapore is to succeed in the new millennium.

Furthermore, at a time when more Singapore companies are establishing themselves overseas and more Singaporeans are working in foreign countries, cultural sensitivity and willingness to learn become more critical. Even though the majority of Singaporeans are ethnically Chinese, this does not mean that doing business in China will automatically be easy. This is true even in the case of Hong Kong, where close to 98 per cent of the population is Chinese.

Possible Changes in the Immediate Future

What are some of the implications of the Asian financial crisis and the current economic environment on HRM practices in Singapore? A summary of the changes and continuities over the period since the late 1990s is presented in Table 1. As Yuen (1997) did not provide a similar table, it has been compiled by the present author based on his knowledge and personal observations. It is difficult to pinpoint which of the changes are due to the Asian crisis or intensified globalization. While the 1997–98 economic crisis may now be over, intensive global competition especially from China will continue to exert its impact on company growth and survival. It would appear that increased labour flexibility and cost competitiveness remain the two utmost concerns that any employer has to tackle.

There is likely to be less adherence to rigid rules given the need to develop a more flexible workforce. Adaptability is not restricted to individual employees but also concerns organizations and the government. What worked in the past may not be valid any more. On the other hand, we expect those common values and norms that have proved valuable to the nation's success will continue to evolve. These include the practice of tripartism, national unity, racial and religious harmony. Tripartism is the cornerstone of years of industrial peace and labour–management cooperation in the country. Both industrial and social harmony is indispensable for securing foreign investments.

The employment system in Singapore is likely to evolve into one that pays much less attention to lifelong jobs. In the face of severe competition, organizations will have to continue to restructure and

TABLE 1

ASSESSMENT OF HRM CHANGES AND CONTINUITIES

Dimensions	Presence	Change
Rules: adherence to	%	+
Behaviour: common values and norms	✓	+
Key managers: personnel/specialists v. line/general	✓	++
Personnel selection	✓	++
Payment systems	✓	++
Work conditions: harmonized	%	+
Contracts: individual v. standardized	✓	+
In-house training	%	+
Right to hire and fire	✓	+
Strategic role for personnel manager	%	+

Key: (*Practice*)
  ✓ present
  % present to some degree

  (*Degree of change in past 4 years*)
  ++ major change
  + change
  0 none

Source: adapted from Storey (1992).

introduce new work processes. They will have to focus on their core competencies and outsource where appropriate. They will have to be more selective in staffing, for example, more freedom in personnel selection, more contract and part-time jobs, use of individual contracts and preserve their right to hire and fire. More and more companies will be using performance-based pay and promoting employees based on merit.

While the strategic role of HR professionals is likely to become more crucial, they will have to identify those added values they can create and develop measures to evaluate their own performance (Ulrich, 1997). At the same time, because of decentralization of decision-making and better access to information and data, line managers' roles will increase. They will have to deal with more employee-oriented matters and stay pro-active in managing HRs.

As far as individual employees are concerned, they will have to be more active in charting their own future. Singaporean workers have been reminded many times by ministers and leading unionists that they should constantly upgrade their skills, accept changes and prepare to work for more than one employer in their lifetime. Perhaps the biggest challenge for organizations in this new employer–employee relationship is how to motivate employees and generate commitment when they are no longer willing to guarantee long-term job security (Cappelli, 1999).

Indeed, balancing the interests of employers and their counterparts will require mutual understanding and action. Organizations should seek to become more family friendly (such as by offering flexible work arrangements), support employee training and development and harmonize work conditions. The biggest test will come when organizations are downsizing or restructuring. Whenever possible, they should be more compassionate towards those affected. The government has provided various incentive schemes to encourage employers to upgrade the skills of their employees. The Ministry of Manpower can play an important role in championing workers' interests and help redress their complaints and grievances. Workers, professionals and executives alike have to ensure that their employment adds value to their employers. They will need to be more receptive to constantly upgrading themselves and engage in lifelong learning.

DISCUSSION

Why Changes Have Occurred

As the title of this essay suggests, the issue is not whether there will be any change but how far and why. The Singapore economy is highly dependent on developments in the external environment, especially the economic health of the US. As an example, Singapore's high dependence on electronics exports to the US and the industry's shorter product life cycles imply that the country is likely to experience more frequent ups and downs in future (*The Straits Times*, 18 March 2002). That is why, like the case of Taiwan, there is an urgent need to broaden Singapore's economic base. Apart from developing its manpower capabilities, the country has to speed up its effort to attract MNCs that provide cutting edge technologies, R&D experience and management expertise. New and promising areas that can add a competitive edge to Singapore's economic base include product design, product development, management education, life sciences, e-commerce, process engineering, pharmaceutics, bio-tech and value-added logistics.

Meanwhile, competition from Malaysia has intensified. Malaysia is set to compete with Singapore in becoming another transportation hub in the region. It is expanding its seaport facilities and rail network in the State of Johor – the southern most part of mainland Malaysia and directly opposite Singapore. With lower wages and cheaper land, together with an improved infrastructure, the Johor seaport is likely to become a formidable competitor in the near future.

China's emergence as a key economic power provides both threats and opportunities to East and South East Asia. While its economic potential makes it the single largest recipient of foreign direct investment (FDI) in Asia and hence deprives other parts of South East Asia of more FDI, its growing middle class also presents a huge source of demand for overseas products and services. On balance, commentators agree that many Asian countries should benefit from China's admission to the WTO and its right to hold the 2008 Olympic Games. Singapore is also taking advantage of these latest developments and continues to reinforce its presence in China. These include management education and consulting, hotel and tourism, logistics management, infrastructure, supermarkets, food processing, transportation and port facilities as well as other niche services. The importance of the China market is further reflected in the trend that more and more tourists arriving in Singapore are from China. In addition, Chinese firms can make use of Singapore's financial infrastructure and its knowledge and networking experience in this part of the region.

One example of the big changes that should be highlighted here is the consolidation of the banking sector. For years, the banking sector in Singapore has been dominated by the four big local banks – United Overseas Bank (UOB), Overseas Union Bank (OUB), Oversea–Chinese Banking Corporation (OCBC), and the Development Bank of Singapore (DBS). As a result of the introduction of new technologies and mergers and acquisitions, the number of white-collar workers needed after automation (for example, the use of automated teller machines and other self-banking alternatives) and organizational restructuring (such as closing branches and elimination of duplicated functions) are reduced.

Examples of recent 'marriages' include those between Keppel Bank and Tat Lee Bank, DBS and Post Office Savings Bank, UOB and OUB as well as OCBC Bank and Keppel Tat Lee Bank. The figures on retrenchments speak for themselves. In January 1999, Keppel Tat Lee Bank cut close to 300 workers, while in August 2001, DBS laid off 160. UOB axed 435 workers in December 2001, while OCBC Bank announced in March 2002 that it will cut 229 staff. Not only are local banks adjusting to the need for cost-cutting and 'right-sizing'. Japanese and US financial institutions in Singapore are also involved in organizational restructuring. Last but not least, the implementation of a new cheque-clearing system in September 2002 may affect another 1,000 or so employees in clerical and executive positions. (*The Straits Times*, 17 March 2002).

Key Issues for HRM

We can approach this question by looking at two levels: HRM at the national level and HRM at the firm level. We first begin with a discussion on HRM at the national level.

The Singapore government has been an indispensable driving-force for the strategic development and utilization of HR in the country. It has done this within a well-established tripartite framework of government, employers and unions (Wan, 1996; Yuen, 1997). The CSC has spelt out its vision of developing Singapore's human capital into a world-class workforce in the twenty-first century. To compete successfully in the new millennium, the country has to take a two-prong approach. Firstly, it has to maximize the full potential of its domestic workforce. One way is to make sure that the education system produces a workforce that is adaptive to new challenges and opportunities. Secondly, it has to strengthen the attractiveness of Singapore to overseas talents (professionals, entrepreneurs, managers, skilled workers, athletes and artists).

The educational curriculum from primary school up to university level is being reviewed and revamped. Independent thinking, creativity and entrepreneurial spirit are currently emphasized. To broaden the cosmopolitan outlook in schools, especially at the tertiary level, foreign teachers are recruited and exchange students are welcomed. More scholarships for overseas students to study in Singapore are also in place. Vocational/technical training and continued education for adults are not ignored. A fifth polytechnic has opened and a fourth university is planned. In view of the country's need for more business/management manpower, the Singapore Management University opened its doors to students in July 2000.

Demographic shifts also affect the ability of Singapore companies to access the limited labour pool. The country's workforce is ageing fast. In 1989, Singapore already had a larger proportion of its population aged 65 and above than Thailand, Malaysia, Indonesia and the Philippines. By the year 2025, those aged 65 and above in Singapore are expected to rise to 17 per cent, the highest percentage of aged persons in any ASEAN country. Increased life expectancy combined with a declining fertility rate prompted the government to increase the minimum retirement age from 55 to 60 in 1993. The present retirement age is 62 and the long-term target is 67.

Another response to the tight labour market has been efforts to increase the employment of women. The labour force participation rate of women in 2001 was 54.3 per cent. While this figure is comparable with that of Japan, the US and Britain, the Singapore government has been very active in encouraging women to join and remain in the workforce. As a major employer in the country, it has come up with numerous solutions to address problems encountered by the growing number of dual career families.

A third response to the generally tight labour market is to develop more flexible work arrangements, such as flexi-hours, job sharing, part-time work and home-based work. While part-time work has become more common over the years, Singapore still lags behind other developed countries. Some employers in the manufacturing sector have reservations about employing part-time workers on the grounds that they need a longer time to be trained. Employers also perceive that full-timers are more productive and more committed.

To further augment Singapore's talent pool, the country has been aggressively marketing itself overseas as a hub for finance, research, e-business, e-learning, bio-medical science and a bridge for those who aim to expand their businesses in this part of the world. Because of Singapore's high standard of living, religious, social and political stability, as well as the government's determination to welcome foreign expertise, it has been able to attract people from far and near. Those Singaporeans who have been working abroad are also encouraged to return and contribute. Another targeted group is former expatriates who have worked in the country and those international students who have studied here.

In the long term, the possibility of structural unemployment in Singapore is real. When the economy is fast moving towards one that is more high-tech and knowledge-based, structural unemployment can occur when workers, after remaining unemployed for a long time, find it hard to gain fruitful employment. This labour mis-match happens when there are new jobs available but individuals do not have the skills or knowledge required to fill them. In the past, it has been lower-educated workers (be they production or service workers) who were more likely to encounter this problem. Increasingly, in a restructured economy, executives, managers and professionals alike have to continuously sharpen their knowledge and skills in order to stay employable.

In respect of HRM at company level, we first examine the practice of HRM in Singapore firms, followed by foreign companies. For the sake of the present analysis, one can divide local firms into two main categories – small and medium enterprises (SME) and large local companies. SMEs are defined by the Singapore Productivity and Standards Board as 'companies with at least 30 per cent Singapore equity, fixed productive assets of not more than S$15 million in manufacturing, or staff strength of not more than 200 in a commerce or service sector'. Many large local companies were formally state-owned established by the government to jumpstart the development of a specific sector (for example, shipbuilding, ship repair, airline, telecommunications, oil refining, port infrastructure, property, manufacturing, defence science, power supply, finance and banking). Besides these government-linked companies, most of the other large local companies are successful local family businesses which have grown in size over time. Foreign firms are Singapore-based MNC subsidiaries as well as joint venture companies with more than 70 per cent foreign capital (Yuen, 1997).

While large local companies comprise only a very small proportion of the total companies, they employ about one-quarter of the workforce. SMEs on the other hand formed the bulk of the companies (87 per cent) in 1998 but employ only 46 per cent of the workforce. Singapore SMEs are mainly found in the commerce and services sectors rather than in manufacturing. They mainly serve domestic customers and are generally not export-oriented (Chan, 2001).

Chinese ownership dominates the bulk of the local SMEs. In the early days, the management style of these Chinese enterprises was characterized by a strong leader who made most of the decisions and expected loyalty from employees. Management practices in general were poorly developed and it was not until after Singapore became independent in 1965 that more advanced HR practices were introduced by the MNCs (Chew and Teo, 1991).

SMEs have, and still play, a critical role in the Singapore economy. Despite their economic significance, they find it hard to compete with the much larger government-linked companies and the MNCs with regard to recruitment and employee retention. It is hard for the SMEs to compete with the big players when it comes to pay, fringe benefits, training opportunities, career prospects and marketability (Teo and Poon, 1994).

As in many other countries, the more established government-linked companies and large family enterprises today employ more professional staff. With a sizeable number of MNCs operating in Singapore, it is not uncommon to find the bigger local companies and financial institutions importing Western and Japanese management concepts and practices, for example, productivity and performance, consensus and consultation in decision-making, information sharing and quality control. The rapid growth of the private sector since the early 1990s witnessed more of the local firms becoming public companies and listed on the Singapore Stock Exchange. Many of them have also established their presence in overseas markets, a consequence of the nation's effort towards regionalization and 'going global'. With better management capabilities and good corporate governance, it is foreseeable that large local enterprises will have an important role in the Singapore economy alongside their foreign counterparts.

With high unemployment in the 1960s, the urgent need to accelerate the country's manufacturing base explained the arrival of more and more MNCs. These MNCs were regarded as the main engine propelling Singapore's export-oriented industrialization. Because of the lack of suitably qualified Singaporeans at that time, these MNCs had to rely on their own nationals to work as expatriates. Localization was slow even though the larger MNCs, especially the Americans, were willing to take on local graduates and train them (Wong, 1992).

With the arrival of MNCs from different countries over the years, Singapore has a chance to experience management practices that have been developed and tested in other parts of the world (Wong, 1991). The major MNCs operating in Singapore are those from the US and Japan. For instance, Seagate, a large American company, is Singapore's second largest employer. Other European and Asian MNCs are also gaining importance.

As expected, not all foreign subsidiaries fully transfer their head office management practices to Singapore. In general, US subsidiaries are better able to implement their home country's management practices locally than are Japanese firms. The former have far fewer expatriate staff than their Japanese counterparts. Japanese subsidiaries, on the other hand, tend to believe that they cannot transfer their home country's practices to the local context without drastic modifications. For example, much job-hopping among Singapore workers discourages the practice of lifetime employment and all that this entails. Moreover, Japanese management practices reflect their country's language and unique culture (Chew, 2000). Communications with the Japanese head office are usually carried out in Japanese and few Singaporeans can speak the language fluently.

To date, MNCs are still crucial to the Singapore economy in terms of their contributions to the country's employment, direct exports, technological transfer and capital investment. They are given a relatively free hand in importing and modifying their management systems.

Convergence or Divergence

Our discussion so far tends to point towards a convergence rather than a divergence of HRM in Singapore. In the Singapore context, there is broad consensus at the national level in terms of political and social stabilities, racial and religious harmony as well as good tripartite relations between the government, the employers and the unions. The outcome of these in the HRM arena is reflected in industrial peace, wage moderation, higher productivity and a skilled workforce.

National HR strategies are geared towards a pragmatic response to opportunities and threats in the ever-changing global environment. These strategies are formulated at the national level with inputs from the key stakeholders. A typical example is the NWC which is charged with the responsibility to 'formulate guidelines on wage policy' and to 'recommend adjustments in wage structure to be consistent with Singapore's economic development.' Even though NWC recommendations are only guidelines, employers and unions generally accept them as a base for reference or further negotiations. Ever since its formation in 1972, this spirit of tripartism at the NWC remains alive and well.

Promotion of tripartism for the purpose of achieving higher productivity and faster economic growth can also be seen in tripartite representation in statutory boards and other government agencies such as the CPF Board, Economic Development Board, Vocational and Industrial Training Board, the Industrial Arbitration Court, the NPB, the 1986 ERC and the 1998 CSC. Tripartism in Singapore is successful mainly because the principle of forging co-operation and consensus is supported by all the parties involved. The very close relationship between political leadership and the labour movement has also led to the adoption of 'responsible' trade unionism.

At the company level, one would also expect a certain degree of convergence. The newer generation of ethnic Chinese, Indian and Malay managers tend to put emphasis more on managerial professionalism as opposed to seniority and blind loyalty. Many of these younger generation managers have studied or even worked abroad and later return to work for their father. The way they run their businesses will not be entirely the same as that of the older generation. In the larger local companies and MNC subsidiaries, the use of modern management concepts and techniques will be more pronounced.

 The question is whether the Singapore workforce is ready to accept the influx of new ideas and new practices. So far, the answer is generally yes. The pressure of globalization, technological change, economic restructuring and intense competition from neighbouring countries for overseas direct investments dictate that labour-intensive and low value-ended industries will continue to leave Singapore. To survive and compete, companies have to win over their workers, import 'good' HR practices (be they Western or Asian), restructure work processes, emphasize quality and nurture good organizational citizenship behaviour. These require cooperation, trust and action from both management and the managed.

CONCLUSION

Many of the strategies adopted by the Singapore government since the People's Action Party came to power are still relevant to the present day context – good government, first-class infrastructure, a strong emphasis on education, meritocracy, equal opportunity for all, pragmatism, high savings rate, fiscal prudence, conducive business climate, international orientation and low inflation (*The Strategic Economic Plan*, 1991). Not only do these contributing factors help to explain the fast recovery from two recessions, they will continue to play a crucial role in shaping the country's future.

We expect those common values and norms that have proved valuable to Singapore's unity and success will continue to evolve. With respect to the employment system, it will continue to evolve into one that pays much less attention to lifelong jobs. In the face of severe competition, organizations will have to continue to restructure and introduce new work processes. More and more companies will be using performance-based pay and promoting employees based on merit. While the strategic role of HR professionals is likely to become more crucial, they will have to identify those added values that they can create and develop measures to evaluate their own performance. As far as individual employees are concerned, they will have to be more active in charting their own future. In a restructured economy, executives, professionals, rank and file workers and managers alike have to continuously sharpen their knowledge and skills in order to stay employable.

The Singapore experience provides a vivid example of how a country can achieve both near full employment and social justice at the same time (Sen, 1997). We do not imply that the road ahead will be easy. Indeed, President Nathan's address to the opening of Singapore's tenth parliament highlighted the challenges ahead: 'The next few years will present us with the most severe challenges in our nation's history... tougher competition, because of globalization... adapting to China's emergence and economic transformation... a troubled region.' (*Business Times*, 26 March 2002)

China will continue to be the big magnet for foreign investments. More firms will relocate their labour-intensive activities to nearby countries like Malaysia, Indonesia and Thailand. Over time, there will be more high value-added companies coming to establish themselves in Singapore. Building up a competent and knowledge-based workforce is indispensable if the country wants to benefit from new investments and stay ahead of its competitors.

REFERENCES

Anantaraman, Venkatraman (1990), *Singapore Industrial Relations System*. McGraw-Hill, Singapore.

Arun, Mahizhnan and Lee, Tsao Yuan (eds.) (1998), *Singapore: Re-Engineering Success*. Oxford University Press.

Bae, Johngseok, Chen, Shyh-jer, Lawler, John J., Wan, Tai Wai, and Roh, Hyuntak (2001), 'Human Resource Strategy and Firm Performance in Pacific Rim Countries: A Comparative Study of Korea, Taiwan, Singapore, and Thailand'. Paper presented to the *Global Management Conference*, Barcelona, Spain.

Business Times, a Singapore newspaper, various issues.

Cappelli, Peter (1999), *The New Deal at Work*. Boston, MA: Harvard Business School Press.

Chan, Lem Kok (2001), 'Singapore SMEs: Issues and Development', Occasional Paper, Centre for Business Research & Development, Faculty of Business Administration, National University of Singapore.

Chew, Irene (2000), 'Singapore' in Jai B. P. Sinha (ed.), *Managing Cultural Diversity for Productivity – the Asian Ways*. Tokyo: Asian Productivity Organization.

Chew, Irene and Teo, Chu Ying (1991), 'Human Resource Practices in Singapore: A Survey of Local Firms and MNCs', *Asia Pacific Journal of Human Resource Management*, Vol.29, No.1, pp.30–38.

Chow, Kit Boey (1999), 'The Singapore Economy: Recovering from the Financial Crisis' *Occasional Paper*, Centre for Business Research and Development, Faculty of Business Administration, National University of Singapore.

Hofstede, Geert (1980), *Culture's Consequences: International Differences in Work-Related Values*. Beverly Hills, CA: Sage.

Lim, Chong Yah and Chew, Rosalind (ed.) (1998), *Wages and Wages Policies: Tripartism in Singapore*. River Edge, N.J: World Scientific.

Low, Linda (2000), 'Political Economy of Human Resource Challenges and Changes in the Post-Asian Financial Crisis', *Research and Practice in Human Resource Management*, Vol.8, No.1, pp.23–40.

Ministry of Manpower (1999), *Manpower 21: Vision of a Talent Capital*. Singapore.

Ministry of Trade and Industry (1986), *The Singapore Economy: New Directions*. Singapore: Ministry of Trade and Industry.

Ministry of Trade and Industry (1991), *The Strategic Economic Plan: Towards A Developed Nation*. Singapore: Ministry of Trade and Industry

Ministry of Trade and Industry (1998), *Committee on Singapore's Competitiveness*. Singapore: Ministry of Trade and Industry.

Sen, Aryee (1997), 'Inequality, Unemployment and Contemporary Europe', *International Labour Review*, Vol.136, No.2, pp.155–72.

Storey, J. (1992), *Developments in Management of Human Resources*. London: Routledge.

Tan, Chwee Huat (1999), *Employment Relations in Singapore*. Singapore: Prentice Hall.

Teo, Hee Ang and Poon, Teng Fatt James (1994), 'Career Choice of Undergraduates and SMEs in Singapore', *The International Journal of Career Management*, Vol.6, No.3, pp.20–26.

The New Paper, a Singapore newspaper, various issues.

The Straits Times, a Singapore newspaper, various issues.

Ulrich, Dave (1997), *Human Resource Champions*. Boston: Harvard Business School.

Wan, David (1996), 'Developing Human Resources and Labour Flexibility in Singapore', *International Employment Relations Review*, Vol.2, No.1, pp.77–90.

Wan, David (1999), 'Competitive advantage through people – the Singapore experience' in A.R. Nankervis, R. Compton and T. McCarthy (1999), *Strategic Human Resource Management*. Australia: Nelson ITP, pp.690–700.

Wan, David and Ong, Chin Huat (2000), 'The Asian Economic Crisis and its Aftermath: Re-Engineering Human Resource Competitiveness in Singapore', *International Human Resource Issues*, Vol.1, No.1, pp.18–27.

Wong, Evelyn (1992), 'Labour Policies and Industrial Relations' in L. Low and M. H. Toh (eds.), *Public Policies in Singapore*. Singapore: Times Academic Press.

Wong, Kwei Cheong (1991), 'The Style of Managing in a Multicultural Society – Singapore' in J. M. Putti (ed.), *Management: Asian Context*. Singapore: McGraw-Hill, pp.78–94.

Yuen, Chi Ching (1997), 'HRM Under Guided Economic Development: The Singapore Experience', Asia Pacific Business Review, Vol.3, No.4, pp.133–51.

The Post-Asian Financial Crisis: Changes in HRM in Taiwanese Enterprises

YING ZHU

Taiwan's economy experienced sustainable growth between the 1960s and the late 1990s. Even during the 1997–98 Asian financial crisis, Taiwan's economy still maintained a moderate growth without the negative outcomes experienced in other Asian economies. However, this does not mean that there is no problem within the Taiwanese economy. In fact, many potential problems exist and could lead to a crisis if an adequate adjustment cannot be made. Government policy has been singled out as an important factor in such adjustment. However, a flexible and progressive management system is also an important factor for the survival and success of individual firms and the economy as whole. This essay is based on recent research into the changing elements of human resource management (HRM) in Taiwanese enterprises since the Asian crisis. Using information from earlier research by Chen (1997) the changes in HRM that are taking place are considered.

CONTEXTUAL FACTORS AND ISSUES

Political and Historical

Since the 1960s, Taiwan has experienced many political and economic developments. On the political front, pressure for democratization had become overwhelming in the late 1980s and early 1990s. While the Nationalist Party (KMT) initially retained control of most government institutions, it continued to lose electoral support, culminating in its final defeat by the Democratic Progress Party (DPP) candidate in the 2000 presidential elections (Wang and Cooney, 2002). The changes to the political environment had a profound influence on business and the economy. For instance, the leadership and reform of state-owned enterprises (SOEs) had a new agenda following the replacement of the KMT by the DPP in central government. Union movements became stronger and more influential in political decision making. Individual citizens had more freedom of political participation and association.

As Lee (1995: 101) claims, during the past two decades, the political system became more complex and government policy shifted towards a more pro-labour orientation following the process of democratization. The outcome was that the government amended several labour laws in the 1980s, including the Collective Agreement Law in 1982, the Labour Disputes Law and the Labour Insurance Act in 1988, and the Vocational Training Act in 1983 (Lee, 1995:101; Chen, 1998:155– 6). It also enacted new laws such as the Labour Standards Law in 1984 (amended in 1996), the Employment Service Act in 1992, and the Equal Rights in the Workplace Act in 1993 (Lee, 1995: 101; Chen, 1997: 155– 6).

The government also expanded the range of worker benefits through the creation of a social welfare system. For instance, the National Health Insurance Law of 1994, the Law for the Protection of People with Mental and Physical Disabilities of 1997, and the Rules for the Implementation of the Payment of Unemployment Insurance Benefits of 1998 were implemented in the 1990s (Wang and Cooney, 2002). Some of them, for instance, the rules on unemployment benefits, were responses to the effects of the Asian financial crisis.

Economic

The different stages of economic development are accompanied by different management patterns. In Taiwan, for instance, economic development since the 1960s can be divided into two stages: the export expansion period between 1961 and 1980 and the technology-intensive industries expansion period from 1981 to 1997 before the Asian crisis (Lee, 1995; Zhu et al., 2000).

During the export expansion period, the government encouraged labour-intensive industries, such as textile and food (Chen, 1997). SOEs played a monopolistic role in industries such as petroleum, transportation, sugar, and electronics. The average gross national product (GNP) growth was above 8 per cent and the unemployment rate was about 2 per cent during this period (Chen, 1997). On the other hand, during the technology-intensive industries expansion period, GNP growth maintained a level above 5.5 per cent and unemployment was below 2 per cent (DGBAS, 1996).

Labour Markets

In the labour market, important changes have taken place in the past two decades (Chen, 1997, Lee, 1995, Zhu et al., 2000, and Wang and Cooney, 2002). In the 1980s, after over three decades of rapid industrial expansion, the supply of land and labour were limited, causing a rapid increase in labour costs and land prices. As a consequence, many labour-intensive industries relocated from Taiwan to low-cost countries, especially in South East Asia and Mainland China. The government policy also shifted from developing labour-intensive industries to encouraging the development of technology-intensive and service industry in order to maintain the momentum of economic development. In order to relieve the problem of shortage of labour, the government began to allow foreign workers from South East Asia to work in Taiwan in 1989. The policy was that a company could employ foreign workers, up to 30 per cent of its total employees (Zhu and Warner, 2001: 140). In fact, the total number of legal foreign workers reached 220,000 in mid-1996 (Chen, 1997: 153). In addition, due to the restructuring of industries, the labour force employed in the manufacturing sector decreased while workers employed by the service industry increased. For example, among the total labour force, 27.08 per cent worked in the manufacturing sector and 50.71 per cent in the service sector in 1995 (Chen, 1997: 153).

1997 Asian Financial Crisis and Reactions

At the end of 1997, when foreign exchange turmoil started in South East Asia, speculative foreign funds were transferred from Asian regions to other places as safe havens, and countries such as Thailand, Indonesia, South Korea, and the Philippines with insufficient foreign reserves were hit hard by the loss of credit confidence. Hence, when the Thai baht was allowed to float in accordance with worsening economic conditions in July 1997 (as part of a correction of an overvalued currency), the Thai baht's value began to fall, causing a contagion effect on other currencies in East and South East Asia (ICFTU, 1998).

When the Asian crisis started, Taiwan still maintained a GDP growth of 6.7 per cent (Hoover, 1998: 4). Private-sector investment was up by 14 per cent (Hoover, 1998: 4), including a near doubling of foreign investment largely due to western firms turning to Taiwan as an investment safe haven. Its relatively stable macro-economy, characterized by $83 billion in official foreign exchange reserves, little foreign debt, and a trade surplus, showed that Taiwan maintained one of the better performing economies in the region (Hoover, 1998: 4). In 1998, however, the negative impact of the Asian crisis became more obvious. Real GDP growth dropped to 4.8 per cent (DSMEA, 1999). Foreign direct investment fell by 20 per cent (Wang, 1999: 65). The trade surplus declined 28 per cent (You, 1999: 35) and the value of exports fell by 9 per cent (Chen, 1999: 24). The fluctuation of the financial market and the huge bad debts of the banking system led to an unstable domestic economic environment. Over 5000 small and medium-sized enterprises (SMEs)[1] became bankrupt and unemployment reached 2.9 per cent. The total number of unemployed increased from 220,000 to 280,000 within a year (*Commercial Times*, 1999). The government tried to ease the problem by providing a loan of NT$5 billion to help SMEs to overcome their current difficulties (*China Times*, 1999). However, the business environment was still enveloped in uncertainty and anxiety.

Current Economic Situation

Taiwan's economy is emerging as expected from the contraction in 2001. Export growth has been particularly strong, exceeding expectations. Stronger demand from US computer hardware makers translates into more business for Taiwanese semi-conductor and electronic component productions. The statistics show that, at the end of 2002, Taiwan's economic growth reached 3.24 per cent, a mild recovery compared with a contraction of 2.18 per cent growth in 2001 (*Taipei Times*, 2002). However, the economic recovery did not produce a sizeable number of new jobs. In fact, unemployment was still rising and the recent data shows that the rate of unemployment reached 7.5 per cent (a total of 765,000 unemployed people) in November 2002 (*News of Xinhuanet*, 2002). In January 2003, the government released details of an NT$70 billion package to provide temporary jobs to unemployed workers through a scheme involving public works, educational and other projects (*Taipei Times*, 2003).

On the other hand, foreign direct investment fell 16 per cent between 2001 and 2002 (*Wells Fargo Economics*, 2002). However, Taiwanese investment in Mainland China was up 26 per cent during the same period and most of the investment was in the manufacturing sector (*Wells Fargo Economics*, 2002). Hence, Taiwan has to continuously rely on larger service sector investments to replace lost manufacturing investment.

Generally speaking, the changes in the labour market (Rowley, 1998), the challenges of the Asian crisis (Berger and Borer, 1997; Orru, Biggart and Hamilton, 1997; Godement, 1999) and more broadly, global economic competition did not produce a consistent HRM response by enterprises. The responses by enterprises are investigated in the next section by a consideration of the changes in HRM policies and practices in 14 Taiwanese enterprises. These enterprises represent various types of ownership, namely foreign subsidiaries (FS), joint ventures (JV) between Taiwanese and foreign capital, Taiwanese private enterprises (TPE) and SOEs. They also represent both SMEs and Large Enterprises (LE), and cover a number of major business sectors including infrastructure, manufacturing, trade, market and financial services.

CHANGES IN HRM

The research on which this essay is based was carried out in 1999 and 2000 in the four major Taiwanese industrial and commercial cities, namely Taipei, Taichun, Tanian and Kaohsiung. In addition, a more recent questionnaire survey was conducted among case study enterprises in the middle of 2002 for more up-to-date information about changes. The 14 case study enterprises were recommended and selected under the assistance of the Economic Ministry, covering a wide range of variables, such as ownership, size, business sector and location. An intensive qualitative case study approach was used in all instances, employing a semi-structured set of in-depth interviews with a senior manager, and the personnel manager if there was one. Additionally, meetings with employees were also held where appropriate. Company documents were collected for background information. A profile of the case study enterprises is presented in Table 1.

The case study enterprises had the following characteristics:

1. *Ownership*: there were four types of ownership, namely four FSs (i.e. F1 to F4), one JV (F5), seven TPEs (F6 to F12), and two SOEs (F13 and F14);
2. *Size*: seven enterprises were SMEs (i.e. F4, F5, F7, F8, F9, F10 and F12) (see Note 1 for the definition of SMEs) and seven were LEs (i.e. F1, F2, F3, F6, F11, F13 and F14);
3. *Business sectors*: five enterprises were engaged in both manufacturing production and trade activities (i.e. F3, F5, F7, F8 and F10), six enterprises were involved only in manufacturing production (i.e. F1, F2, F6, F11 and F13), two enterprises were in market and financial services (F4 and F12) and one was in the infrastructure sector (i.e. F14).

Major Changes Taking Place

Using the ten dimensions of HRM (see Tables 2 and 3), there were some variations but also some common features between the types of enterprise studied. The similarities between these enterprises of similar size suggest the need to tabulate the groups separately between SMEs and LEs.

TABLE 1

ENTERPRISE PROFILE IN TAIWANESE FIRMS SAMPLED

Firm	Ownership[1]	Age (year)	Location	Business	Size[2] (employees)	Turnover (US$mil)	Market (%)	
F1	FS (US)	12	3 (Kaohsiung, Taipei & China)	Electronic manufacturing	650	82	100	overseas
F2	FS (Dutch)	35	1 (Kaohsiung)	Electronic manufacturing	2,660	234	100	overseas
F3	FS (Japan)	15	5 (Kaohsiung & Taipei)	Electronic manufacturing & trading	1,000	88	80 / 20	overseas / domestic
F4	FS (US)	16	3 (Taipei, Taichung & Kaohsiung)	Financial analysis	30	7	100	domestic
F5	JV (Taiwan–Japan)	37	5 (Tainan, Taichung, Kaohsiung, Malaysia & China)	Auto-parts manufacturing & trading	550	32	50 / 50	overseas / domestic
F6	TPE	30	2 (Kaohsiung & Philippines)	Electronic manufacturing	3,768	281	40 / 60	overseas / domestic
F7	TPE	24	1 (Tainan)	Sun-glasses manufacturing & trading	12	1.2	100	overseas
F8	TPE	30	9 (all in Taiwan)	Pottery manufacturing & trading	100	3.1	100	domestic
F9	TPE	12	1 (Tainan)	Optical glasses manufacturing	31	1.5	20 / 80	overseas / domestic
F10	TPE	11	2 (Taichung & China)	Furniture manufacturing & trading	30	4.1	70 / 30	overseas / domestic
F11	TPE	42	2 (Tainan & China)	Plastic manufacturing & trading	1,500	697	50 / 50	overseas / domestic
F12	TPE	35	4 (3 in Taiwan & 1 in China)	Business survey & analysis	200	7	25 / 75	overseas / domestic
F13	SOE	55	24 (22 in Taiwan & 2 in overseas)	Sugar manufacturing & trading, and other multi-business	8,048	1,853	20 / 80	overseas / domestic
F14	SOE	55	> 100 branches in Taiwan & 4 in overseas	Electricity generation & supply	28,992	8,388	100	domestic

Notes: 1. FS: foreign subsidiary; JV: joint venture; SOE: state-owned enterprise; and TPE: Taiwanese private enterprise.
2. The size of employment is the number of employees in Taiwan excluding the overseas operation.

TABLE 2

ASSESSMENT OF HRM IN TAIWANESE LEs

Dimension	Presence						
	F1	F2	F3	F6	F11	F13	F14
Rules: adherence to	✓	✓	✓	✓	✓	✓	✓
Behaviour: common values and norms	✓	✓	✓	✓	✓	✓	✓
Key managers: personnel/specialists v. line/general	✓	✓	%	%	%	✓	✓
Personnel selection	✓	✓	✓	✓	✓	✓	✓
Payment systems	✓	%	%	%	✓	%	%
Work conditions: harmonized	✓	✓	✓	✓	✓	✓	✓
Contracts: individual versus standardized	✓	✓	✓	✓	✓	✓	✓
In-house training	✓	✓	✓	✓	✓	✓	✓
Right to hire and fire	✓	✓	✓	✓	✓	%	%
Strategic role for personnel manager	✓	✓	%	%	%	✓	✓

Key: (*Practice*)
✓ present
% present to some degree
✗ not present
Source: adapted from Storey (1992).

TABLE 3

ASSESSMENT OF HRM IN TAIWANESE SMEs

Dimension	Presence						
	F4	F5	F7	F8	F9	F10	F12
Rules: adherence to	✓	✓	✓	✓	✓	✓	✓
Behaviour: common values and norms	✓	✓	✓	✓	✓	✓	✓
Key managers: / personnel/specialists v. line/general	%	%	✗	✗	✗	✗	%
Personnel selection	✓	✓	✓	✓	✓	✓	✓
Payment systems	✓	%	✗	%	%	%	✓
Work conditions: harmonized	✓	✓	✓	✓	✓	✓	✓
Contracts: individual versus standardized	✓	✓	✓	✓	✗	✗	%
In-house training	✓	✓	✗	✓	✓	✓	✓
Right to hire and fire	✓	✓	✓	✓	✓	✓	✓
Strategic role for personnel manager	%	%	✗	✗	✗	✗	%

Key: (*Practice*)
✓ present
% present to some degree
✗ not present
Source: adapted from Storey (1992).

There is a fairly even pattern of characteristics among the first two dimensions examined. All case study enterprises, including both LEs and SMEs, applied adherence to rules and common values and norms. Since 1998, changes did occur among the majority of enterprises. However, the dimension of the importance of line managers in LEs seems to be more significant than in SMEs. In fact, LEs had always emphasized the strategic role of line managers, and hence, there was basically no change in LEs in this respect. However, line managers played less significant roles in SMEs in the past, due to the active involvement of owners in the traditional family-oriented business environment. In recent years, some professional managers who were not family members of the business might be recruited by some SMEs in order to improve business performance. On the other hand, the dimension of personnel selection had been widely adopted among all case study enterprises, and there was an increasing tendency for line managers to have more power in personnel selection.

In addition, there were some variations under the dimension of payment systems. Among these 14 enterprises, only four (F1, F4, F11 and F12) were practising individual performance pay in full. Among them, two were US investments; one was a large TPE and one was a small TPE in the service sector. Due to the corporate culture of harmony in Taiwan, it was very difficult for most enterprises to implement fully individual performance pay. Therefore, group-oriented performance pay and relatively equal bonus pay were the main payment systems among the case study enterprises. In addition, the harmonized work conditions were very important among these companies due to traditional Confucian cultural influence.

There were two small TPEs (F9 and F10) that did not have individual contracts. In fact, only an informal contract was made by verbal agreement. In addition, a number of SMEs did not have collective contracts, as indicated by standardized contracts. For the other firms with both individual contracts and a collective contract, the latter provided a basic guarantee of the general conditions and welfare. Individual contracts covered more personal-oriented and detailed issues such as wages, working hours, duration of contract, welfare and other benefits, responsibility of both sides and reasons for discharge. The conditions and welfare of individual contracts were generally above the level stipulated by the collective contract.

Most firms, SMEs in particular, paid attention to both previous and current types of training due to its low costs and because it was directly linked to the needs of production. For most LEs, especially technologically-oriented firms, professional training and overseas training were also important to maintain advanced skills among the key employees. Professional training included training arranged by professional training organizations or universities. Generally speaking, trainees were key employees with special skills and techniques or managers. In order for companies to be able to develop certain new products or adopt new technology, these key people took a full-time training programme for a period of time (between one to three months). If the training could not be provided in Taiwan, overseas training was necessary for key staff members to obtain the advanced technology. A large number of FSs adopted overseas training for their key staff in their headquarters such as in Japan, the US and Europe for one to three months. As for the large TPEs and SOEs, they normally established exchange training programmes with foreign companies in order to provide overseas training in the advanced areas for their own key staff members. However, professional training and overseas training were not the usual methods for a large number of SMEs due to their relatively low technological orientation and concerns about the costs of training.

In addition, most firms had the absolute right to hire and fire workers, except the two large SOEs. Taiwan is experiencing an economic slowdown with an official unemployment rate of 7.5 per cent (*News of Xinhuanet*, 2002). Most SMEs have difficulty in retainimg their business in Taiwan. A large number of them have moved offshore, mainly located in Mainland China. The cessation of business operations in Taiwan, entirely or partially, leads to increases in lay-offs of employees. For most SMEs and private LEs, the right to hire and fire workers became part of managerial autonomy in the past four years. However, among the SOEs, the right to hire and fire workers by management was constrained due to the lack of clear vision on the process of reform and possible privatization. So far, there has not been much change in SOEs in this rspect.

Most LEs saw that the personnel manager's role was crucial for the development of business in both the short and long term. As for F1, F2, F13 and F14, personnel managers were members of company boards and directly involved in decision-making. The other three LEs also provided the opportunity for personnel managers to participate in certain decision-making processes, such as designing strategic plans for recruitment, job designing and training to accommodate the changes in production and management systems. In contrast, most SMEs provided a limited role for the personnel manager. Some SMEs did not even have a personnel manager and HRM strategy seemed not to be important for a company's development.

Industrial Relations

The trade union movement in Taiwan remained subservient to the government for a long time. Up to 1987, the KMT guided most unions by local government control over the nomination and election of union officials, by fostering KMT branches at workplaces, and by 'supervision' by larger affiliates of the sole national union peak council, the Chinese Federation of Labor (CFL) (Frenkel et al., 1993: 164).

When martial law was lifted, the union movement emerged and more independent unions were established. The amended Trade Union Law in 1975 required unions to be established in workplaces with more than 30 employees in most sectors (Lee, 1988: 188–91). However, the reality is that even now a large number of enterprises with more than 30 employees are without union organization. Among the case study enterprises, the majority of the SMEs did not have trade union organization (see Table 4). Only two enterprises had enterprise unions among the seven SMEs. Although two SMEs had a high union density of 90 per cent under the leadership of a part-time trade union official, the major tasks of unions in these firms were rather narrowly defined, such as communicating and assisting management, organizing annual union meetings and making collective agreements with management once every three years (actually, only one firm had a collective contract). Union–management meetings were held as required by both sides.

In contrast, a majority of LEs had union organizations on site. Among the case study LEs, except for one firm (F1), the remaining six

TABLE 4

INDUSTRIAL RELATIONS IN TAIWANESE ENTERPRISES

Dimension	Firms													
	F1	F2	F3	F4	F5	F6	F7	F8	F9	F10	F11	F12	F13	F14
Industrial relations														
Trade union	✗	✓	✓	✗	✓	✓	✗	✗	✗	✗	✓	✓	✓	✓
Union density (%)	✗	90	90	✗	90	90	✗	✗	✗	✗	90	90	100	100
Full-time officials	✗	1	½	✗	½	1	✗	✗	✗	✗	½	½	>20	>30
Union meetings/a	✗	2	2	✗	2	2	✗	✗	✗	✗	2	2	2	2
Collective contract	✗	✓	✓	✗	✗	✓	✗	✗	✗	✗	✓	✓	✓	✓
Union–management meetings	✗	AR	AR	✗	AR	AR	✗	✗	✗	✗	M	AR	M	M
Grievance procedure	✗	✓	✓	✗	✓	✓	✗	✗	✗	✗	✓	✓	✓	✓

Key: (*Practice*)
   ✓ present
   % present to some degree
   ✗ not present
   AR as required
   M monthly
Source: adapted from Storey (1992).

firms all had unions, with a very high union density between 90 per cent and 100 per cent. Certainly, union organization and activities are different between private firms and SOEs. The four private LEs had their own enterprise union with a limited role. According to the Chairman of F11, the union should maintain within the enterprise an 'invisible' presence. In fact, the reason for these firms to have unions was because of the enforcement of the Labour Law and the Trade Union Law by the government. These large firms were too prominent to ignore state policy. However, in reality, the trade unions only played a marginal role, such as communicating with the managers, negotiating collective agreements once every three years, conciliating disputes and organizing annual meetings (Wang and Cooney, 2002). Unions were not part of the decision-making processes of these enterprises.

Unions in the large SOEs were also hardly independent. The unions within SOEs were established for a long time as part of official trade union organizations under the rule of KMT (see Ng and Warner, 1998). They had a strong membership-base and bureaucracy. For instance, F13 had 19 union branches with 29 full-time officials. All employees of SOEs were members of unions. During the interviews with the two SOEs, a strong sense of a dual role for unions in SOEs was provided by both management and union leaders. For instance, the functions of unions in F13 were described as: on the one hand, the union should represent workers and protect workers' interests. Through the involvement of enterprise decision-making, annual meetings with management and negotiation with management on the collective contract, the union officials could bring workers' concerns and grievances to management. On the other hand, unions could help their enterprises to develop. By providing and assisting training programmes for workers, promoting the relevant government policies and assisting management to improve quality and productivity, unions were seen as a useful bridge between workers and management to guarantee smoother industrial relations (see Thurley, 1988).

From the case study enterprises, we may note the ambiguous nature of the unions' role in Taiwanese enterprises, no matter whether they are private or public organizations. It demonstrates a lack of independence, being marginal and having a 'dual-role'. These are major characteristics of Taiwanese trade unions.

DISCUSSION

Why Changes Have Occurred

The changes of the macro-economic environment, due to the Asian crisis, have been an important stimulus to organizational and HRM changes in Taiwanese enterprises. This study examines these responses by looking at individual firms, using a case study approach. The pattern of organizational responses introduced in these enterprises has exhibited a variety of different characteristics. Most have implemented strategies towards enhancing the individual firms' competitiveness.

Relocation of some of the production processes from Taiwan to other Asian developing countries such as Mainland China, the Philippines and Malaysia has been a major shift of business operational strategy (Zhu and Warner, 2001). Nowadays, many FIEs carry out regional production strategies and see Taiwan as only a part of their regional production sites. Reorganization and restructuring of production systems between Taiwan and other Asian countries by multinational companies (MNCs) become more important than ever before.

Other changes related to the crisis, particularly in the TPE sector, include giving up low value-added products and moving to high value-added products, reducing business scale and business items by concentrating the core business sector on competitiveness, outsourcing some of the business and only employing new employees where they are casual workers (Zhu and Warner, 2001).

Lifetime employment status will be ended soon in the formerly centrally important Taiwanese SOEs. In addition, the privileged position of their monopoly over the economy will be diminished and competition with other FIEs and TPEs in the market will push the current SOEs to reposition and reorganize their organization and production systems, including their management systems. So far, there have been some initiatives to make most subsidiaries of large SOEs eventually become economically independent. However, due to the change of political landscape marked by the power shift from KMT to DPP, uncertainties of leadership changes and reform processes in SOEs reduce the momentum of SOE restructuring.

Convergence or Divergence

The current theoretical debate on the trend of HRM development between convergent and divergent paths can be divided into several streams.

1. Globalization causes convergence in HRM with the views based on universal theories (Appelbaum and Batt, 1994; Pfeffer, 1994; Delery and Doty, 1996). The central proposition is that world-wide trends and forces (political, economic, social and technological) tend to induce convergence of national systems, including HRM, towards uniformity (see Rowley and Bae, 2002: 523).

2. Reasons for change and convergence other than globalization are based on institutional theory. Certain practices are adopted not because of 'effectiveness', but other specific social constraining forces (McKinley et al., 1995). Those changes then eventually gain legitimacy that reflects institutional environments.

3. In contrast to the convergence approach, the divergence approach questions the validity of such universal beliefs, by using case studies across the Asian economies (Rowley, 1998). Other research also found that divergence remains at national and international levels, as these forces are mediated by different institutions with their own traditions and cultures (Bamber and Lansbury, 1998: 32). Therefore, this study may help us to gain further clarification of those debates.

In fact, the restructuring of industries under the pressure of globalization has led to a number of consequences, such as the relocation of factories, downsizing or retraining employees (Warner, 2002: 392). These shifts have influenced the enterprise-level HRM practices, such as labour-hiring flexibility, fixed-term employment contracts (rather than lifetime employment), performance-based compensation and rewards, training and career development, and commitment and motivation towards organization and work. Those so-called Western-style HRM practices may be found in certain firms in Taiwan, in particular in MNCs. However, the question is whether the general trend of such development is towards the 'convergent' or 'divergent' path (see Rowley, 1998). Based on the findings of the case studies, it is hard to posit a full degree of convergence, but a degree of 'relative convergence' (see Warner, 2002). The trends towards globalization can only strengthen these tendencies towards greater similarities in HRM policies and practices over the coming decades, although we can expect that each country's apparent distinctness will remain visible.

Key Issues for HRM

The key issues relating to HRM changes can be identified by comparing this survey with the previous research of Chen (1997) offered here.

First, the fundamental change is the general economic environment: a transformation from the situation of economic boom to economic recession. Therefore, several key economic indicators changed between these two periods from high economic growth and demand for extra labour (including foreign labour) to low economic growth and increasing unemployment. In that sense, the labour market environment changed from demand-driven to over-supply of labour. This requires HRM policy to be flexible at both national and enterprise levels in order to prepare adequate skilled labour force, train laid-off workers for re-employment and develop long-term HRM strategic plans.

Second, foreign investment and MNCs have a profound impact on adopting international standardized HRM practices. This issue, however, was not illustrated in the previous research. The case studies suggested that in FIE management, the philosophy is different in Taiwanese-owned enterprises compared with European or US-owned firms or JVs, with more individualist values being predominant. FIEs are more likely than domestic firms to have individual-based rewards systems.

Third, the larger the enterprise, the more likely are formal management practices to be carried out. The data suggested that size measured by the number of employees in the company is an extremely important factor. Larger firms are more likely to implement the ten dimensions than SMEs, though SMEs also experienced some substantial changes in the past four years.

Fourth, irrespective of sector, in order to be more competitive in both domestic and international markets, most firms applied such HRM practices as adherence to rules, common values and norms, importance of line-managers and freedom of personnel selection and so on.

Finally, for the future the most important issue is how different enterprises adopt new initiatives and strategies to cope with the recent economic crisis and global competition. Ownership seems to be an obvious influence on adopting different management initiatives. As for JVs and FSs, Taiwan is part of regional/global production and trade strategy; rationalization of production divisions within the East Asian region and reduction of costs by adopting different means are the dominating initiatives that have been carried out by most JVs and FSs. As for TPEs, relocation of production to Mainland China and South East Asia and concentration on more service-oriented activities such as design and sale are the most practical options. As for SOEs, 'downsizing' and privatization will be the major outcome of the reform in the future and consequently HRM may play a crucial role in such transition. Relevant changes of management systems and HRM will be carried out in order to cope with the restructuring of the former 'public' organizations.

Implications for Theory Development

This research may be 'meaningful' in terms of understanding the theoretical arguments about the trend of HRM development towards a possibly hybrid 'cross-vergent' phenomenon where national cultural systems are blended with broader economic ideologies. Certainly, East Asian development has been explained in culturalist terms that argue that cultural factors determined the successful outcome of economic development in this region (Redding, 1995). However, three inter-related issues may work here:

1. Cultural factors influence the formation of certain management patterns and related mindsets, for example Confucianism is crucial for many elements in East Asian management concepts and practices, and Taiwan is part of that.
2. Culture is not isolated and unchangeable, but constantly changing, being modified, and transforming
3. Social norms including political, economic, and historical factors also influence managerial thinking and reshape the outcome of managerial approaches and practices.

The example of Taiwanese uniqueness is summarized in Table 5. It demonstrates the HRM changes and continuities in Taiwan under the influence of cultural norms and as well as political, economic and historical norms. All HRM dimensions, except two (namely key managers – personnel/specialists versus line/general – and in-house training) changed, though these changes were not as large as in other Asian countries. Hence, these findings are consistent with the general arguments made in the introduction of this publication that each country in the East Asian region tries to do its best to improve its performance and competitiveness following the Asian crisis, although different HRM patterns have been seen to be effective ways to achieve these goals.

CONCLUSION

It is clear that HRM in Taiwan is now in flux. This change has been mainly due to the Asian crisis, the changes in the labour market, growing exposure to foreign influences and the increasing degree of competition in world markets (see Orru et al., 1997; Berger and Borer, 1997; Godement, 1999) that is being felt throughout the whole economy. In recent years, the state's policies towards organized labour have become more favourable. In order to remain competitive, firms have had to seek new, appropriate business and HRM strategies but these have varied from one kind of firm to another. The adoption of international standardized HRM practices is one such move that is

TABLE 5

ASSESSMENT OF HRM CHANGES AND CONTINUITIES

Dimensions	Presence	Change
1. Rules: adherence to	✓	+
2. Behaviour: common values and norms	✓	+
3. Key managers: personnel/specialists v. line/general	✓	0
4. Personnel selection	✓	+
5. Payment systems	%	+
6. Work conditions: harmonized	✓	0
7. Contracts: individual v. standardized	%	+
8. In-house training	✓	0
9. Right to hire and fire	✓	+
10. Strategic role for personnel manager	%	+

Key: (*Practice*)
        ✓ present
        % present to some degree
        ✗ not present

        (*Degree of change in past 4 years*)
        ++ major change
        + change
        0 none
Source: adapted by Storey (1992).

now becoming more general in Taiwan, in particular among MNCs operating there. Hence, it is possible to claim that there will at least be a degree of 'relative convergence' or 'cross-vergence' given the evidence presented above. The trends towards globalization may in many significant respects only strengthen tendencies towards greater similarities in HRM policies and practices in the future. However, each society's apparent distinctness will surely remain visible due to their unique cultural tradition and social, political and economic environments.

NOTE

1. SME applies to companies with capital of less than NT$60 million and employees fewer than 200.

REFERENCES

Appelbaum, E. and Batt, R. (1994), *The New American Workplace: Transforming Work Systems in the United States*. Ithaca, NY: ILR Press.
Bamber, G. and Lansbury, R. (eds.) (1998), *International and Comparative Employment Relations*. London: Sage.
Berger M, and Borer, D. (eds.) (1997), *The Rise of East Asia: Critical Visions of the Pacific Century*. London: Routledge.
Chen, S.J. (1997), 'The Development of HRM Practices in Taiwan', *Asia Pacific Business Review*, Special Issue, Vol.3, No.4, pp.152–69.
Chen, S.J. (1998) 'The Development of HRM Practices in Taiwan', in C. Rowley (ed.)

Human Resource Management in the Asia Pacific Region: Convergence Questioned, London: Frank Cass, pp.152–69.

Chen, Y.B. (1999), 'The Outlook of Taiwan's Economy in 1999', *Economic Outlook*, Vol.61, pp.24–9.

China Times (1999), 'Government Supports SMEs to Overcome Economic Crisis', Taipei, 17 Feb. 1999, p.3.

Commercial Times (1999), 'It Becomes More Easier to Break the Rice-bowl of Labour', Taipei, 27 Feb. 1999, p.2.

Delery, J.E. and Doty, D.H. (1996), 'Modes of Theorizing in Strategic HRM: Tests of Universalistic, Contingency, and Configurational Performance Predictions', *Academy of Management Journal*, No.39, pp.802–35.

DGBAS (1996), Monthly Bulletin of Manpower Statistics, Taiwan Area, Republic of China, Oct. Taipei: Executive Yuan, Directorate-General of Budget, Accounting and Statistics.

DSMEA (1999), Domestic and Foreign Express Report of Economic Statistics Indicators, Taipei: Department of Statistics Ministry of Economic Affairs.

Frenkel, S, Hong, J.C. and Lee, B.L. (1993), 'The Resurgence and Fragility of Trade Unions in Taiwan' in S. Frenkel (ed.), *Organized Labor in the Asia-Pacific Region: a Comparative Study of Trade Unionism in Nine Countries*, Ithaca, New York: ILR Press, pp.162–86.

Godement, F. (1999), *The Downsizing of Asia*, London: Routledge.

Hoover, J. (1998), 'In the "Year of the Tiger", One Tiger, Taiwan, Stands Its Ground', *Business America*, Sept., pp.5–13.

ICFTU (1998), ICFT–APRO Statement on Asian Economic Crisis, International Confederation of Free Trade Unions and Asian and Pacific Regional Organisation, Singapore, 10–11 , 1998.

Lee, J.S. (1995), 'Economic Development and the Evolution of Industrial Relations in Taiwan, 1950–1993' in A. Verma, T.A. Kochan and R.D. Lansbury (eds.), *Employment Relations in the Growing Asian Economies*, Routledge: London, pp.88–118.

Lee, J.S. (1988), 'Labor Relations and the Stages of Economic Development: The Case of the Republic of China' in Proceedings of the Conference on Labor and Economic Development, Taipei: Institution for Economic Research, China Productivity Center, pp.177–204.

McKinley, W., Sanchez, L. and Schick, A.G. (1995), 'Organizational Downsizing: Constraining, Cloning, Learning', *Academy of Management Executive*, Vol.9, No.3, pp.32–44.

News of Xinhuanet (2002), 'Taiwan's Unemployment Rate Reached a Historical Peak with 7.46%', 24 Dec. 2002.

Ng, S.H. and Warner, M. (1998), *China's Trade Unions and Management*. London: Macmillan and New York: St Martin's Press.

Orru, M., Biggart, N.W. and Hamilton, G.G. (eds.) (1997), *The Economic Organization of East Asian Capitalism*. London: Sage.

Pfeffer, J. (1994), *Competitive Advantage Through People*. Boston, MA: Harvard Business School Press.

Redding, G. (1995), *The Spirit of Chinese Capitalism*. Berlin: De Gruyter.

Rowley, C. (ed.) (1998), *Human Resource Management in the Asia-Pacific Region: Convergence Questioned*. London & Portland, OR: Frank Cass.

Rowley, C. and Bae, J.S. (2002), 'Globalization and Transformation of Human Resource Management in South Korea', *International Journal of Human Resource Management*, Vol.13, No.3, pp.522–49.

Storey, J. (1992), *Developments in the Management of Human Resources*. London: Routledge.

Taipei Times (2002), 'Business Briefs: Economy Set to expand', Taipei, 24 Dec., p.11.

Taipei Times (2003), 'Premier Provides Details of New Employment Scheme', Taipei, 3 Jan., p.3.

Thurley, K. (1988), 'Trade Unionism in Asian Countries' in Y.C. Jao, D.A. Levin, S-H. Ng and E. Sinn (eds.), *Labour Movement in A Changing Society*. Hong Kong, Centre of Asian Studies, University of Hong Kong, pp.24–31.

Wang, S.W. (1999), 'Review and Outlook of Taiwan's Economy in 1999', *Economic Outlook*, Vol.61, No.1, pp.64–7.

Wang, H.L. and Cooney, S. (2002), 'Taiwan's Labour Law: The End of State Corporatism?', in S. Cooney, T. Lindsey, R. Mitchell and Y. Zhu (eds.), *Law and Labour Market Regulation in East Asia*. London and New York: Routledge, pp.185–214.

Warner, M. (2002), 'Globalization, Labour Markets and Human Resources', *International Journal of Human Resource Management*, Vol.13, No.3, pp.1–15.

Wells Fargo Economics (2002), 'Country Reports: Taiwan', *Wells Fargo Economics*, Dec., pp.28–30.

You, M.J. (1999), 'Domestic Economy: Review and Outlook', *Taiwan Economic Research Monthly Journal*, No.12, pp.1–10.

Zhu, Y., Chen, I. and Warner, M. (2000), 'HRM in Taiwan: An Empirical Case Study', *Human Resource Management Journal*, Vol.10, No.4, pp.32–44.

Zhu, Y. and Warner, M. (2001), 'Taiwan Business Strategies vis-à-vis the Asian Financial Crisis', *Asia Pacific Business Review*, Vol.7, No.3, pp.139–56.

HRM in Thailand:
A Post-1997 Update

JOHN J. LAWLER and VINITA ATMIYANANDANA

Among the most dominant images on the road into Bangkok from the airport are hundreds of pairs of concrete pillars extending for several miles, each of which is two to three stories high and connected by a crossbeam. These are the remnants of the ironically named 'Hopewell Project' (after the Hong Kong company that undertook the project), intended as a rapid transit system to link Bangkok to its northern suburbs. The project failed many years ago. Now labelled by some as 'Thailand's Stonehenge,' it stands as a poignant reminder of the heady days of 8 and 9 per cent economic growth enjoyed in Thailand prior to the 1997 Asian financial crisis and the subsequent impact of the crisis. But despite significant setbacks, as reflected in the Hopewell Project, the Thai economy has shown signs of resilience and appears, at this writing, to be staging a gradual, if not dramatic, recovery.

The 1997 crisis and its aftermath have been the products of a number of forces (Phongpaichit and Baker, 1998), but certainly management practices in Thailand played a major role. The period since 1997 has seen efforts at innovation and reform in the managerial arena, including changes in human resource management (HRM) policies and practices. To date, these shifts, while promising, are still incomplete, particularly in locally-owned companies. This essay builds on an earlier assessment of HRM practices in Thailand (Lawler et al., 1997), focusing on what has transpired in the wake of the crisis. As with the other essays in this collection, we relate HRM practices and changes in the Thai system to the various HRM dimensions proposed by Storey (1992).

CONTEXTUAL FACTORS AND ISSUES

Political and Historical

Once a series of principalities with populations that shared similar languages, cultures, and ethnic origins, Thailand became a unified country several hundred years ago. Unlike all other South East Asian countries, it avoided colonization at the hands of a European power, although it was under Japanese domination during World War II. Thailand was an absolute monarchy until a revolution in 1932 led to the establishment of a constitutional monarchy (and ultimately to a change in the country's name from 'Siam' to 'Thailand'). Yet in practice Thailand was ruled by a succession of military dictators for most of the post-revolutionary period. With rapid economic growth and the emergence of a significant middle class, the country has operated as a parliamentary democracy since the late 1980s. A notable exception was a military coup in 1991 that ended in bloody popular uprising in 1992 and restored democratic rule. There are multiple political parties in Thailand, most of which are built around a particular leader rather than specific ideologies or philosophies. The king, though having limited authority, is highly respected throughout the country and has played an instrumental role in promoting the country's economic and political development.

The Thai population is largely a mixture of ethnic Thais and individuals of Chinese heritage. Thais of Chinese extraction constitute the largest ethnic minority, amounting to between 15 and 20 per cent of the population. However, unlike other South East Asian countries, where the Chinese and indigenous communities often do not intermingle and often harbour mutual mistrust and hostility (for example, Indonesia, Singapore and Malaysia), the Sino-Thais are largely assimilated into Thai society (with the exception of some isolated Chinese communities in northern Thailand that are composed mainly of descendants of followers of the Chiang Kai-shek that fled China in 1949). There is considerable intermarriage and most Sino-Thais speak Thai as their first language; the Sino-Thais have adopted Thai culture. Nonetheless, there is a clear recognition of ancestry, which often is critical in business matters. Most major locally-owned Thai companies (apart from state-owned enterprises) were established, and continue to be controlled, by entrepreneurial Chinese families. Despite strong attachment to Thailand and Thai culture, Chinese families, and particularly those involved in business, retain strong connections to other Chinese within Thailand and with Chinese communities elsewhere in the region. Chinese approaches to management thus tend to dominate in the private sector, at least in locally-owned companies.

Thailand is an overwhelmingly Buddhist country, with 95 per cent of the population belonging to this religious group. Thais profess Theravada Buddhism, which differs in many respects from the type of Buddhism practised in China, Korea, Japan, Singapore and Vietnam. It is a more introspective form of Buddhism and probably promotes a more passive acceptance of life events and fatalism. Theravada Buddhism is also dominant in the Sino-Thai community; Confucianism does not play the same role in Thailand as it does in much of East Asia. So a strong preoccupation with personal accomplishment, linked in particular to the Confucian ethic, is not particularly central to Thai identity. While many of the values that are important in places such as China, Korea, Japan and Taiwan – humility, deference to superiors, loyalty to the group, reliance on social networks and preferential treatment of network members, pursuit of harmonious relations and avoidance of conflict and maintaining face – are central values in Thai culture, Thais would also be more focused on issues such as quality of life. Thus the concept of *sanuk*, which literally means 'to have fun', is integral to most aspects of Thai life.

Thais are neither apt to show unflinching commitment to their employers nor do they accept the sort of high stress levels at work that seem common in Japan and Korea. Managers have often noted to the authors in conversation the need to incorporate elements of *sanuk* into the daily working life in order to have a motivated and productive workforce. Of course, values vary as a function of factors such as income, age, education, and location (younger, better educated, and more affluent urban dwellers, particularly those in the Bangkok area, are apt to have less traditional values and be more Westernized and individualistic).

There are other ethnic and religious groups in Thailand, including Indians, Muslims (mainly in southern Thailand), members of various mountain tribe groups (principally in north-western Thailand), and, more recently, immigrants for Myanmar (Burma) and Cambodia. But these groups play a generally limited role in Thai society. However, there is a long-standing separatist movement among the Muslims in the southern provinces adjacent to Malaysia. The level of violence in this region has increased in recent years and has been primarily directed at police and government officials in the Muslim-majority provinces, few of whom are themselves Muslims.

Economic

The Thai economy began a sustained take-off in the 1980s. This was built largely on foreign direct investment (FDI), especially emanating from Japan after the yen appreciated substantially. Japanese companies moved considerable amounts of labour-intensive, low value-added production offshore, mainly to low wage countries in East Asia. Thailand also formulated an export-oriented development policy, with its Board of Investment (BOI) patterned to some extent after the

Japanese Ministry of International Trade and Investment (MITI), and sought to generate patterns of investment that would promote and sustain economic development. Enterprise zones were established and foreign investors were granted preferential treatment.

For a period in the early 1990s, Thailand was the *Wunderkind* of economic development, with double-digit growth and low inflation, and arguably the world's highest rate of economic growth. Yet the stresses of development began to take their toll. One of Thailand's greatest weaknesses was an infrastructure that failed to expand at a pace equivalent to economic growth. Legendary traffic jams and gridlock that quite literally would bring almost the whole of Bangkok to a halt were only a part of the problem. The port facilities were unable to handle the massive increase in imports and exports and dock workers and customs officers were rumoured to make small fortunes in 'tea money' (bribes) to facilitate movement of shipments. There were often 'blackouts' in Bangkok and other metropolitan areas because of insufficient electrical power, and reaching someone by telephone at peak usage hours was often impossible as a consequence of overloaded telephone exchanges. The AIDS epidemic, which threatened the country throughout much of the 1990s, and severe environmental degradation, are other examples of the problems that were at least exacerbated by overly rapid development.

Development officials worked feverishly to expand airports, port facilities, highways, electricity generation capacity and communication infrastructure. The rapid growth in this period seemingly generated a consciousness of unlimited potential, with increasing borrowing from the foreign sector and investment in ill-conceived business ventures. This largely set the stage for the 1997 financial crisis, though economic problems began to emerge prior to 1997, as evidenced, for example, by the collapse of the Hopewell project referred to above.

Labour Markets

Although Thailand has a generally high level of literacy, educational attainment is still a problem, even by regional standards. Only about 30 per cent of the Thai population has more than an elementary school education and many workers, particularly those over 30 years of age, have only a few years of formal schooling. Thailand has been, and remains, very much a labour-surplus economy. Economic growth lured large numbers of rural people to Bangkok, which grew from a population of four or five million in the 1970s to perhaps 12 million today. Thus there are significant numbers of people in urban areas in the secondary and tertiary labour markets, many waiting for jobs in the primary sector. Although the government has been promoting higher levels of educational attainment, particularly at the lower end of the distribution, by policies such as gradually increasing mandatory schooling, Thailand suffers from a labour force that is ill-equipped to function in the high-technology sector and other high-value added, capital intensive industries. The country also has perpetual shortages of engineers, scientists, and other types of key professionals. Thailand has many plants that manufacture basic types of computer chip, but most of these are at the lower end of the market. Also it lacks the high technology initiatives and clusters found in neighbouring countries such as Malaysia and Singapore. The labour force is thus another infrastructure problem for Thailand.

1997 Asian Financial Crisis and Reactions

The Asian crisis first affected Thailand, then moved to many other Pacific Rim countries. It was largely precipitated in Thailand by large external debts incurred by investors and consumers who seemingly failed to recognize the limits of the economy's potential. Perhaps most significant was the real estate 'bubble'. Construction projects, particularly for commercial space in Bangkok, far exceeded potential capacity, with projects often funded with little concern for financial viability, as reflected in Sheridan's (1999: 180) characterization of banking in Thailand:

> When a man applies for a loan, the first thing the proverbial Thai banker asks is: Do I know this person....what connections do I have with him, what connections can I build with him? The first question is not: What is the credit-worthiness of this loan application, does it satisfy objective rules and criteria, is the business plan convincing?

Of course, reliance on personal connections in business transactions is commonplace throughout East Asia (Hamilton, 1996). And networking has often been seen as a fundamental strength of Asian societies and markets. However, in extreme circumstances, such as Thailand in the mid-1990s, such cultural practices can seemingly have catastrophic consequences, especially when personal connections lead to favouritism without proper regard for the economic merits of a project or transaction.

Declining property values brought about by overbuilding, coupled with chronic problems with Thailand's overburdened infrastructure, declining FDI (which had been attracted to China, Vietnam and other emerging markets) and other factors, led to serious balance of payments problems and rapidly dwindling foreign reserves. With traders sensing its vulnerability, the Thai baht came under speculative assault and the Bank of Thailand spent huge amounts defending the currency and endeavouring to maintain the existing exchange rate. As foreign exchange balances fell dangerously low, Thailand had little option but to devalue its currency and seek help from the International Monetary Fund (IMF), which provided several billion dollars in emergency loans.

The IMF loans shored up the Thai economy to some extent, though gross domestic product (GDP) continued to decline until at least 2001 (*Far Eastern Economic Review*, 2001). But IMF help came at a price. The IMF demanded that the government implement austerity programmes, including reductions in government spending, increased taxation, and reforms in banking and commercial practices to promote greater transparency and accountability. Recessionary conditions continued through the end of the decade, along with high unemployment and business failures. The policies imposed on Thailand by the IMF often rankled, in part as a perceived affront to national sovereignty and in part as a consequence of the cultural insensitivity of some policies. For example, the IMF insisted on the establishment of a 'social safety net' to protect unemployed workers, although the Thais maintained that strong family connections were generally sufficient to help those experiencing financial difficulty. The IMF also insisted that educational expenditure be redirected from higher education (which largely benefited the country's elite) to primary and secondary education (thus improving Thailand's relatively low level of educational attainment). While a desirable move, this still had the effect of angering the beneficiaries of higher education (which is actually fairly open to lower-class individuals who are able to complete high school).

Current Economic Situation

By 2002 the Thai economy had stabilized and GDP had begun to grow, though at a quite modest rate (about 2 per cent per year) compared to the early 1990s. Certainly the reforms introduced by the government of Prime Minister Chuan Leekpai in the wake of the 1997 crisis laid the foundation for this recovery, but the subsequent liberalization of economic policy on the part of the Thaksin Shinawat government, which many feared might bring about another boom–bust cycle, was seemingly leading to more controlled and sustainable growth. And while Prime Minister Thaksin has been criticized for his apparently less than enthusiastic support of democratic ideals, he has maintained peace and avoided military confrontation with neighbouring Burma, despite a series of provocative actions by the Burmese government, including numerous incursions into Thai territory by the Burmese military and allied militia groups. Certainly this stance aided economic recovery. Another factor has been the relationship between the Thai and Chinese economies. With the size and openness of the Chinese market, coupled with China's rapid growth, Thailand (along with most other economies in the region) had found itself at a severe disadvantage in attracting FDI and in competing with Chinese-produced goods. Indeed, the movement of FDI away from Thailand and into China undoubtedly played a role in Thailand's economic difficulties in 1997. Yet in the longer term, the success of the Chinese economy would seem to be generating considerable opportunity for neighbouring economies, including Thailand. There is now greater trade with China, Chinese companies are investing in Thailand, and Thailand's vibrant tourist industry has significantly benefited as a favoured location for Chinese vacationers. Much of the growth that took place in Thailand in the 1990s was driven by Japanese investment. With Japan's declining fortunes, China may now serve a similar role in bolstering the Thai economy.

By early 2003, Thailand's economy was experiencing meaningful recovery from the events of 1997, with economic growth nearing 4 per cent and the long awaited recovery seemed to be under way, despite a general slowdown in the world economy. Many of the infrastructure problems noted above had been largely solved. A system of expressways now crisscrosses Bangkok and helps to move traffic reasonably rapidly. There are still traffic jams, but much less severe than in the 1990s (though lower levels of economic activity may explain this). There are now completed, or soon to be completed, mass transit systems in Bangkok (including an operating 'skytrain' and a subway system in the final stages of construction). Thailand is considered a leader in efforts to contain the AIDS epidemic, which is no longer a major threat.

Though economic growth was much slower than was the case a decade earlier, it was probably more sustainable, though Thailand's fortunes are still tied to the performance of global markets and major trading partners, especially America and, increasingly, China. We can relate conditions to the labour market dimensions discussed in the original review by Rowley (1997, Table 4). By late 2002, most labour shortages, which was the case for skilled labour and professionals pre-1997, had largely been eliminated. The Thai unemployment rate was in the range of 6–7 per cent, a figure that undoubtedly understates true unemployment as workers returned to their villages from Bangkok and other urban areas or otherwise left the labour market. College graduates reported continuing difficulty finding jobs. Thus, there were general surpluses in the labour market in most occupations. Market volatility would seem to have been low, with the economy growing are a very modest pace. There were uncertainties and potential disruptions of the Thai economy. With the economies increasing linkages to Chinese economy, any major disruption in China would clearly affect Thailand. As this is being written, the severe acute respiratory syndrome (SARS) epidemic is a major problem in Asia, particularly China. Although to this point SARS has not affect Thailand, the disruption it as brought to the Chinese economy could substantially affect the Thai economy. If SARS were to become endemic in East Asia and not readily treatable, the implications for Thailand, and the rest of the region, are apt to be sobering.

Uncertainty regarding global economic conditions would also be a potential source of volatility. In addition, a bombing that occurred in Bali in October 2002, killing nearly 200 largely Western tourists, created threats to Thailand as well; indeed, there were many warnings that Thailand might be a target of action by Islamic extremists, either domestic or foreign. Any major terrorist strike, in Thailand or even in a neighbouring country, could be economically devastating given the country's heavy reliance on tourism. Indeed, the warnings had a significant negative impact on tourism in late 2002 and early 2003, normally the 'high season' in the industry.

Direct state involvement in the Thai economy is generally low. There are still many state-owned enterprises in Thailand, but these are gradually being privatized and, under World Trade Organization (WTO) regulations, cannot be subsidized by the state. Indirect state involvement is higher. These would include economic reforms mandated by the IMF that make, for example, banks and other financial institutions more accountable to the government. The BOI endeavours to promote investment in the country and targets certain industries and geographical areas. Thus Thailand continues to have some type of industrial development policy, though not so strong and as focused as, say, in the case of Singapore (Yuen, 1997). Labour unions are very limited in the private sector and have been greatly weakened in recent years in state-owned enterprises (Lawler and Suttawet, 2000). Although there is a variety of ethnic groups in Thai society, overall it is relatively homogeneous. The largest single group is the ethnic Chinese, but in contrast to the rest of South East Asia, the Chinese are quite well assimilated in Thailand. There is immigrant labour, from Burma and other neighbouring countries, as well as Thai Muslims who feel estranged from mainstream society. However, these groups are small and relatively marginalized (except, as noted, for the Muslims in the southernmost provinces). Similarly, there are mountain tribe groups in the North, but these are largely agrarian, semi-nomadic and not significantly involved in the industrial sector. Thus cultural diversity in the labour force is not a major issue in Thailand, as most workers in the modern sector are either ethnic Thais or assimilated Thai-Chinese.

CHANGES IN HRM

Major Changes Taking Place

Lawler et al. (1997) differentiated between two types of domestically owned, private sector firms: family enterprises and Thai-owned corporations. The former tend to be smaller or medium-sized enterprises that rely on the conventional management practices of Chinese-style family enterprises (not surprising, given that the Thai entrepreneurial community is largely composed of ethnic Chinese or Chinese intermarried with native Thais). In such organizations, HRM practices are generally simple and informal, with personal relationships being very important in hiring, the determination of wages, salaries, bonuses, and promotions. Pay is often linked to demographic and status-related factors, rather than either the external labour market or internal equity. Training and development are quite limited. Thai-owned corporations have generally grown out of family enterprises (though some are privatized state enterprises). Normally as such firms grow, they become more globally active, and require capital from external investors (particularly through the sale of stock). These companies often continue to have significant involvement in management by members of the founding family, though their size means that professional managers must also be hired. The rise of graduate business education in Thailand has meant that this new cohort of managers, including those from the new generation within founding families with MBAs and other degrees in management, have increasingly professionalized these companies, often applying techniques based on Western business practices. We noted in the earlier essay that these companies still have HRM systems that are rooted in personal connections, though greater reliance on technical and strategic approaches to HRM are observed.

The other major category discussed was subsidiaries of foreign multinational companies (MNCs). American-based, and, to an increasing extent, European-based MNCs, have subsidiaries that typically apply rationalistic and systematic approaches to HRM based on notions of international 'best practices.' Subsidiaries of Japanese-based MNCs have, in Thailand, tended to utilize some, but not all of the methods found in parent company operations in Japan. For example, pay may be based to a large extent on seniority and there may be considerable internal development, but policies such as 'lifetime employment' and participative decision making would not appear to be so common.

Although there are a fairly limited number of English-language studies dealing with HRM policies and practices in Thailand, there are some recent studies that are helpful in understanding post-1997 developments. For example, Pyatt et al. (2001) used interviews and qualitative analysis to examine the changing nature of locally-owned enterprises in both Hong Kong and Thailand. They identified a typology of approaches to management in these companies. What they termed the 'country-net architecture' is equivalent to the traditional family enterprise. They also identified an 'international architecture,' which is quite similar to what we have called the Thai-owned (or domestic) corporation. However, they also observed an emerging organizational form, the 'transnational architecture,' which, though family controlled, is much more akin to Western transnational or MNCs. These companies are rooted in traditional values and Asian business networks, but are much more global in focus, utilize strategic planning and other more advanced management techniques, are more interconnected with non-Asian and non-Chinese organizational networks, and can be expected to utilize more sophisticated and rationalized employment practices. Although Pyatt et al. (2001) provide no estimate of the distribution of companies by these categories, the import of their study is that the transnational architecture is evolving, still relatively rare, and more common in Hong Kong than in Thailand. However, to the extent this form evolves, it should increase the prevalence of more progressive human resource (HR) strategies in Thai-owned companies.

Chainuvati and Granrose (2001) report the results of a survey study of career planning and development for managers in Thailand. Their principal finding is that, while Thai managers were generally found to have well thought-out career plans, most Thai companies had only very limited career planning and development policies (even at the managerial level). Such policies and practices were found to be more common, however, in subsidiaries of American-based MNCs. For example, annual performance reviews and career development efforts were much less frequently observed in Thai-owned than American-owned firms. Chainuvati and Granrose (2001) speculate that this deficiency could be an important problem for Thai organizations in the post-1997 era, as firms will need to become more performance-driven. Better career planning plus use of methods such as mentoring and subsidization of participation in external training and educational programmes were means identified by the authors as potentially contributing to success in this area, though they do not show evidence of such a transition underway.

In contrast to limited career development efforts, Dubey-Villinger (2001b) observes that training has, in some ways, both increased and improved in Thailand in the post-1997 era. The government, for example, has implemented a number of programmes intended to upgrade the skills of lower-level employees, especially those displaced by the 1997 crisis. This is important in light of Thailand's relatively low level of HR development (HRD) relative to neighbouring countries (for example, only about 30 per cent of Thais have more than an elementary school education). Private sector initiatives in the hotel and hospitality industry, a leading industry given Thailand's position as a major tourist destination, have been quite extensive. However, the same does not seem to be true in the case of the banking and finance industry, where HRM activities have often been curtailed or outsourced to save money. This is especially troubling given the role this sector played in precipitating the onset of the country's financial difficulties in 1997. More generally, there seems to be some division of opinion regarding the role of HR in organizational training and development. There was a belief in Thailand that the 1997 crisis might lead to a more strategic approach to HRD and a greater role in Thai organizations for HRD professionals; the reality seems to be that HRD functions have shifted towards line management (Akaraborn and McLean, 2002).

A general theme in analyses dealing with Thailand's future is the need to enhance the country's competitiveness in light of decline in the post-1997 era (Lawler et al., 1997). The dominant managerial system in Thai-owned firms is one that can best be characterized as benevolent paternalism (Chainuvati and Granrose, 2001) and Thai cultural values emphasize collectivism and intra-group harmony, deference to authority, humility, self-restraint, and consideration for others (Dubey-Villinger, 2001a). But such values might be expected to be inconsistent with the implementation of what are termed 'high performance work systems' (HPWS), methods that require decentralization, employee empowerment, skill training and development, and often some level of intra-personal competitiveness. The importance of HPWS is argued to be related to their potential to make organizations more flexible and responsive in the face of enhanced competitive pressures related to globalization, rapid technological change, and the turbulence of the contemporary business environment. HPWS are also seen as helping to increase organizational learning capabilities.

Research regarding the impact of HPWS in Asian organizations has, in fact, shown that, despite cultural difficulties that might be expected in their implementation, this approach can contribute to organizational effectiveness in Asian organizations. Bae et al. (forthcoming) found that HPWS generally enhanced the organizational performance of firms in Asian countries and this effect was unrelated to factors such as the fit between organizational and HR strategies or the size of the firm. In addition, these effects were quite strong in indigenous firms, outpacing effects in subsidiaries of MNCs. Especially relevant here is that Bae et al. contrasted the effects of HPWSs in four Asian economies: Thailand, Korea, Taiwan, and Singapore. Despite the expectation that HPWS would have generally the weakest effects in Thailand (given the more advanced levels of economic development in the other three locations), the effects were positive in Thailand and the strongest of any of the locations. The authors speculated that part of this might have to do with the novelty of HPWS in Thailand and also that the values of urban workers, particularly younger ones, may, as with many other Asian countries, be becoming more individualistic and 'Westernized,' especially as a consequence of economic development.

The processes by which HPWS might be effective in the Thai context is illustrated in a case study of Sun Valley Thailand, a poultry processor owned and operated by the US-based Cargill Corporation (Lawler and Atmiyanandana, 2001). When started as a 'greenfield' site in the early 1990s, the plant, while profitable, had several problems, including high turnover, high absenteeism, and lower than expected productivity. The company implemented numerous changes in its HRM policies and practices that address the needs of the largely female workforce (including a variety of 'family friendly' initiatives). Most interesting here was the use of HPWS techniques in the poultry production farms. Workers who were responsible for the care and maintenance of the sheds in which chickens were raised were provided strong incentives to reduce poultry mortality rates. These workers had considerable discretion in certain areas to address this problem. They received very substantial bonuses for achieving mortality reduction goals. Despite the fact that most of these workers had fairly low educational levels, came from rural backgrounds, and held very traditional values, some degree of empowerment, coupled with performance-based incentives, did have quite positive results. Yet a significant factor in the success of what the company accomplished is that it did so in a culturally informed and sensitive manner. The system itself was designed largely by Thai HR managers and although high performance work system techniques were utilized, these were supplemented by an emphasis on a benevolent, paternalistic approach to leadership, particularly at the level of the first-line supervisor. The company selected supervisors who could be empathetic with their subordinates and establish a kind of big sister or big brother relationship with subordinates.

Further insights into the nature of HRM policies and practices in Thailand can be seen in the results of survey work conducted by the authors and others in 1998 and 1999. The lead HR managers in a random sample of approximately 100 companies, both locally owned and subsidiaries of MNCs, were asked to complete a questionnaire focusing on the HR policies and practices in the firm, as applied in the case of non-managerial, non-professional employees (for instance, production workers). The questions focused on several dimensions of HR strategy, including staffing, training, rewards, employee involvement, employee empowerment, and the views of the respondents as to top management's perceptions of the importance of HR as a source of value and competitive advantage to the firm. These scales were all structured such that higher values were consistent with HPWS. Thus, as the rewards scale increases, the firm relied more on pay for performance and incentive systems; likewise, increases in the staffing scale means the firm tended to be more selective in employment decisions and provided greater job security. The higher the value of the training scale, the greater the firm invested in and emphasized training and development for lower level employees. The higher the value of the empowerment scale, the more autonomy and discretion lower level employees generally had in carrying out their jobs. These data were collected as part of a larger, multi-country study; research methods and further results of this study are reported in Bae et al.

Table 1 compares the average values of each of these scales for Thai-owned companies relative to Thai-based subsidiaries of foreign MNCs. The subsidiaries of MNCs were pooled, as the sample size was not large enough to differentiate based on the MNC country of origin. However, most MNC affiliates were American or European-owned. We found statistically significant differences in several cases. Management in locally-owned firms seemed to have a generally less positive view of the value of human resources (at least in the case of lower-level employees) than management in MNC subsidiaries. Similarly, the extent to which local firms utilized highly selective staffing techniques, provided extensive training, and empowered lower level employees was significantly less than for MNC subsidiaries. In general, it would seem that local companies still maintained HR systems that were significantly more traditional (i.e., based on the conventional family-enterprise approach) and distinct from HPWSs than those of MNC subsidiaries. The work cited above as to the impact of HPWSs on company performance in Asian countries (Bae et al.) suggests that this is apt to have a negative impact on the competitiveness of these firms.

Table 2 compares locally-owned firms in Thailand with locally-owned firms in three other important regional economies: Korea, Taiwan and Singapore. All three of these countries are significantly more economically developed than Thailand and are places in which there has been considerable concern with industrial restructuring and the introduction of newer and more sophisticated HR policies and

TABLE 1

HRM DIMENSIONS: THAI-OWNED VS. MNC SUBSIDIARIES
(Means and Standard Deviations)

	Management Perceptions of HR value	Staffing	Rewards	Employee influence	Training	Empower-ment
MNC Subsidiaries (*n*=37)	4.77 (1.14)	5.06 (0.67)	4.71 (0.46)	3.89 (0.76)	4.26 (1.02)	4.35 (0.67)
Locally Owned (*n* = 74)	4.2603 (1.03)	4.75 (0.81)	4.55 (0.62)	3.79 (0.92)	3.79 (1.12)	4.11 (0.78)
t-value	2.38[a]	2.03[a]	1.39	0.55	2.13[a]	2.11[b]

a Significant at the 0.05 level (2-tailed test)
b Significant at the 0.10 level (2-tailed test)

TABLE 2

HRM DIMENSIONS: LOCALLY OWNED FIRM IN THAILAND VS. LOCALLY
OWNED FIRMS IN KOREA, SINGAPORE AND TAIWAN
(Means and Standard Deviations)

	Management Perceptions of HR Value	Staffing	Rewards	Employee influence	Training	Empower-ment
Non-Thai Locally-Owned (*n*=318)	4.41 (1.01)	4.86 (0.87)	4.21 (0.78)	4.15 (1.01)	3.82 (1.05)	3.74 (0.66)
Thai Locally-Owned (*n* = 74)	4.26 (1.03)	4.75 (0.81)	4.55 (0.62)	4.79 (0.93)	3.79 (1.13)	4.11 (0.78)
t-value	1.18	0.99	–3.55[a]	2.84[a]	0.15	–4.13[a]

a Significant at the 0.05 level (2-tailed test)

practices. This has been most evident in Korea, where there was much concern regarding implementation of the 'new HRM' (Bae, 1997). These efforts at reform in Korea reflect the long-standing apprehension in Korean governmental circles regarding the impact of globalization on the ability of Korean *chaebol* to remain internationally competitive (Ungson et al., 1997), a concern apparently justified by the problems that beset Korean companies during the economic crisis (McLean, 2001). Larger-scale and internationally active Taiwanese companies are also apparently moving more in the direction of replacing more traditional family-enterprise approaches to workforce management with techniques based on international 'best practices' (Huang, 2001). Yet local Thai firms seem to be somewhat ahead of local companies in these other three economies with respect to empowerment efforts and pay-for-performance.

Assessment of HRM Changes and Continuities

Here we consider post-1997 developments in Thailand in comparison to the various HRM dimensions proposed by Storey (1992) and used as an integrating mechanism in this symposium (Table 3). It is clear that companies in Thailand have had a tendency to promote adherence to rules, but Thai culture makes rule adherence somewhat relaxed. This may be less so in MNC subsidiaries than in locally-owned companies. Our assessment is that there is a significant movement toward greater flexibility in general in Thai-based companies, though this probably varies by level. It is still the case that the vast majority of rank-and-file workers have relatively low education and training, so the extent to which these workers can be 'empowered' in the sense suggested by the HPWS literature is questionable (although we saw this to some extent in the Cargill case discussed above, Lawler and Atmiyanandana, 2001). Common values and norms are very much present in Thai companies – either through a corporate culture in the case of MNC subsidiaries or through the cohesiveness engendered by Thai culture in locally-owned firms. This has probably not changed much in recent years. HR managers are widespread in Thai companies and the increasing professionalization of management, including the HRM field, is prpbably enhancing their role to some extent. Personnel selection is still not so well integrated. Firms seem keen on investing in efforts to find the right employees, but usually this involves a focus more on job fit than organizational fit.

In regard to payment, job evaluation methods are widespread, at least in the larger and more sophisticated companies. Many have adopted the Hay system, for example. Perhaps even more common in most Thai-owned companies has been pay systems based not so much on internal equity as personal characteristics (age, gender, social background, connections). However, movement toward performance-based pay, at both the individual and group levels, is quite evident. This approach is common among managers and often professionals; it seems to be extending to rank-and-file workers as well. There has been little in the way of collective bargaining in the Thai private sector and that remains the case (Lawler and Suttawet, 2000). A major development would seem to be that Thai companies, both local and MNC affiliates, are emphasizing continuous training effort, necessitated by frequently changing market conditions, global competitive pressures, and current shortages for many types of skilled workers. One senses that many companies in Thailand increasingly view training as an 'investment' rather than a 'cost'. There are effectively few legal limitations on Thai employers to hire and fire workers at will, though cultural constraints are such that most employers would prefer to avoid discharges if possible. There were massive lay-offs in conjunction with the 1997 crisis, however. Many companies now would seem to be adapting a 'core-peripheral' approach to workforce management, often relying heavily on contract labour to absorb the shocks of market variability. So in that sense, there would seem to be greater employer freedom in adjusting to market changes through workforce expansion and contraction. Finally, the HR field seems to be assuming a more strategic role in organizations, but this varies considerably by type of firm. The impact is likely greatest in MNC subsidiaries and much less so in most Thai-owned companies. The strategic role for HR managers in Thai-owned companies is probably greater in publicly-owned Thai corporations than in family enterprises and in high technology companies (such as computers and telecommunications).

Possible Changes in the Immediate Future

The process of change in the HRM area in Thailand would seem to be generally fairly slow, especially within locally-owned companies. We believe that there will be a tendency toward greater adaptation of HPWS and related methods by the larger Thai companies, although these changes might often be somewhat cosmetic. Anecdotally, at least, many Thai managers who have talked to the authors believe Thai cultural influences will continue to dominate within the local companies, so that major changes, if they do occur, will only be implemented in the long term. On the other hand, we anticipate much more rapid change in this direction within subsidiaries of MNCs, a process which is already apparently well underway in many of these companies.

TABLE 3

AN ASSESSMENT OF HRM CHANGES AND CONTINUITIES

Dimension	Presence	Change
1. Rules – adherence to	%	++
2. Behaviour – common values and norms	✓	0
3. Key managers – personnel/specialists v. line/general	%	+
4. Personnel selection	✓	0
5. Payment systems	%	++
6. Work conditions – harmonised	%	++
7. Contracts – individual v. standardised	%	0
8. In-house training	%	++
9. Right to hire and fire	✓	0
10. Strategic role for personnel manager	%	+

Key: (*Practice*)
✓ present
% present to some degree
✗ not present

(*Degree of change in past 4 years*)
++ major change
+ change
0 none

Source: adapted from Storey (1992).

DISCUSSION

Why Changes Have Occurred

The impact of the 1997 crisis on Thailand was quite profound. Thailand's depreciation of its currency in July of that year marked the onset of the crisis that spread regionally. Although the much-feared regional – and possibly global – economic meltdown never materialized, the crisis has led to a sea change in Asian business. China is emerging as the dominant economic power in the region, while Japan's position continues to erode as its economy stagnates. China is also displacing Japan as the major trading partner with other East Asian economies. Economies that were once the engines of Pacific Rim growth – Taiwan, Korea, Hong Kong, Thailand, Singapore, Malaysia – must now play a more reactive role, with much diminished growth. Yet these economies have, for the most part, recovered from the 1997 crisis.[1] Thailand's economy is once again growing (albeit at a much lower rate than in the pre-1997 period) and the government has announced that it planned to complete repayment of its IMF emergency loans in 2003, which is two years earlier than scheduled.

Changes have occurred in many of these economies both at the governmental and managerial levels. There is a greater call for accountability and transparency, generating reforms in commercial law (for example, tougher bankruptcy laws) and in corporate governance (for example, a greater voice for investors, greater accountability to stakeholders). Along these lines, the Stock Exchange of Thailand has issued guidelines requiring all listed companies to adopt corporate governance policies that incorporate several specific provisions. These pressures, along with the forces of globalization, have pushed many companies – locally-owned as well as multinational – towards benchmarking management practices against international 'best practice'.

These changes are evident in HRM policies and practices in Thailand. As we have discussed above, companies we have surveyed in the post-1997 period in Thailand tend to exhibit approaches to HRM more consistent with flexible HPWS than with more traditional approaches. Although subsidiaries of MNCs are generally ahead of locally-owned companies in this respect, the data we have presented show that Thai companies (at least larger, globally active ones) are apparently more apt to use HPWS-related methods.

Our survey findings are supported anecdotally. The authors conducted informal interviews with a number of Thai HR managers in early 2003. Most of these individuals worked for MNC subsidiaries, but were aware of developments in Thai-owned firms similar to their own. They generally indicated forces affecting their own companies – both the 1997 crisis and the enhanced competitiveness of the world economy – are pushing them to adopt what are seen as international 'best practices' in the HRM area (for example, pay for performance, greater emphasis on training, more worker discretion or, at least, participation). They also sensed this was occurring within larger Thai-owned firms, particularly those utilizing more sophisticated technologies or operating in more competitive emerging industries. Yet they also noted that they thought that such adaptations were not always as complete as in MNC subsidiaries. That is, some of the defining qualities of Thai culture, such as heavy reliance on social networks, paternalistic management, deference to authority, and concern for harmony and face, continued to play a much more important role in Thai-owned companies, even the larger Thai corporations, than in MNC subsidiaries. So while there is apparently increasing convergence to global best practice in the HRM area in Thailand, further work needs to be conducted to understand the extent to which these changes are substantive rather than superficial and adopted for the sake of appearance. For example, Hoecklin and Payne (1995: 5) quote one leading Thai executive who suggested that, regardless of the outward form, traditional Thai values would continue to dominate action, at least in Thai-owned organizations:

> We are born with *krieng jai* and *bunkhun* (traditional Thai values relating to deference and reciprocity). They are inside our heart. But inevitably in the future the cultures from the USA and Europe will come in and mix. But we are not afraid that we will lose our values. The majority of Thai managers – more than 95% – are (and will remain) typically Thai.

Convergence or Divergence

As stated above, it is our belief that there are clear convergence forces at work within Thailand, particularly within MNC subsidiaries. Changes are less pronounced, and moving at a slower place, yet evident in locally-owned companies.

Key Issues for HRM

Thailand confronts many concerns relevant to HRM. A large concern must be upgrading skills and training of the labour force, if Thailand is to be able to compete in higher technology industries that will be critical to national competitiveness in coming years. Another important issue will be the need for Thai companies to be more flexible and competitive in coming years, which will necessitate the introduction of HRM methods that are not particularly well suited to Thai culture (for example, greater worker empowerment and independence in the workplace, greater emphasis on merit and performance in all HRM-related decisions).

Implications for Theory Development

What has occurred in Thailand has implications for theory development, particularly relating to the 'convergence-divergence' debate. Prior to 1997, it would seem that national HRM systems in East and South East Asia were often strongly influenced by local culture and that there was a general tendency for these systems to be grounded in local culture, at least in the case of locally-owned companies. Certainly this was so for Thailand, as suggested in the work of Lawler et al. (1989) and Isarangkun Na Ayuthaya and Taira (1977). But as we have now seen, there is increasing, albeit incomplete, movement in the direction of global 'best practice' in the HRM area. This means, in many respects, greater interest in, if not full adoption of, western HRM practices, particularly those linked to HPWS, and greater organizational flexibility. We anticipate that MNC subsidiaries operating in Thailand will increasingly adopt this approach to HRM (precluding any unforeseen changes in the world economic order). And, as we have observed, Thai companies can be expected also to move in this direction, but perhaps at a slower rate and as a function of the type of company.

CONCLUSION

In our earlier essay (Lawler et al., 1997), we concluded that there were substantial differences in HRM policies and practices across organizations in Thailand related to issues such as country of origin (Western, Asian, Thai-owned) and type of firm (closely held family enterprise versus publicly traded corporation). We did note a growing tendency in foreign-owned and some Thai-owned companies to move away from traditional, Thai-based approaches to HRM towards something akin to the more flexible and responsive American-style HPWS. In post-1997 Thailand, this pressure is even greater and seemingly more widespread. This is not to say that companies in Thailand have fully endorsed the American approach. In fact, it would seem that they have adopted certain features, while trying to retain a certain culturally driven HRM policy. This is not unlike what seems to be occurring in other countries in the region. It will be interesting to see the extent to which such new approaches to HRM will continue and expand.

NOTE

1. Exceptions would be the continuing weakness of the Hong Kong economy and the more recent difficulties experienced by Taiwan that are unrelated to the 1997 crisis.

REFERENCES

Akarabonworn, C.T. and McLean, G.N. (2002), 'The Changing Roles of HRD in Thailand during the Current Economic Crisis', *International Journal of Human Resources Development and Management*, Vol.2, Nos.1–2, pp.64–77.

Bae, J. (1997), 'Beyond Seniority-based Systems: A Paradigm Shift in Korean HRM?', *Asia Pacific Business Review*, Vol.3, No.4, pp.82–110.

Bae, J., Chen, S., Wan, T., Lawler, J. and Walumbwa, F. (forthcoming), 'Human Resource Strategy and Firm Performance in Pacific Rim Countries', *International Journal of Human Resource Management*.

Chainuvati, V. and Granrose, C.S. (2001), 'Career Planning and Development of Managers in Thailand' in J.B. Kidd, X. Li and F.J. Richter (eds.), *Advances in Human Resource Management in Asia*. London: Palgrave.

Dubey-Villinger, N. (2001a), 'Thai Business Culture: Hierarchy and Groups, Initiative and Motivation' in J.B. Kidd, X. Li and F.J. Richter (eds.), *Advances in Human Resource Management in Asia*. London: Palgrave.

Dubey-Villinger, N. (2001b), 'Training in Thailand: Trends and Cases from the Service Sector' in J.B. Kidd, X. Li and F.J. Richter (eds.), *Advances in Human Resource Management in Asia*. London: Palgrave.

Far Eastern Economic Review (2001), *Asia 2002 Yearbook*. Hong Kong: Review Publishing Company.

Hamilton, G. (1996), *Asian Business Networks*. Berlin: Walter de Gruyter.

Hoecklin, L.A. and Payne, M. (eds.) (1995), *Managing Cultural Differences: Strategies for Competitive Advantage*. New York: Addison Wesley.

Huang, T. (2001), 'Human Resource Management in Taiwan' in P.S. Budhwar and A.D. Yaw (eds.), *Human Resource Management in Developing Countries*. London: Routledge.

Isarangkun Na Ayuthaya, C. and Taira, K. (1977), 'The Organization and Behavior of the Factory Work Force in Thailand', *The Developing Economies*, Vol.15, pp.16–36.

Lawler, J., and Atmiyanandana, V. (2001), 'Case Study: *Cargill Sun Valley (Thailand)*'. Champaign, IL: Gender in Agribusiness Project, University of Illinois.

Lawler, J., Siengthai, S. and Atmiyanandana V. (1997), 'HRM in Thailand: Eroding Traditions', *Asia Pacific Business Review*, Vol.3, No.4, pp.190–6.

Lawler, J. and Suttawet C. (2000), 'Labour Unions, Globalization and Deregulation in Thailand', in C. Rowley, and J. Benson (eds.), *Globalization and Labour in the Asia Pacific Region*. London & Portland, OR: Frank Cass.

Lawler, J., Zaidi, M.A. and Atmiyanandana V. (1989), 'Human Resource Strategies in Southeast Asia: The Case of Thailand' in A. Nedd, G. Ferris, and K. Rowland (eds.) *Research in Personnel and Human Resources Management* (Supplement 1). Greenwich, CN: JAI Press.

McLean, G. (2001), 'On Human Resource Development and Human Resource Management in the *Chaebols* of South Korea in Response to a National Economic Crisis', in J.B. Kidd, X. Li, and F.J. Richter (eds.), *Advances in Human Resource Management in Asia*. London, Palgrave.

Phongpaichit, P., and Baker, C. (1998), *Thailand's Boom and Bust*. Bangkok: Silkworm Books.

Pyat, R., Ashkanasy, N., Tamaschke, R. and Grigg, T. (2001), 'Transitions and Traditions in Chinese Family Businesses: Evidence from Hong Kong and Thailand' in J.B. Kidd, X. Li, and F.J. Richter (eds.), *Advances in Human Resource Management in Asia*. New York, Palgrave, pp.80–104.

Rowley, C. (1997), 'Introduction: Comparisons and Perspectives on HRM in the Asia-Pacific', *Asia Pacific Business Review*, Vol.3, No.4, pp.1–18.

Storey, John (1992), *Developments in the Management of Human Resources*. Oxford: Blackwell.

Sheridan, G. (1999), *Asian Values, Western Dreams: Understanding the New Asia*. Crows Nest NSW, Australia: Allen-Unwin.

Ungson, G., Steers, R. and Park S. (1997), *Korean Enterprise: The Quest For Globalization*. Boston: Harvard Business School.

Yuen, Chi-Ching (1997), 'HRM under Guided Economic Development: The Singapore Experience', *Asia Pacific Business Review*, Vol.3, No.4, pp.133–51.

Conclusion:
Changes in Asian HRM –
Implications for Theory and Practice

JOHN BENSON and CHRIS ROWLEY

This volume has explored the degree of change and continuity in Asian human resource management (HRM). The specific aim was to explore changes since 1997. In this period many Asian countries experienced the direct effects of the Asian financial crisis. There was also a substantial economic downturn in the US, which impacted on Asian exports, low levels of growth, as in Japan, dramatic changes in direction and increases in foreign direct investment (FDI), particularly in China, and a range of social and political changes. As a consequence, much of what has been written about Asia in that period is outmoded and may well be irrelevant.

To provide a unified approach to investigating change in the Asian region we built on the earlier collection by Rowley (1997) which explored the question of whether the changes taking place in Asian HRM were leading to a convergence towards what may be termed the 'Western HRM' model. By extending this work and exploring the same economies, this has allowed us to make more balanced judgements and to explore change in the context of its implications for theory development and HRM practices. For theory, the key issues were why such changes are occurring and was this leading to the application of a similar model of HRM throughout the region. In other words, are we now witnessing a period of convergence of practices or are key national differences maintaining or leading to distinct HRM systems? For practitioners, both in Asia and elsewhere, this raises a multitude of questions concerning 'best practice', the relevance of national cultures and the ability to transfer and successfully transplant human resource (HR) practices.

As discussed earlier, the volume includes a variety of Asian countries that represent the divide between developed and developing countries and also the differences in size. These are important criteria when exploring HRM change in country settings. In addition, we adopted a model of change that explores change at the levels of architecture, policy and practice. This meant that superficial change at the practice level was not equated equally with changes in the architecture that underpins a system. To answer the questions raised above, this piece is divided into three parts. The next section provides a summary and analysis of the individual contributions. Following this a comparative analysis is provided which will locate both the level of change and the key components of that change. The contribution concludes by discussing the implications for theory and practice.

OVERVIEW OF CHANGES

China: the Forward March of Change

The key issues for HRM in China have been related to the elimination of the 'iron rice bowl' and the transition to market-driven employment practices, not just in large firms but also across the wide range of businesses now to be found. The weight of tradition and inertia has been a drag on such a process but the change is now more noticeable, particularly as the state sector withers away. Recruitment is more dependent on the market rather than on allocation by the labour bureaux and selection is increasingly based on merit. Reward systems remain complex but are more performance driven. Motivation of employees is now based on material rewards rather than a pledge of job security and benefits in kind. Training is more systematic, at least in larger firms, even if development is less de rigueur. In short, the 'long march' from personnel management to full-blown HRM is under way, with some changes to the basic architecture of the system.

Hong Kong: Erosion of the Public–Private Sector Divide?

A number of significant changes have occurred in the management of HR in Hong Kong in the past five years. First, employment security has declined as firms across all sectors cut the number of employees. Second, pay freezes and/or pay reductions have become widespread and fringe benefits have been cut while the use of discretionary performance bonuses has spread. Third, employees are expected to work harder, upgrade their skills and become functionally more flexible. Fourth, employment relations have been affected by the political transition as well as the Asian crisis. This was most clearly illustrated by the post-handover government repealing a collective bargaining bill that had been passed in the final days of the colonial regime. Public sector HRM practices are undergoing substantial modification as a consequence of public sector changes and more recently civil service reforms. The hiving-off of government functions to the private sector, the introduction of a voluntary retirement scheme, a management-initiated retirement scheme for directorate-level officials and the hiring of new staff on contracts without guarantees of moving to permanent terms, are examples of changes that have occurred and that represent partial HRM policy and architectural changes.

Japan: Still Muddling Through?

Important changes have occurred in Japanese HRM. First, wage settlements are becoming more disparate and are linked to the nature of employment. In this period real wages also fell. Second, there has been a gradual shift towards a merit-based appraisal system for wages and promotion in Japanese companies. Third, there has been a clear departure from age and tenure as key criteria for wages and promotion. Whilst this has been a trend for the past two decades, the process has accelerated over the past five years. Finally, there has been a general restructuring of HRM with the speed of change substantially increasing. What may have been considered unique practices five years ago have now become more widely established. Nevertheless, HRM reform is still ostensibly at the level of practice and experimentation. There is little indication that the change is systematic or has occurred at the policy or architectural level.

Korea: Back from the Brink?

The core ideology of the traditional Korean HRM system has changed from 'organization first', 'collective equality' and 'community oriented' towards 'individual respect', 'individual equity' and 'market principle'. The main underlying assumptions of traditional HRM – lifetime employment and seniority-based remuneration – have weakened vis-à-vis flexible employment. Outsourcing, performance pay and redeployment policies have become more popular. Recruitment has changed more towards recruitment on demand and selection based on speciality and creativity. Reinforcing competencies is now achieved by more performance-based promotion, while the retaining of such competencies is aided by the development of flatter structures, team-based design, and the development of professionals. Finally, competencies are seen as replaceable and this has led to increased job mobility and flexible employment. Such changes have created the climate for a rapid recovery from the effects of the Asian crisis and have begun to penetrate both the policy and architectural levels of the HRM system.

Philippines: Sectoral Differences?

The adoption of HRM practices has, until recently, been distinguishable by sector. Export-oriented firms have faced global competitive pressure and have adopted HRM practices different from the domestic firms. Recently these domestic firms have adopted HRM practices that have been more characteristic of those in the export-oriented sector. Such practices have included the increased use of subcontracting, labour contracting and retrenchments, Many of these changes have occurred over the past five years and this suggests that the Asian crisis played a significant role. The realities of falling trade and investment barriers, the privatization of state-owned firms and the deregulation faced by domestic firms, are all a result of the numerous structural adjustment programmes sponsored by the international financial institutions. Yet, as most of the changes in the domestic sector have taken place in the past few years, the degree of change has been relatively small and represents change at the level of practice. Nevertheless, given that many of these changes are due to the systematic removal of regulatory protection it is quite likely that, over time, these changes will represent fundamental policy and architectural shifts. In this case further convergence is likely.

Singapore: Upskilling Routes to Success?

The HRM system is in a state of transition and will continue its evolution to one that pays much less attention to lifelong jobs. In the face of severe competition, organizations will continue to restructure and introduce new work processes. More companies are using performance-based pay and promoting employees on merit. While the strategic role of HR professionals is likely to become more crucial, they will need to identify those added values that they can create and develop measures to evaluate their own performance. Similarly, individual employees will have to be more active in charting their own future. In a restructured economy, executives and managers, professionals, and ordinary workers will need to continually improve their knowledge and skills to stay employable. More firms will relocate their labour-intensive activities to nearby countries while at the same time Singapore will encourage higher valued-added companies to locate in Singapore. These companies will demand a highly skilled and flexible workforce and thus will put more pressure on the adoption of HRM practices. It is therefore likely that the changes identified above will become institutionalized at the policy and architectural levels.

Taiwan: Towards International HRM Standards in Economic Recession

Taiwan has moved substantially towards adopting international HRM standards. Much of the pressure for this change has stemmed from changes in the economic environment; from a period of economic boom conditions to one of prolonged recession. This has led to higher unemployment and a fall in demand for migrant labour. As a consequence, HRM policy has shifted to one emphasizing flexibility at both national and enterprise levels in order to develop the required skills, the training of laid-off workers for re-employment and the refocusing of long-term HR strategic plans. At the same time FDI and multinational companies (MNC) have had a profound impact on HRM and the move to international HR practices. In response to the increased competition and global conditions, firms, irrespective of their size or sector, have began to adopt 'western' HRM practices. This trend will continue in the foreseeable future and it is likely that these changes will influence, in the long-term, the policy and architecture of the HRM system.

Thailand: Adapted Adoption?

The last five years have witnessed innovation and reform in the managerial arena, including changes in HRM policies and practices. These changes are best characterized by the adoption of HRM practices and their subsequent adaptation to the particular Thai context. Nevertheless, it is clear that increasingly companies are exhibiting HRM approaches that are more consistent with flexible, high performance work systems than with the traditional approaches. Rule adherence is somewhat relaxed and common values and norms exist. These approaches, however, are more engendered by Thai culture. HR managers are widespread in Thai companies and the increasing professionalization of these managers is enhancing their role. On the other hand personnel selection still involves a focus on 'job fit' rather than 'organizational fit'. Job evaluation methods are widespread, at least in the larger and more sophisticated companies and some movement has occurred towards performance-based pay. Continuous training is now increasingly emphasized. In contrast there has been little promotion of collective bargaining in the private sector. It is too early to say how far such changes have gone beyond the practice level and if they have penetrated the policy and architectural level.

COMPARATIVE ANALYSIS OF NATURE AND LEVEL
OF CHANGE

The above analysis of HRM changes in the eight case study countries points to convergence of at least some HRM practices at the level of practice. How widespread are these changes and do they represent changes at the HRM policy and architectural levels? Table 1 presents a summary of these changes on ten key dimensions. These dimensions represent three levels of change: system architecture as measured by the beliefs and assumptions underpinning the system, policy choices as measured by strategic qualities and managerial roles, and HRM practices as measured by the key levers.

From Table 1, it is clear that all the countries represented in this study have made substantial moves towards the HRM model in terms of the first level, practice or key levers. Merit-based selection, performance-based pay, employment contracts, harmonized work conditions and continuous in-house training have increasingly become the norm. These are more developed in some countries than others and the pace of change over the past five years has varied considerably. At the level of practice it can therefore be concluded that a more 'Western' HRM model has emerged, albeit in some cases with some unique characteristics.

At the second level of change, policy choices or strategic qualities and managerial roles, less change has been found. With the exception of Japan, few of the other countries have implemented, in full, the HRM model, although all, with the exception of the Philippines, have made some progress in this direction. A more strategic role for personnel managers is emerging and line managers are taking a more active interest in HR issues.

At the third level, system architecture or beliefs and assumptions, most studies in this collection have reported mixed progress over the past five years. While common values and norms seem to be guiding HRM, at least to some extent, it remains unclear as to how far these remain based on traditional customs and practices. Almost with out exception, however, adherence to a set of standardized rules still set the parameters for HRM in the eight case study countries. That is, there is little evidence that a 'can do' outlook or an impatience with rules attitude has been adopted, although some movement in this direction has been detected in all but one of the countries.

Based on these findings, it can be concluded that practices associated with the HRM model have been widely adopted in companies operating in the economies of the eight case studies. Yet such practices have not yet been internalized in policy choices or system architecture. This leaves the HRM systems in these countries

TABLE 1

COMPARATIVE ASSESSMENT OF HRM CHANGES AND CONTINUITIES

Levels/Dimensions	China	Japan	Korea	Thailand	Hong Kong	Philippines	Singapore	Taiwan
System Architecture								
Rules: adherence to	✓(+)	✓(+)	✓(+)	%(++)	%(+)	✓(0)	%(+)	✓(+)
Behaviour: common values and norms	✓(+)	✓(+)	✓(+)	✓(0)	%(+)	✗(0)	✓(+)	✓(+)
Strategic Qualities and Managerial Roles								
Key managers: personnel/specialists v. line/general ✓	(0)	✓(+)	%(+)	%(+)	%(+)	✗(0)	✓(++)	✓(0)
Strategic role for personnel manager	%(+)	✓(0)	%(+)	%(+)	✗(0)	%(+)	%(+)	%(+)
Key Levers								
Personnel selection	✓(+)	✓(+)	✓(+)	✓(0)	✓(+)	✓(0)	✓(++)	✓(+)
Payment systems	✓(+)	%(+)	%(++)	%(++)	%(+)	%(+)	✓(++)	%(+)
Work conditions: harmonized	%(+)	✓(+)	✓(0)	%(++)	✗(0)	%(0)	%(+)	✓(0)
Contracts: individual v. standardized	✓(++)	%(+)	%(+)	%(0)	✓(0)	✓(+)	✓(+)	%(+)
In-house training	✓(+)	✓(+)	✓(0)	%(++)	%(0)	✓(+)	%(+)	✓(0)
Right to hire and fire	✓(++)	✓(0)	%(+)	✓(0)	✓(0)	✓(0)	✓(+)	✓(+)

Key: *(Practice)*   *(Degree of change towards HRM model in 5 years)*
      ✓ present   ++ major change
      % present to some degree   + change
      ✗ not present   0 none

Source: adapted from Storey (1992).

unstable and that the best way to characterize the reform is widespread experimentation with the various component practices of the HRM model. Further, the way the same practice is viewed and implemented can vary, as in the case of non-standard employment in terms of the extent to which it is precarious or stable (Cousins, 1999).

The lack of significant change at the policy and architectural levels also suggests that business structures and some unique cultural attributes remain important constraints on convergence. Notwithstanding the above it is also clear that some reforms in this direction are occurring at these two higher levels which suggest that in the next five to ten years the adoption of the HRM model may have consolidated. On the other hand, this consolidation may develop with each national system forming a unique set of characteristics that represent varying cultural and institutional influences.

IMPLICATIONS

In attempting to understand the changes identified in Asian HRM, this collection addressed four questions. First, why have such changes have occurred? The initial changes were fuelled by globalization and the impact of the Asian crisis which forced firms to become more competitive and efficient. HRM in this context was seen as the appropriate way to improve labour productivity and achieve international 'best practice'. The impact of these factors was not, however, uniform and they were supplemented in particular countries by other more unique factors. In Japan the depressed state of the economy, the ageing workforce, the changing attitudes of younger workers, and a more general loss of faith in the traditional model of Japanese HRM were instrumental in the push for HRM reform. On the other hand, the breakdown of the traditional divide between the public and private sectors in Hong Kong after the handover to China in 1997 were important contextual factors driving change. Other factors included the impact of MNCs (Taiwan and Thailand), the change in the attitudes of managers and workers (China), the removal of regulatory protection (Philippines), strategic choices of management (Korea), and the need to broaden the country's economic base (Singapore).

The second question addressed was whether these changes represented a convergence towards the Western HRM model. All country studies in this collection point to a range of practices that suggest some convergence is taking place. The adoption of the HRM model appears strongest at the level of practice and far weaker at the policy or architectural levels. Yet, even at the HR practice level there is some evidence that embedded custom and practices are constraining convergence. In addition, other factors, such as the stage of economic development and the configuration of technology and management styles, can restrain the onward push of globalization and the convergence to the 'one best way' of managing people internationally. It is therefore concluded that while convergence of practice has occurred it is too simplistic to argue that HRM system convergence is taking place. It would be better to characterize the changes as a transitional stage where the final outcome is difficult to predict and may differ substantially from the HRM model. What is less in dispute is that experimentation with western HRM practices will continue, and in all likelihood will be modified to suit the unique needs of each system.

The third question considered was what are the implications of these changes for HRM. At a practical level a number of issues has arisen from the case studies. These include the issues of improved labour productivity and flexibility, the development of new ways to retain valued employees, the removal of the growing tensions that arise from the adoption of an HRM approach and how to address the paradoxes arising out of the implementation of HRM. The change to HRM practices raises the more important question of how change to policy and architecture will take place. Two scenarios are possible. If change continues in a gradual and continuous fashion, then practice developments will put pressure on reform at higher levels. HRM will then involve considerable experimentation at the policy and architectural levels. It is not immediately clear as to how these changes will occur and what types of policy and systems will be put in place. A large degree of uncertainty will exist and temporary structures will arise to fill the vacuum caused by managerial experimentation. This transitional stage may extend for many years with little indication as to the final outcome. On the other hand, if more radical reform is undertaken and extended to all levels of HRM, then it is likely that, in the transitional period, HR practices will also be affected and make HR more uncertain and difficult to manage. Workers will be alienated in this process and companies will not be able to appeal to the wider norms and values of society to gain the necessary commitment.

The final question concerned implications for the development of HRM theory. The case studies raised a number of issues that will need to be incorporated into any broad theory of HRM. In particular, hybrid systems (Hong Kong, Taiwan) multiple approaches (Philippines), external and internal HRM (China), the superficial and paradoxical nature of change (Korea) and the unitary underpinnings of the HRM approach (Japan), will all need to be considered. This means any generalized model of HRM must be based on context rather than on prescriptive outcomes, able to incorporate a multiplicity of approaches and to recognize the dynamic and inherently unstable nature of HRM. New models of HRM must also accommodate the various levels at which any system operates and develop clearer linkages between these levels. Does change at one level imply increasing pressure for change at other levels or can HRM adapt to accommodate singular events? Equally important is the need to have less focus on convergence as a measure of HRM adoption and the need to place more attention on how systems develop and change to accommodate various cultural, institutional and macro-economic forces.

CONCLUSION

This volume set out to explore the changes in HRM in eight Asian countries since 1997. Such a task was considered important given that many have argued that globalization will lead to the convergence of national systems of HRM. While the earlier volume (Rowley, 1997) concluded that the case studies provided some support for convergence, there was considerable diversity of practice. Some five years later that diversity at the practice level has considerably reduced and a more uniform set of HRM practices has appeared. Yet, much of this development has been limited to the practical aspects of HRM where considerable experimentation and development has taken place, albeit often with 'Asian characteristics'. The case studies provided little evidence to suggest that much of the reform had been converted to policy or institutionalized into the basic architecture of the HRM systems of the eight economies. Indeed, at this level there existed considerable diversity both within and between countries. While this has implications for HRM practice in each country it also has implications for the further development and refinement of HRM theory.

REFERENCES

Cousins, C. (1999), 'Changing Regulatory Frameworks and Non-Standard Employment: A Comparison of Germany, Spain, Sweden and the UK' in A. Felstead and N. Jewson (eds.), *Global Trends in Labour*, Basingstoke: Macmillan, pp.100–20.

Rowley, C. (1997), 'Human Resource Management in the Asia Pacific Region: Convergence Questioned', Special Issue of *Asia Pacific Business Review*, Vol.3, No.4.

Storey, J. (1992), *Developments in the Management of Human Resources*, Oxford: Oxford University Press.

Abstracts

Introduction: Changes and Continuities in Asian HRM *by Chris Rowley and John Benson*

A number of significant events have impacted on Asian countries over the period since 1997 and the Asian Crisis. This means that much of what we know about Asia is outdated and may well be irrelevant. It is for this reason that this contribution re-examines a number of Asian countries to explore how human resource management (HRM) has changed over this period. A model that can be used for a comparative analysis of HRM, and one that allows the various levels of change to be assessed, is presented. This is followed by an overview of the volume's contents with the common focus being on the changes that have occurred over this period.

China's HRM Revisited *by Malcolm Warner*

This contribution discusses the degree to which changes in human resource management (HRM) have taken place in the China since the Special Issue on HRM in the Asia Pacific Region came out in 1997. At that time, we spoke of 'relative convergence' as being the main feature of Chinese HRM; this remains largely the case. As the non-state owned sectors in the Chinese economy expand and state-owned enterprises shrink correspondingly, the impact of World Trade Organization entry will lead to more competition and a greater role for market forces. The greater the impact of these changes on Chinese firms, the more Personnel Management will be replaced by HRM year by year. How rapidly this pragmatic, step-wise path proceeds will depend on how far the new norms become institutionalized and how far managers' as well as workers' mind-sets absorb and integrate them.

HRM in Hong Kong since 1997 *by Stephen W.K. Chiu and David A. Levin*

A diverse set of human resource management (HRM) practices became institutionalized during Hong Kong's industrialization from the 1950s through the 1970s within the context of an open economy, a government disinclined to intervene in business decisions or the labour market and a weak trade union movement. Economic restructuring, labour market changes and rising labour costs during the 1980s and 1990s pressured employers to find more effective ways of using their human resources. We focus on how the economic downturn following the Asian Financial Crisis has impacted on employment practices including employment security, compensation, skill formation, work reorganization and employment relations. We discuss changes in the public as well as private sector and argue that reforms in the former are loosening the rigidities of its highly structured internal labour market system. Public sector employment practices are thus likely to converge increasingly with the 'best practices' of private sector and overseas government HRM systems.

Flexible Labour Markets and Individualized Employment: The Beginnings of a New Japanese HRM System by John Benson and Philippe Debroux

In an earlier study we reported that human resource management (HRM) in Japan was best characterized by continuity with some changes to assessment and pay practices. It is now over five years since we mapped out the changes taking place in Japanese HRM. This contribution reviews some of the changes over this period and considers the future directions of HRM. The essay commences with a discussion of the important contextual factors and issues underpinning HRM including employer proposals for reform. The next section then explores changes taking place in employment, remuneration and evaluation. This is supplemented by a more general assessment of the key changes occurring in Japanese HRM. The essay concludes with a discussion on why such changes are occurring, whether the changes constitute a convergence towards the Western model and the implications for HRM and theory development.

Changes and Continuities in South Korean HRM by Johngseok Bae and Chris Rowley

The operating context of South Korean human resource management (HRM) has undergone radical shifts since we wrote our first piece in 1997 for a similar collection to this. This has undoubtedly influenced the practice of HRM. Therefore, the focus of this piece is to compare the current situation with the past and delineate the amount and type of such change vis-à-vis continuity in HRM. The contextual factors and issues, political and economic background, labour market situation, the 1997 Asian financial crisis and ramifications, are analysed. Then future possible scenarios and key issues are outlined.

Change and Continuity: Recent Developments in HRM in the Philippines by Christopher Skene

There is a tendency in many country studies to investigate a single sector and to imply that the sector is representative of the whole. In the realm of human resource management practices, the case of the Philippines suggests this is not a helpful approach. This essay suggests that, within the Philippines, there are differences between sectors of the economy. The purpose of this paper is three-fold: to build upon Maragtas Amante's 1997 study on HRM practices in the Philippines, to demonstrate differences in HRM practices in the import substitution industrialization (ISI) and export-oriented industrialization (EOI) sectors and to highlight the changes (if any) that have taken place over the past few years. This study suggests that, over the past few decades there has been a great deal of divergence between the ISI and EOI sectors. However, recently there has been evidence that the ISI sector has been adopting HRM practices that have been more characteristic of those in the EOI sector. The reason for this change is that the regulatory protection the ISI sector once enjoyed is no longer available. In addition, the Asian Financial Crisis has contributed to the change by breaking down union resistence that had previously prevented change in the ISI sector.

HRM in Singapore: Change and Continuity *by David Wan*

This essay traces the development of human resource management (HRM) in Singapore from the mid 1990s until the present day, with particular reference to the impact of the 1997 Asian financial crisis. In particular, it explores the changes in employment relations since the publication of Yuen (1997). National HRM concerns and strategies to maximize human capital as Singapore transforms itself and the knowledge economy is highlighted. The issue of convergence versus divergence in the management of human resources (HRs) will be touched upon. Current and future HR challenges that are most likely to impact on the country's competitiveness and economic performance are also explored.

The Post Asian Financial Crisis: Changes in HRM in Taiwanese Enterprises *by Ying Zhu*

The changes in the macro-economic environment, due to the recent Asian crisis, have been an important stimulus to organizational and human resource management (HRM) changes in Taiwanese enterprises. This essay tackles these responses by looking at individual firms, using a case study approach. The pattern of organizational responses introduced in these companies has exhibited a variety of different characteristics. Most have implemented strategies towards enhancing the individual firms' competitiveness. The situation has changed since Chen's research in 1997, marked by differences between a period of economic boom and a period of economic recession. Consequently, key economic indicators and labour market conditions have changed, so HRM practices have evolved too. Generally speaking, the adoption of international standardized HRM practices is one such move that is now becoming more general in Taiwan.

HRM in Thailand: A Post-1997 Update *by John Lawler and Vinita Atmiyanandana*

This essay updates an earlier study of human resource management (HRM) practices in Thailand, focusing specifically on HRM in the post-1997 Asian financial crisis. HRM in Thailand has undergone gradual, but significant, change, with movement away from more traditional styles of HRM and management rooted in personalism and social relationships, toward more flexible employment systems in which employment opportunities are based on merit and performance rather than connections and personal characteristics. These changes are clearly more pronounced in subsidiaries of multinational corporations, particularly those based in Western countries.

Conclusion: Changes in Asian HRM – Implications for Theory and Practice *by John Benson and Chris Rowley*

A number of significant events have impacted on Asian countries over the period since 1997 and the Asian crisis. This means that much of what we know about Asia is outdated and may well be irrelevant. It is for this reason that this contribution re-examines a number of Asian countries to explore how human resource management (HRM) has changed over this period. A model that can be used for a comparative analysis of HRM, and one that allows the various levels of change to be assessed, is presented. This is followed by an overview of the volume's contents with the common focus on the changes that have occurred over this period.

Index